Conceptis Puzzles

An imprint of Sterling Publishing Co., Inc.
www.puzzlewright.com

2 4 6 8 10 9 7 5 3 1

Published by Sterling Publishing Co., Inc.
387 Park Avenue South, New York, NY 10016

Distributed in Canada by Sterling Publishing
c/o Canadian Manda Group, 165 Dufferin Street
Toronto, Ontario, Canada M6K 3H6
Distributed in the United Kingdom by GMC Distribution Services
Castle Place, 166 High Street, Lewes, East Sussex, England BN7 1XU
Distributed in Australia by Capricorn Link (Australia) Pty. Ltd.
P.O. Box 704, Windsor, NSW 2756, Australia

Manufactured in the United States of America

Sterling ISBN 978-1-4027-6583-4

For information about custom editions, special sales, premium and corporate purchases, please contact Sterling Special Sales Department at 800-805-5489 or special-sales@sterlingpublishing.com.

CONTENTS

INTRODUCTION

Calcu-Doku in a Nutshell

Calcu-Doku are math and logic puzzles that require placing numbers in a grid according to certain rules. Each puzzle consists of a grid containing blocks surrounded by bold lines. The object is to fill all empty squares so that the numbers 1 to N (where N is the number of rows or columns in the grid) appear exactly once in each row and column. The numbers in each block produce the result of the operation shown in the upper left corner of the block. In Calcu-Doku, a number *may* be used more than once in the same block (but not more than once in each row or column).

Calcu-Doku puzzles are available in different variants. Single Operation Calcu-Doku uses one math operation, which is either addition or multiplication. Similarly, Dual Operation Calcu-Doku uses two math operations (either addition and subtraction or multiplication and division), while Quad Operation Calcu-Doku uses four math operations (addition, subtraction, multiplication, and division) all at the same time. The math operation used in each block is shown in its upper left corner (except for Single Operation Calcu-Doku, where the operation used applies to every block and is shown above the grid).

Calcu-Doku Techniques

Let's look at a sample puzzle to learn some basic techniques of Calcu-Doku.

Starting With the Givens

Some Calcu-Doku puzzles, especially easy ones, contain blocks consisting of a single square. These are actually given clues and the number to be placed is simply the number in the upper left corner of the single square block, regardless of which math operations are shown above the grid. We can therefore place 2 in the example below.

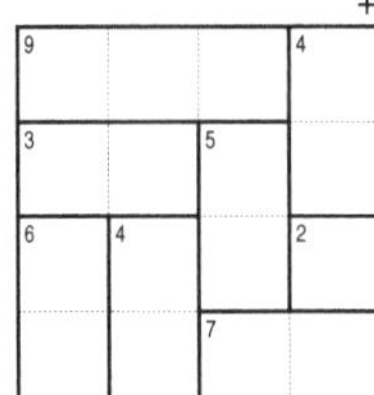

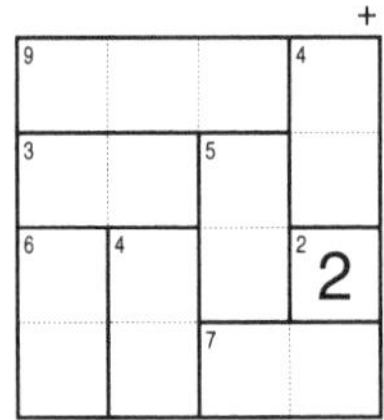

Unique Block Technique

As with kakuro and Sum Sudoku, Calcu-Doku puzzles often have situations where only a single combination of numbers can fit in a block. These situations are useful when starting to solve a puzzle, especially if they appear in straight blocks. Here is one way of using this technique.

In the right column of the Single Operation Calcu-Doku puzzle on the previous page we see a block of two squares with the sum 4. Calcu-Doku rules don't allow the same number to appear more than once in a row or a column, so it couldn't be 2 + 2, even if a 2 weren't already placed in that column. This means the only combination to satisfy the requirement is 1 + 3 or 3 + 1 (though we don't know which one goes where yet). This means that the bottom square in the right column can't be a 1, a 2, or a 3. It must be a 4. Therefore, the number to the left of the 4 must be 7 − 4 = 3.

+

[9]			[4] 31
[3] 12	21	[5]	13
[6]	[4]		[2] 2
		[7] 3	4

Hidden Single Technique

Look at the block that adds up to 3. It must contain a 1 + 2 or a 2 + 1. Knowing that, the box to its right (which contains a small 5) can be filled in using the Hidden Single Technique. This is when there is only one square in a row, column, or block where a certain number can go; in this case there's only one place a 4 can go in the second row. A 1 can then be placed below (5 − 4 = 1).

+

[9]			[4] 31
[3] 12	21	[5] 4	13
[6]	[4]	1	[2] 2
		[7] 3	4

Grid Remainder Technique

At this point we can use a different technique that uses the fact that each row and column adds up to the same number (in this case, 10). You see how the long block in the top row adds up to 9? That means that the square in the upper-right corner must be a 1 (10 − 9). We can place a 3 in the box below the 1 as well.

+

[9]			[4] 1
[3] 12	21	[5] 4	3
[6]	[4]	1	[2] 2
		[7] 3	4

Look at the block that adds up to 6. It can't be a 3 + 3, so it must be 2 + 4 or 4 + 2. Since there's already a 4 in the bottom row, we can tell which goes where.

+

(9)			(4) 1
(3) 12	21	(5) 4	3
(6) 4	(4)	1	(2) 2
2		(7) 3	4

Now it's just a matter of filling in the missing digit in each of the bottom two rows, filling in the block that adds up to 3, and filling in the three missing digits in the top row. Does the big block add up to 9? Of course, the answer is yes.

The completed sample should look like this:

+

(9) 3	4	2	(4) 1
(3) 1	2	(5) 4	3
(6) 4	(4) 3	1	(2) 2
2	1	(7) 3	4

Similar techniques can be used in the multiplication and division puzzles. Note that subtraction and division are always in blocks made up of two squares, with the lower number subtracted from the higher number, or the higher number divided by the lower number. Within each size of puzzle the difficulty increases, so it might be a good idea to have a calculator handy for the last few puzzles in each section. Be sure to visit Conceptis Puzzles online at www.conceptispuzzles.com for more advanced tips and tricks.

Sudoku in a Nutshell

To solve sudoku puzzles, all you need to know is this one simple rule:

> Fill in the boxes so that the nine rows, the nine columns, and the nine 3×3 sections all contain every digit from 1 to 9.

And that's all there is to it! Using this simple rule, let's see how far we get on this sample puzzle at right. (The letters at the top and left edges of the puzzle are for reference only; you won't see them in the regular puzzles.)

The first number that can be filled in is an obvious one: box EN is the only blank box in the center

	A	B	C	D	E	F	G	H	I
J									
K					2		1	8	4
L	9		5		7		2		6
M	1		4	3	9	2		7	
N				7		6			
O		7		1	4	8	9		2
P	3		2		6		8		5
Q	8	4	9		3				
R									

3×3 section, and all the digits 1 through 9 are represented except for 5. EN must be 5.

The next box is a little trickier to discover. Consider the upper left 3×3 section of the puzzle. Where can a 4 go? It can't go in AK, BK, or CK because row K already has a 4 at IK. It can't go in BJ or BL because column B already has a 4 at BQ. It can't go in CJ because column C already has a 4 at CM. So it must go in AJ.

Another box in that same section that can now be filled is BJ. A 2 can't go in AK, BK, or CK due to the 2 at EK. The 2 at GL rules out a 2 at BL. And the 2 at CP means that a 2 can't go in CJ. So BJ must contain the 2. It is worth noting that this 2 couldn't have been placed without the 4 at AJ in place. Many of the puzzles rely on this type of steppingstone behavior.

We now have a grid as shown.

Let's examine column A. There are four blank boxes in column A; in which blank box must the 2 be placed? It can't be AK because of the 2 in EK (and the 2 in BJ). It can't be AO because of the 2 in IO. It can't be AR because of the 2 in CP. Thus, it must be AN that has the 2.

	A	B	C	D	E	F	G	H	I
J	4	2							
K					2		1	8	4
L	9		5		7		2		6
M	1		4	3	9	2		7	
N				7	5	6			
O		7		1	4	8	9		2
P	3		2		6		8		5
Q	8	4	9		3				
R									

By the 9's in AL, EM, and CQ, box BN must be 9. Do you see how?

We can now determine the value for box IM. Looking at row M and then column I, we find all the digits 1 through 9 are represented but 8. IM must be 8.

This brief example of some of the techniques leaves us with the grid at right.

You should now be able to use what you learned to fill in CN followed by BL, then HL followed by DL and FL.

	A	B	C	D	E	F	G	H	I
J	4	2							
K					2		1	8	4
L	9		5		7		2		6
M	1		4	3	9	2		7	8
N	2	9		7	5	6			
O		7		1	4	8	9		2
P	3		2		6		8		5
Q	8	4	9		3				
R									

As you keep going through this puzzle, you'll find it gets easier as you fill in more. And as you keep working through the puzzles in this book, you'll find it gets easier and more fun each time. The final answer is shown below.

Happy puzzling!

	A	B	C	D	E	F	G	H	I
J	4	2	1	6	8	3	5	9	7
K	7	3	6	5	2	9	1	8	4
L	9	8	5	4	7	1	2	3	6
M	1	5	4	3	9	2	6	7	8
N	2	9	8	7	5	6	4	1	3
O	6	7	3	1	4	8	9	5	2
P	3	1	2	9	6	7	8	4	5
Q	8	4	9	2	3	5	7	6	1
R	5	6	7	8	1	4	3	2	9

Calcu-Doku

1

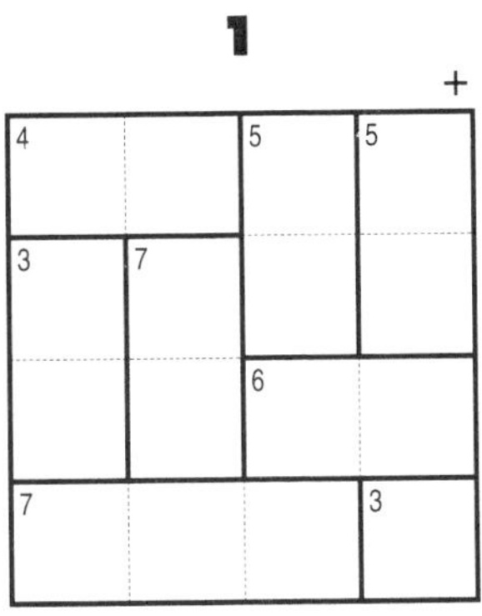

2

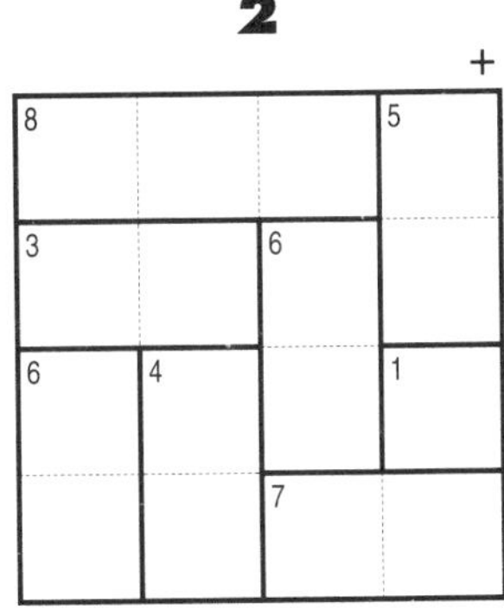

3

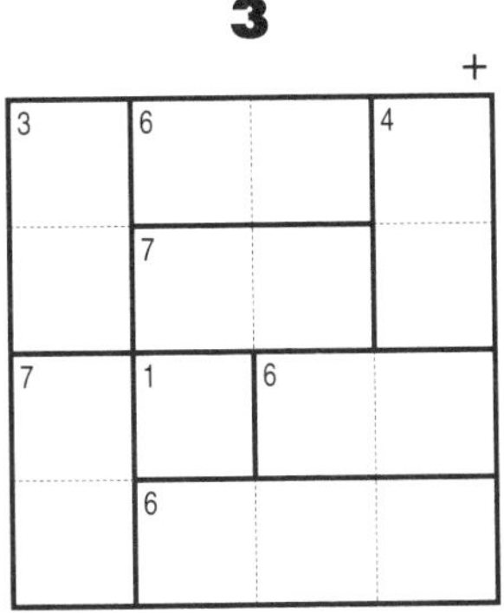

4

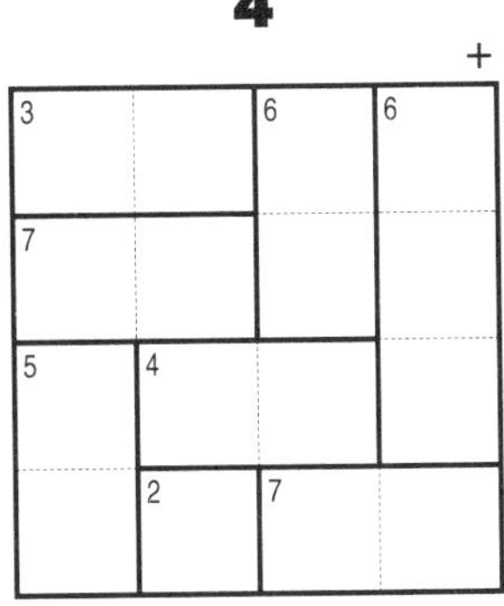

5

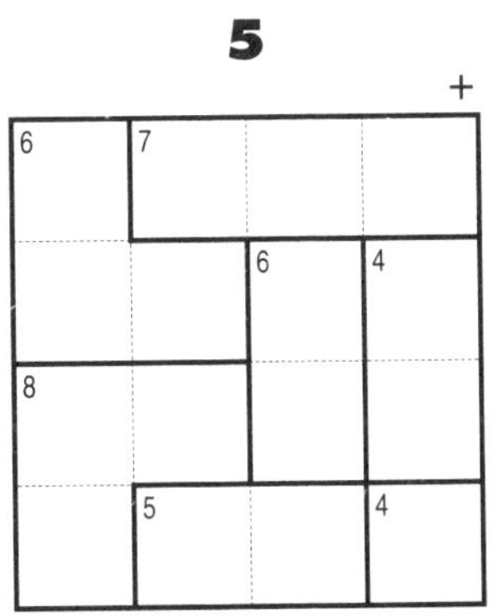

6

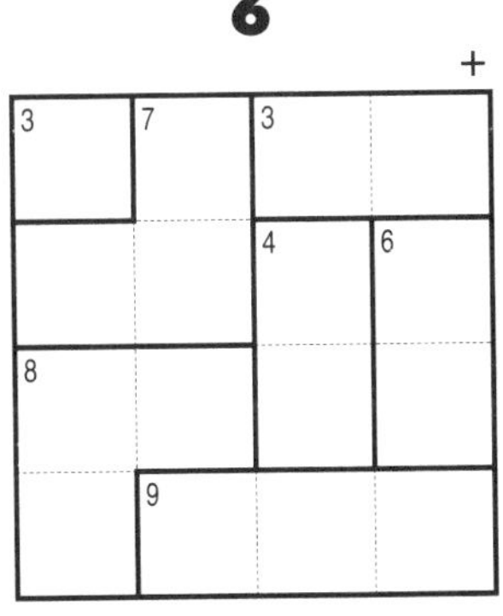

7

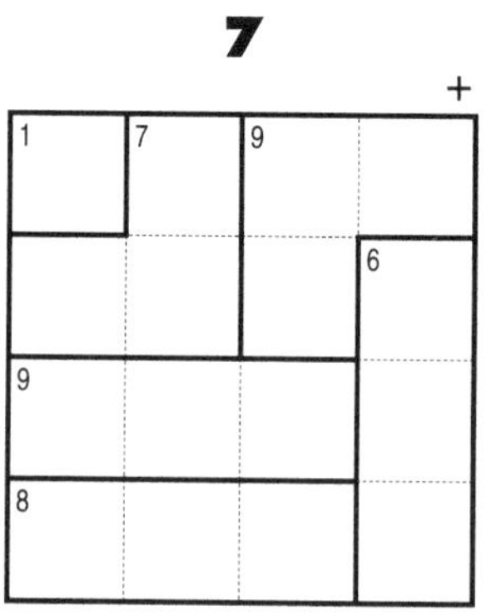

8

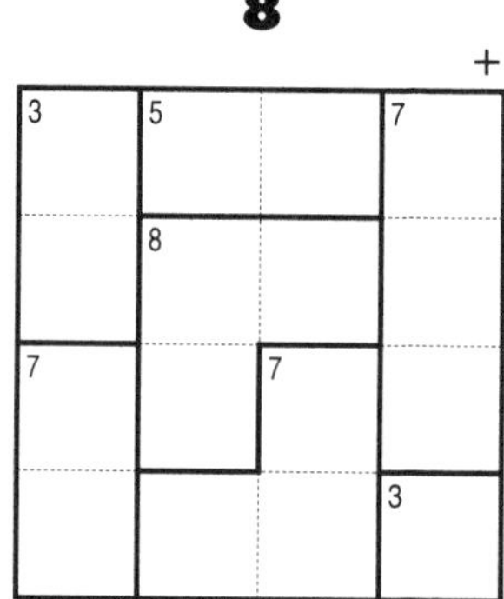

9

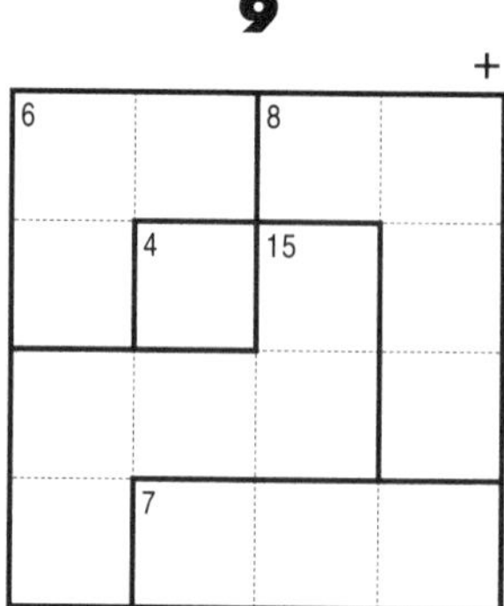

10

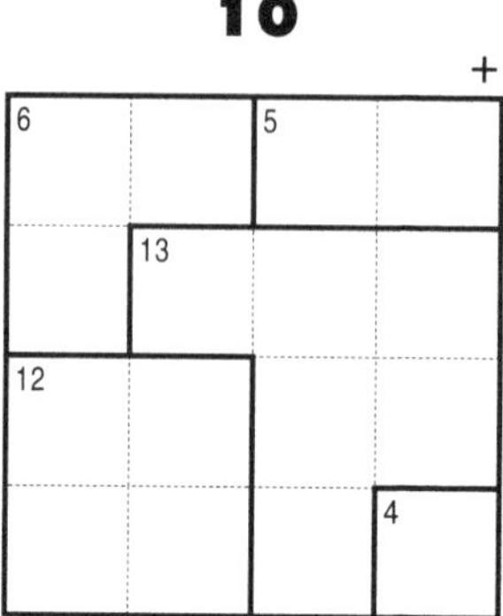

11

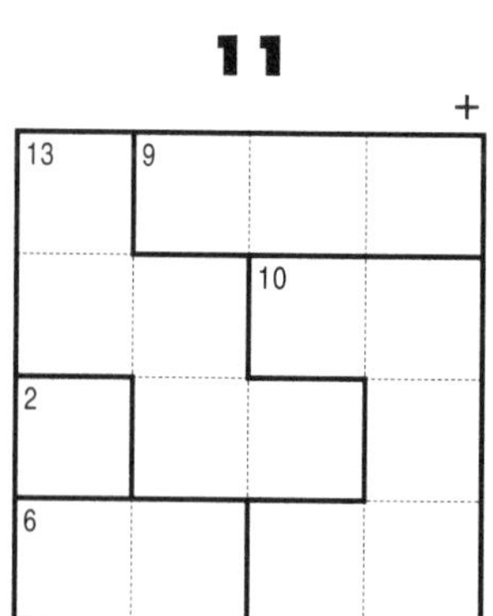

12

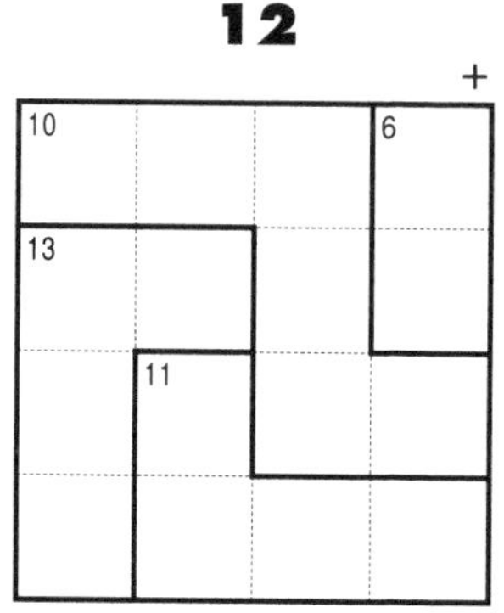

13

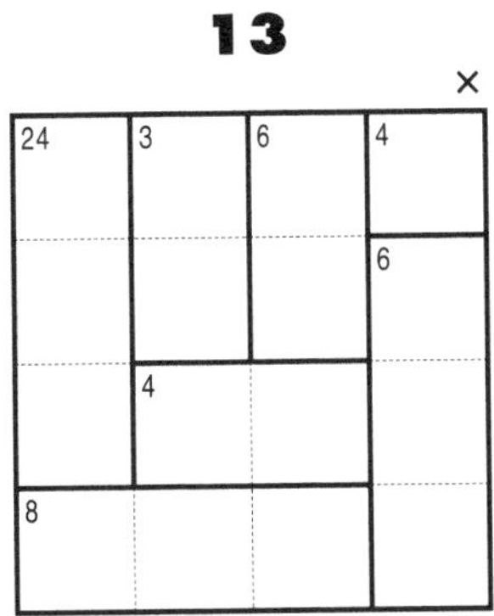

14

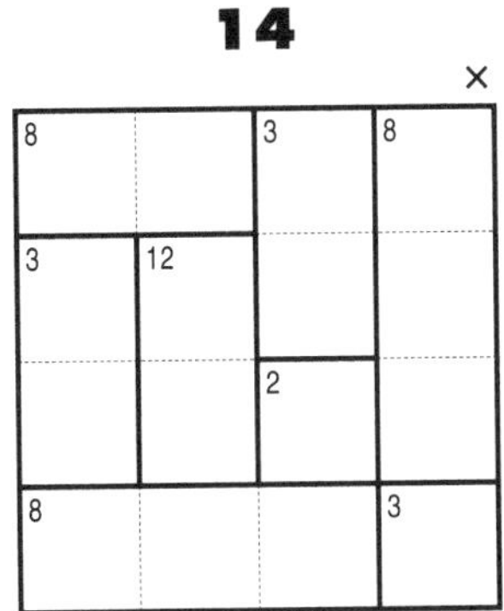

15

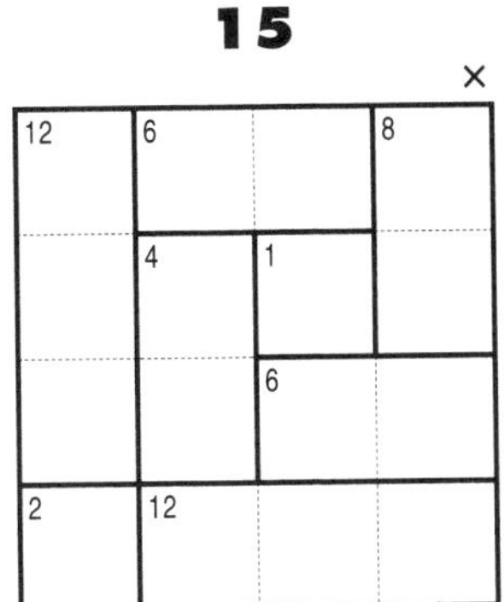

16

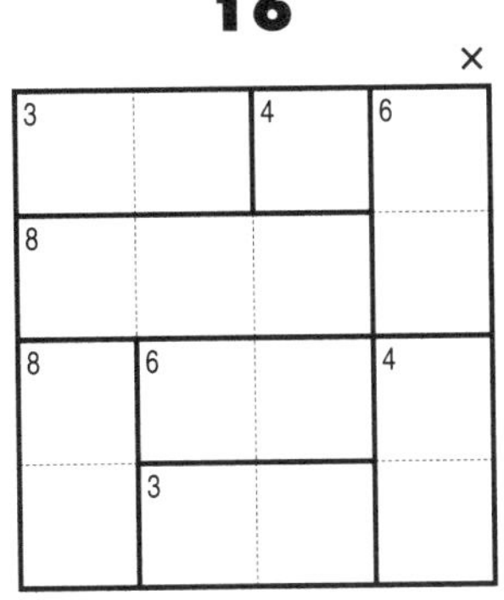

17

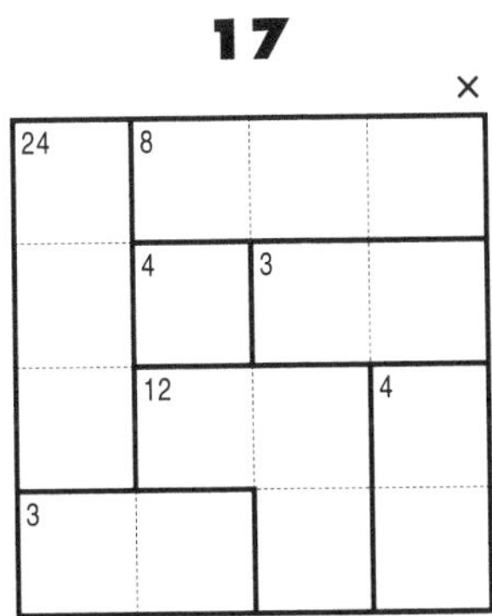

18

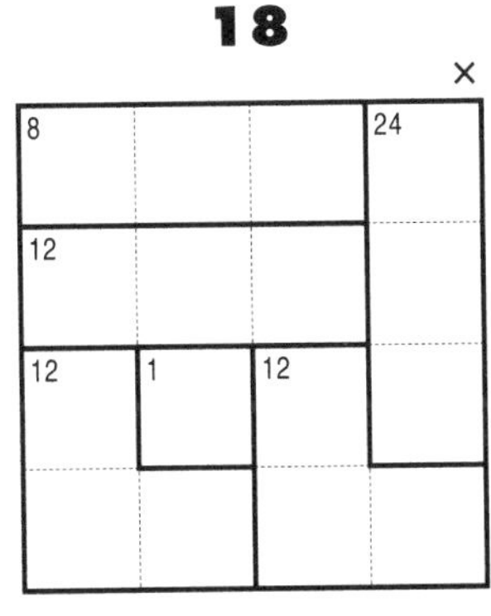

19

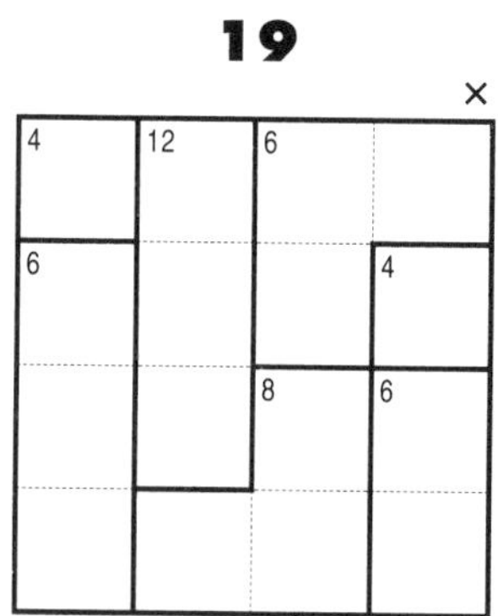

20

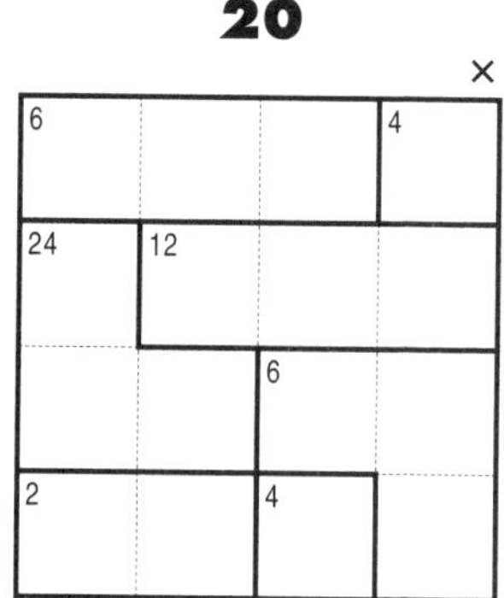

21

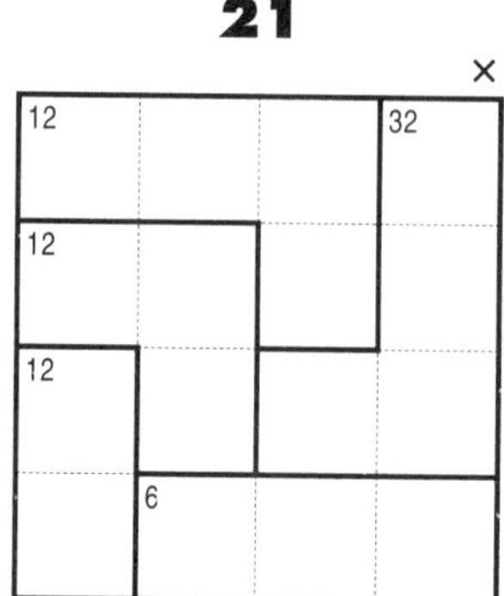

22

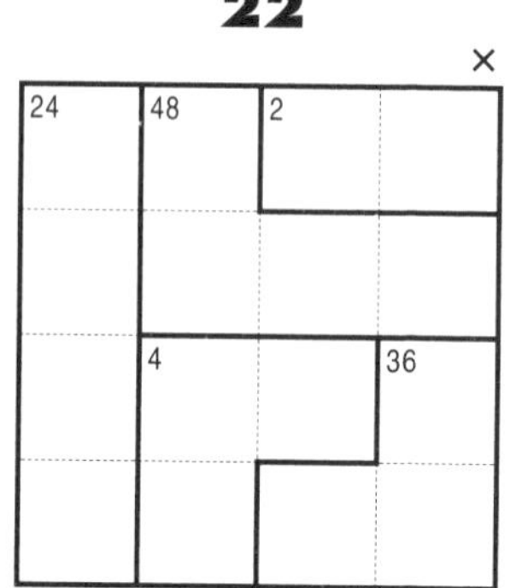

23

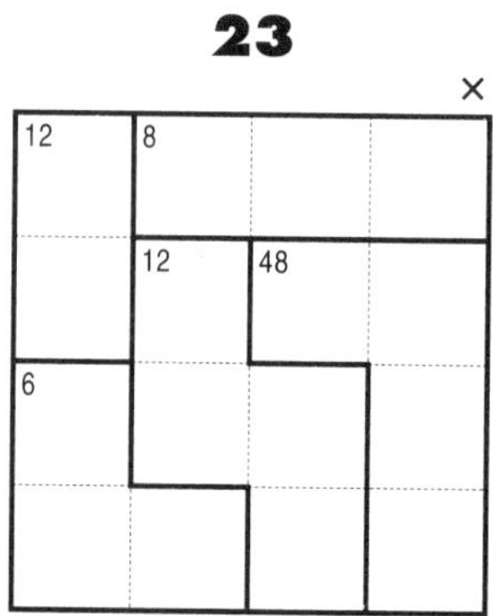

24

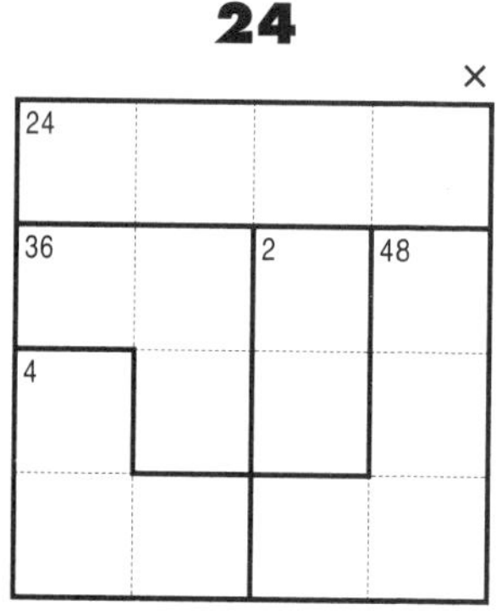

25

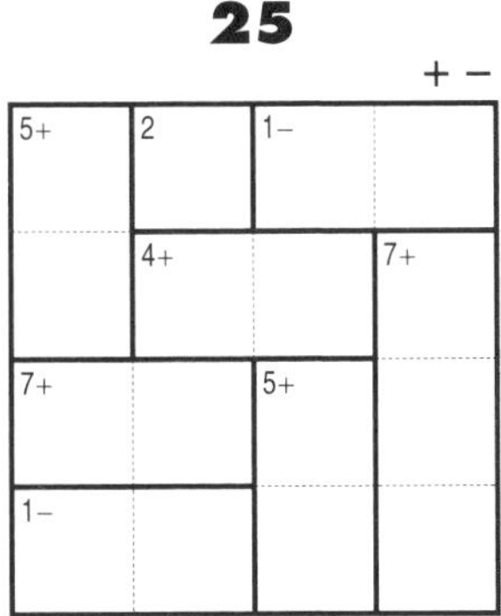

26

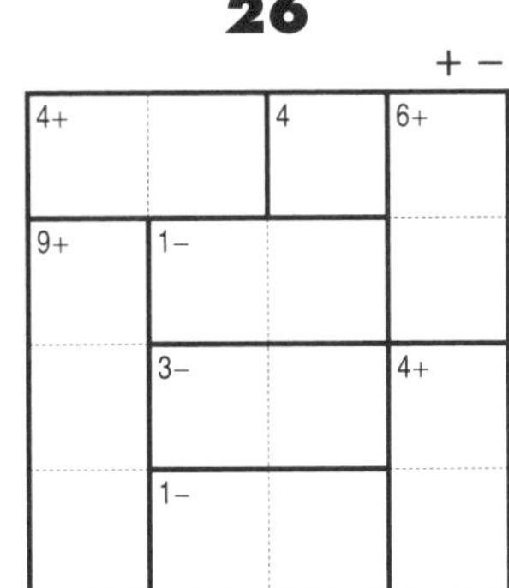

27

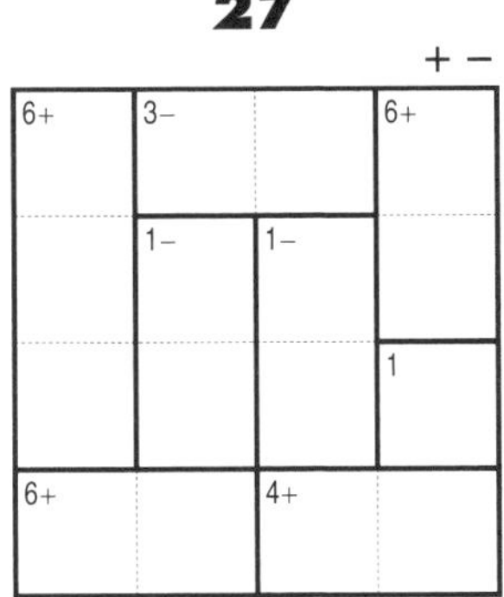

28

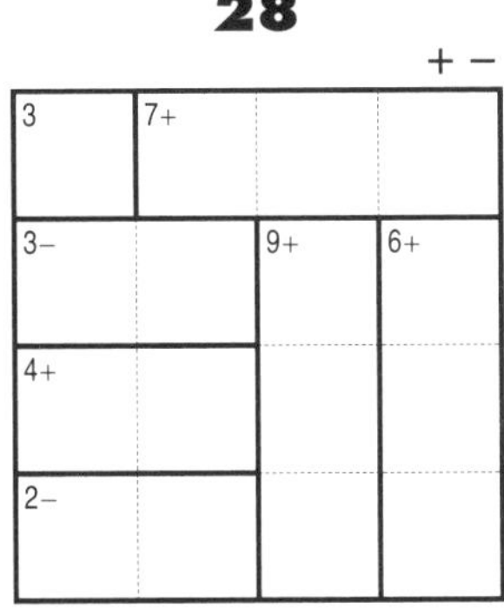

29

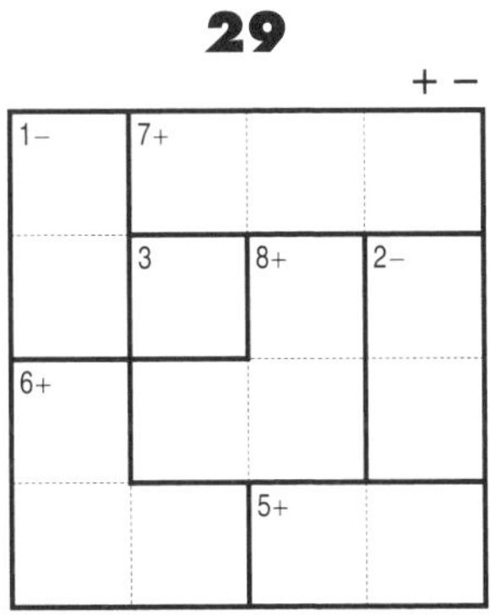

30

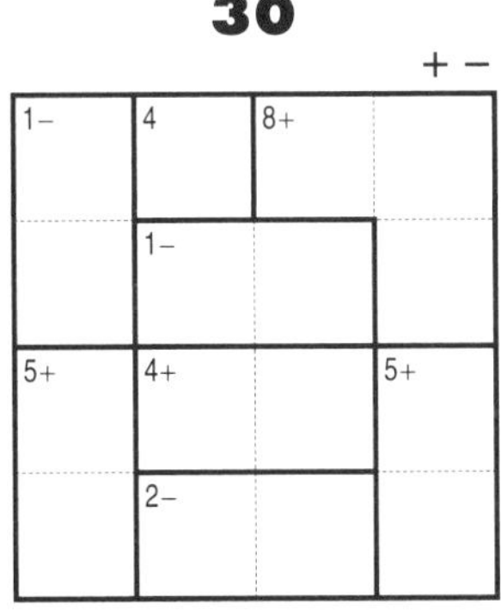

31

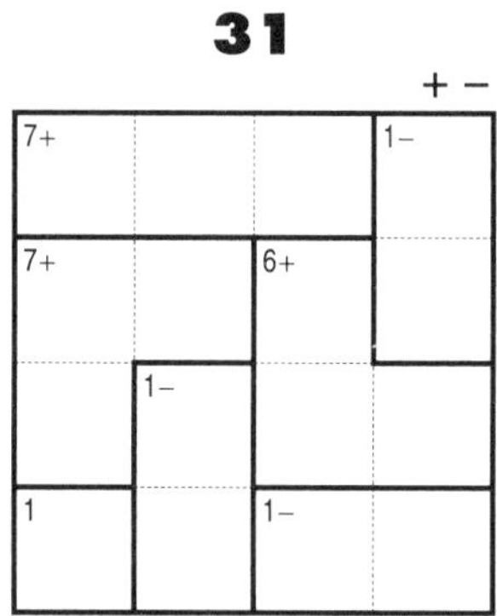

32

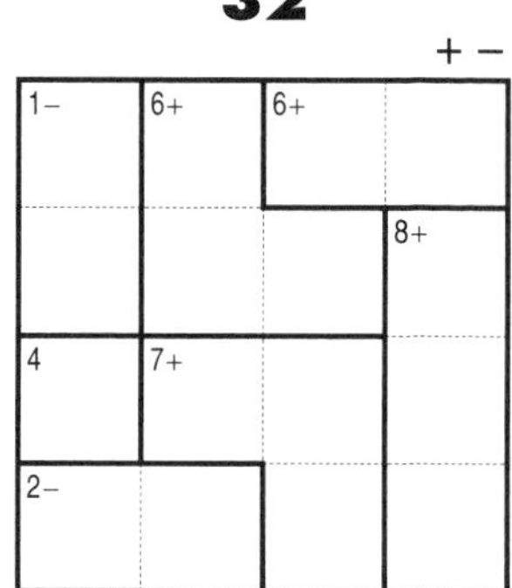

33

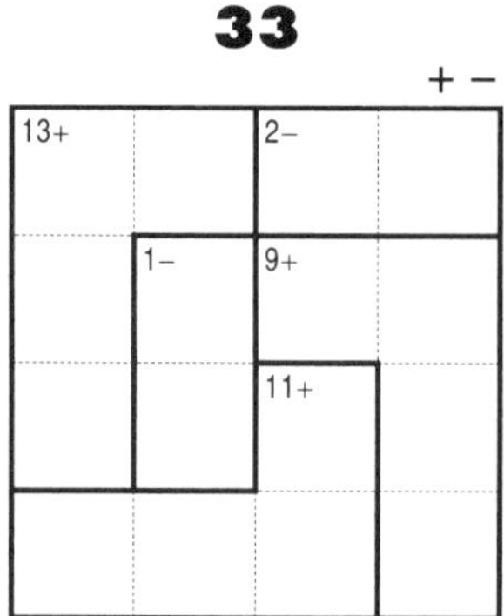

34

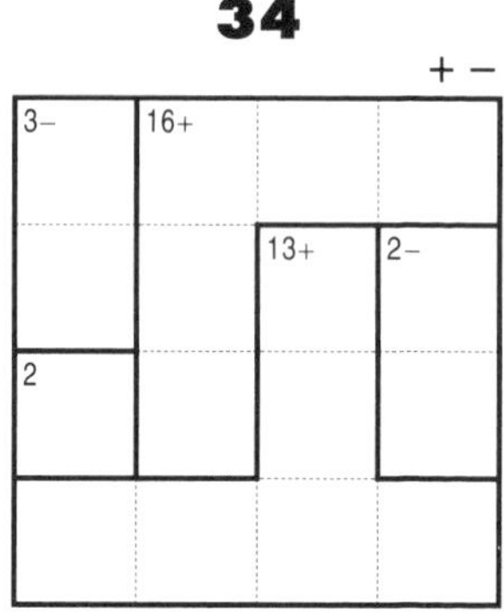

35

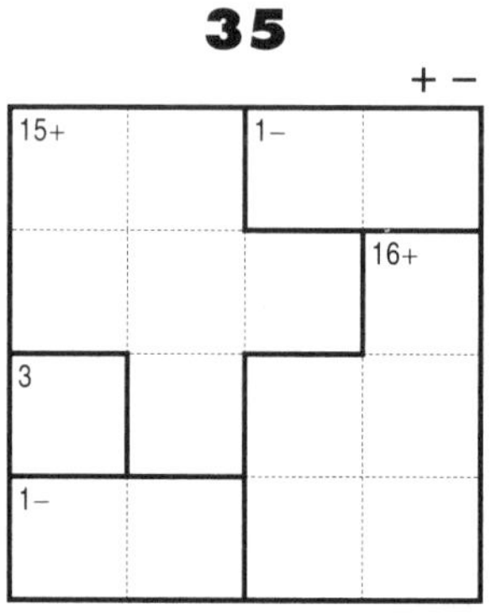

36

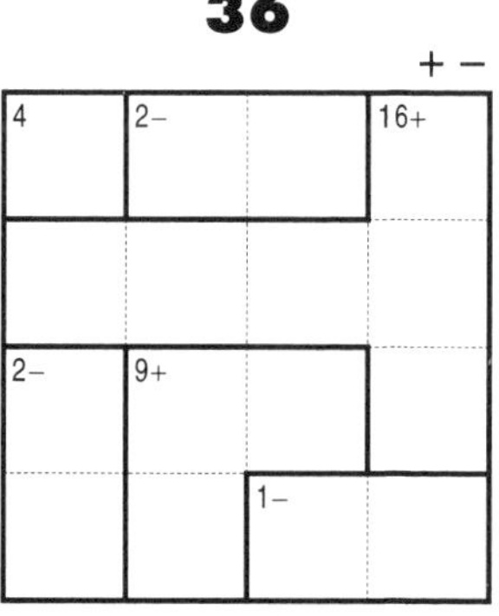

37

× ÷

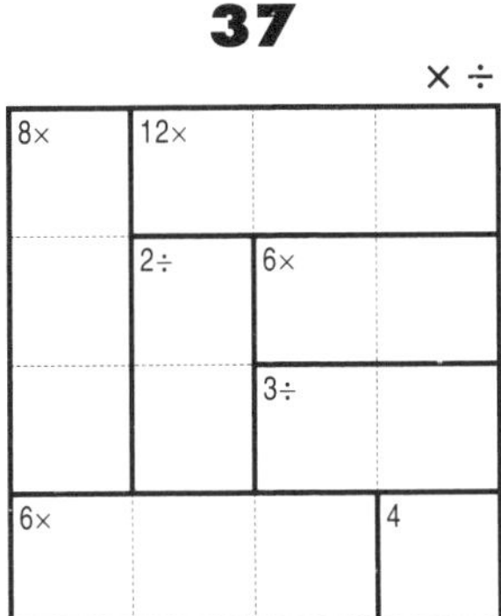

38

× ÷

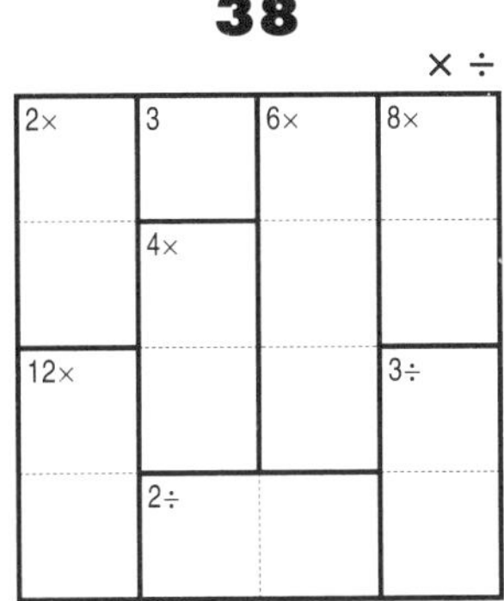

39

× ÷

12×
4÷
2÷
6×
2
12×
3×
2×

40

× ÷

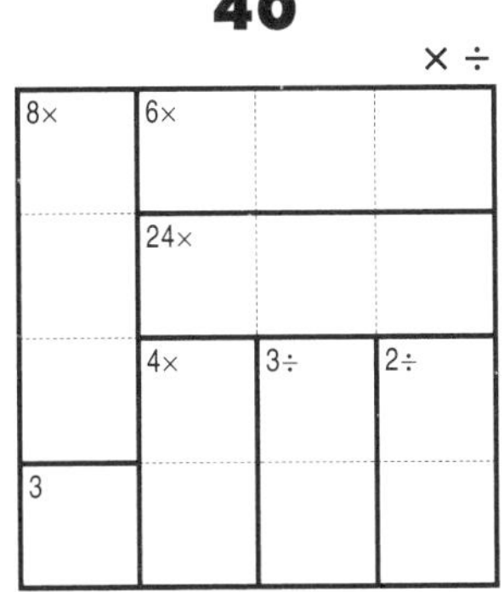

41

× ÷

4÷
6×
24×
2÷
16×
9×
2

42

× ÷

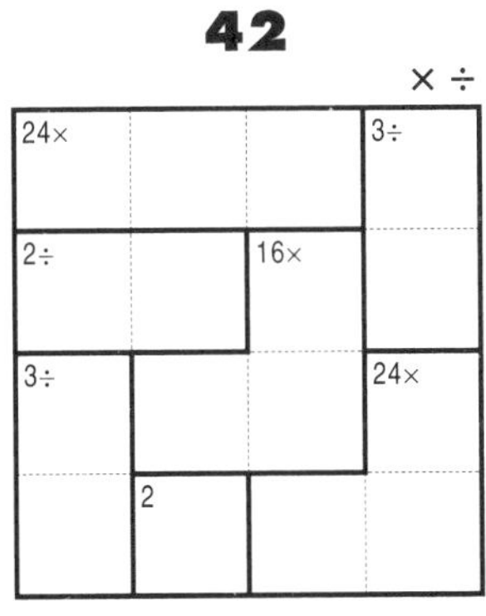

43

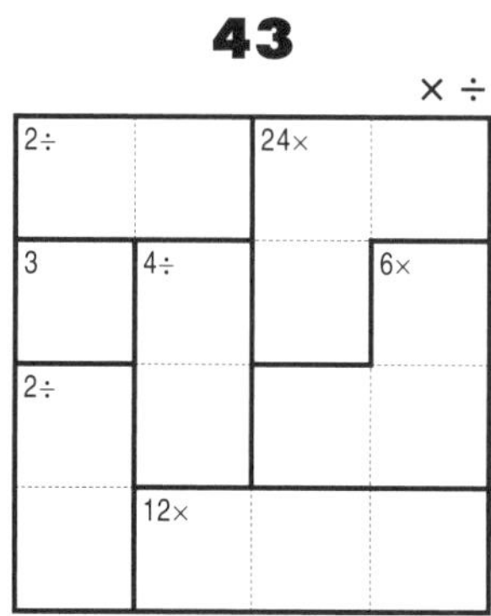

44

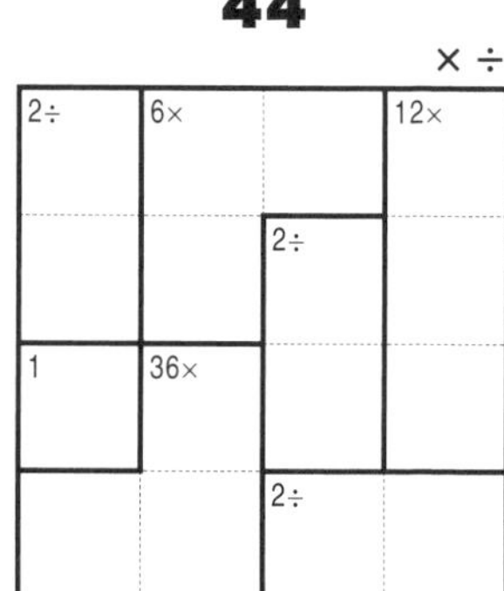

45

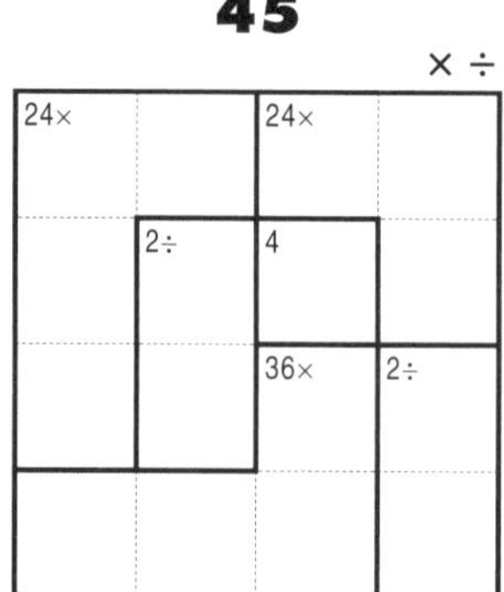

46

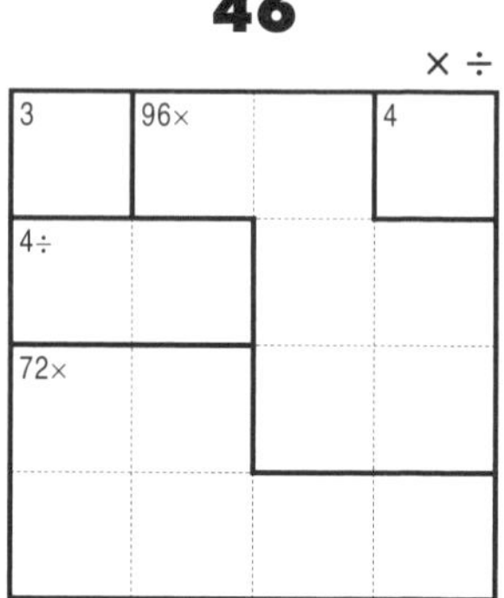

47

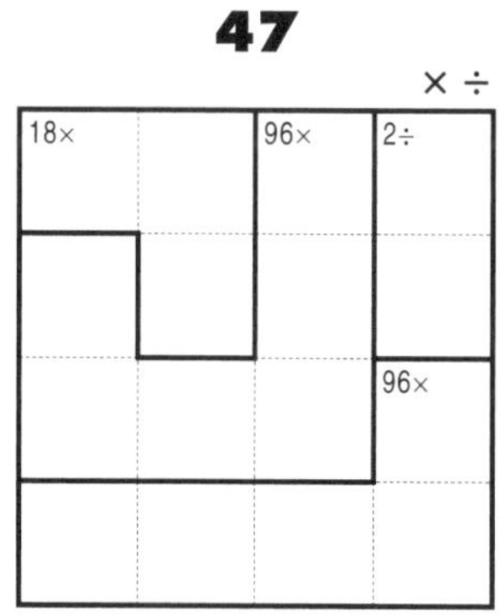

48

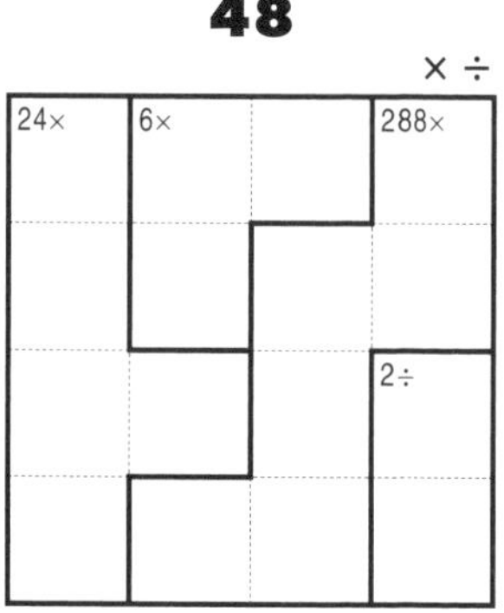

49

\+ − × ÷

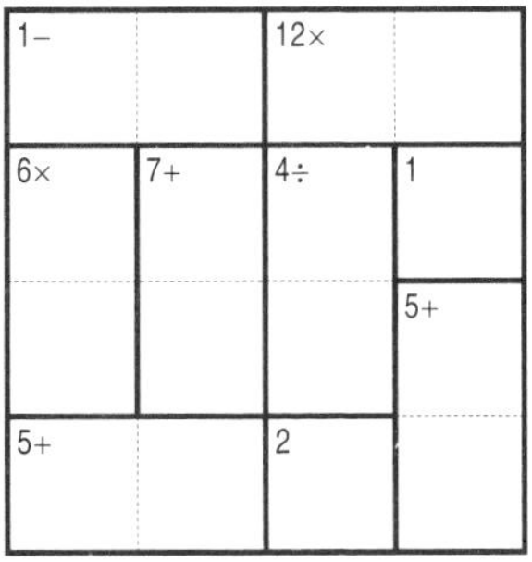

1−		12×	
6×	7+	4÷	1
			5+
5+		2	

50

\+ − × ÷

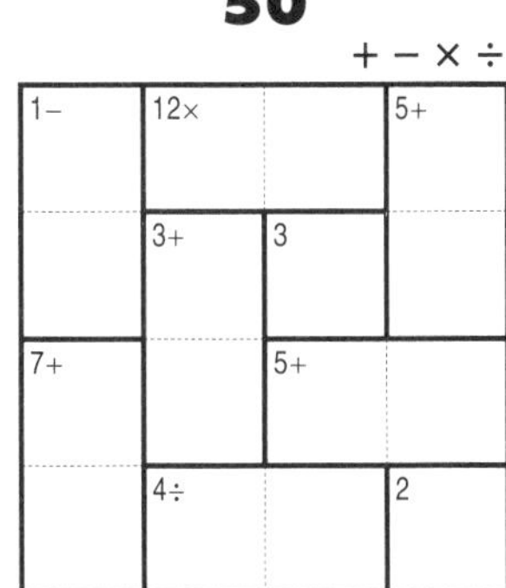

51

\+ − × ÷

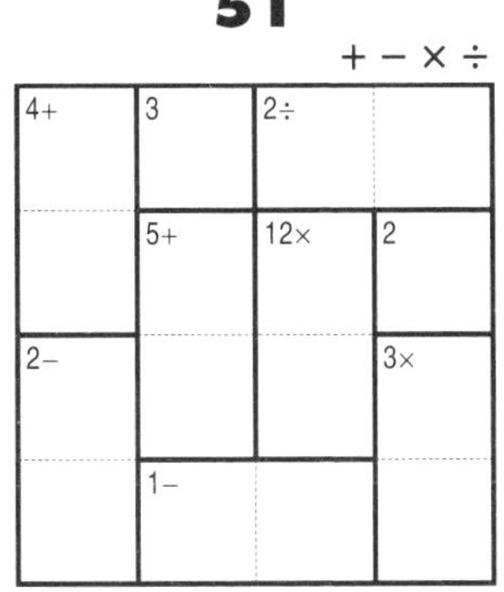

52

\+ − × ÷

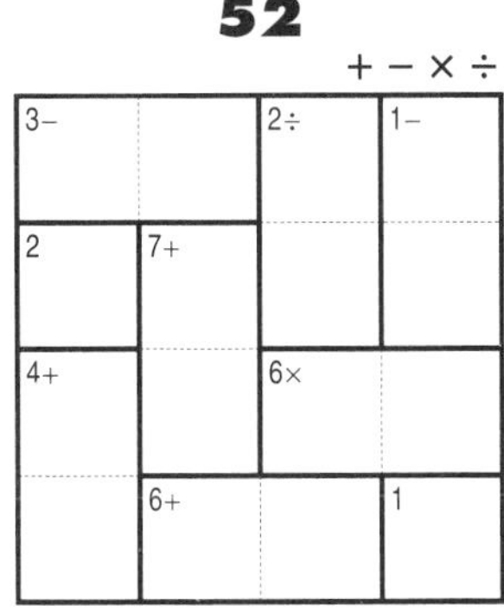

53

\+ − × ÷

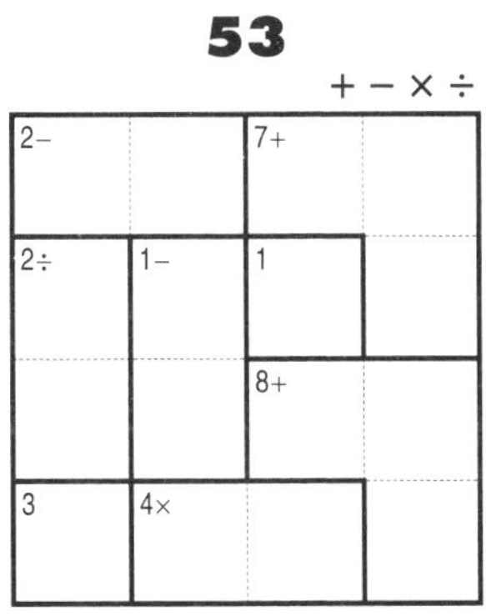

54

\+ − × ÷

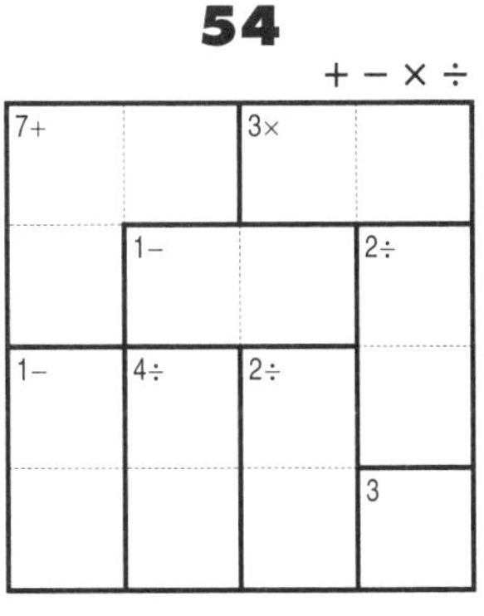

55

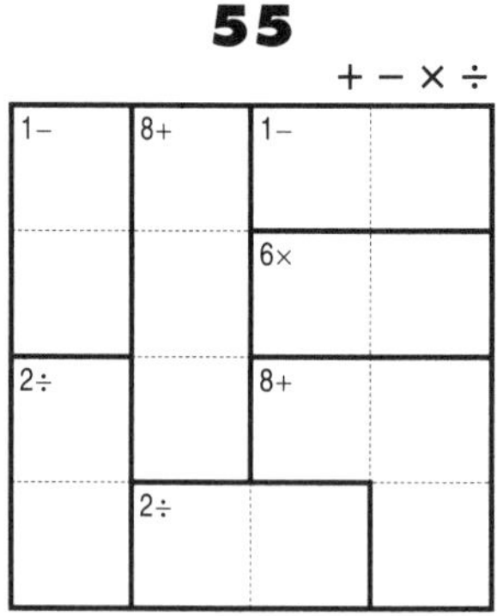

56

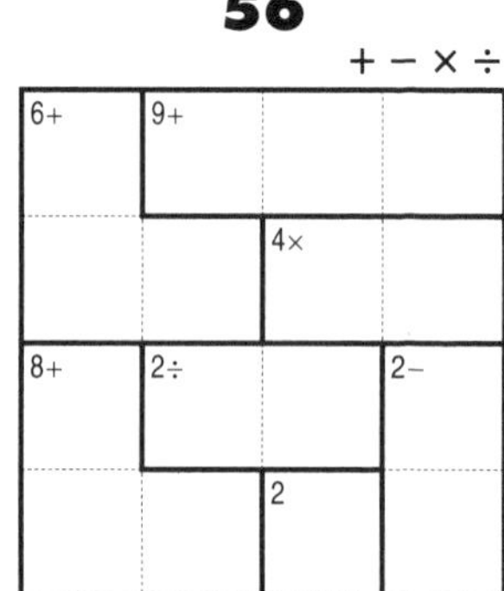

57

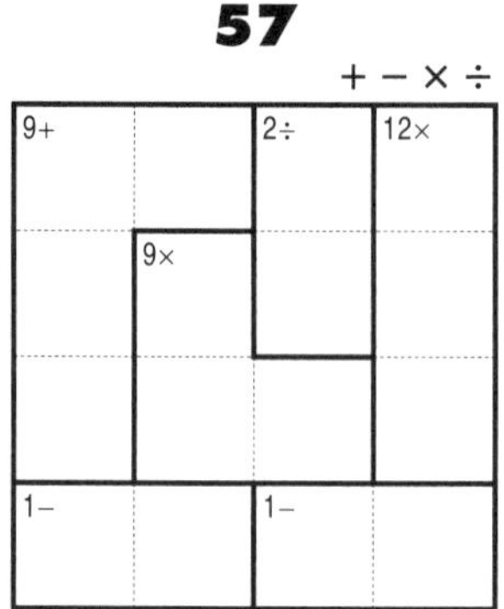

58

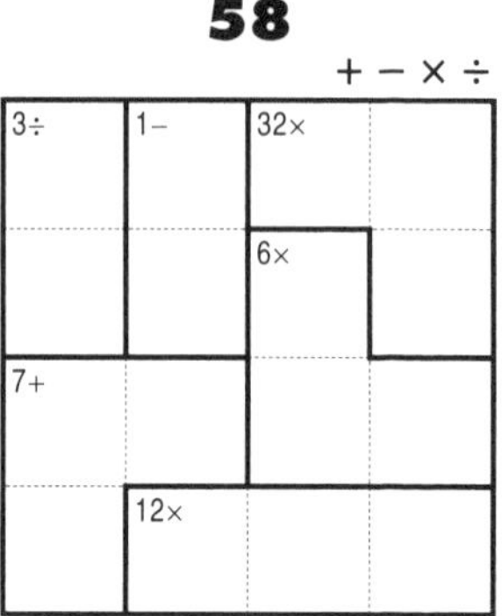

59

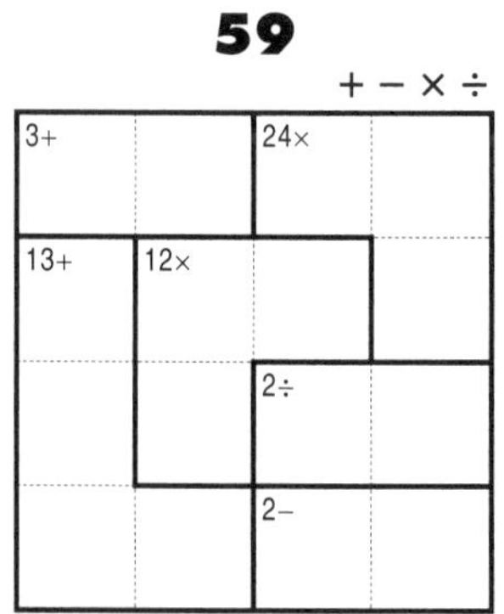

60

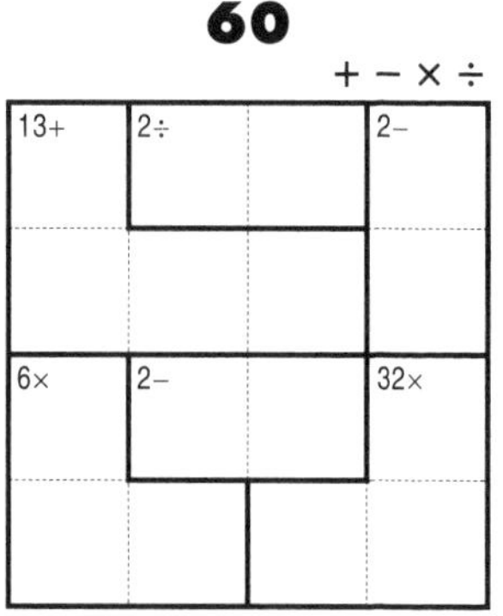

61

62

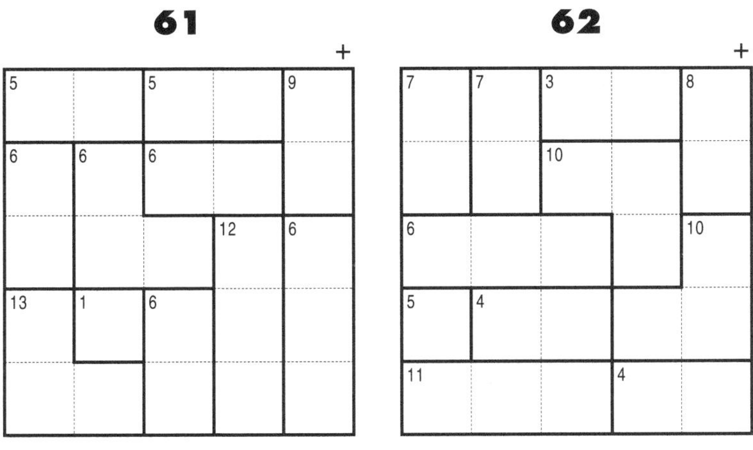

63

64

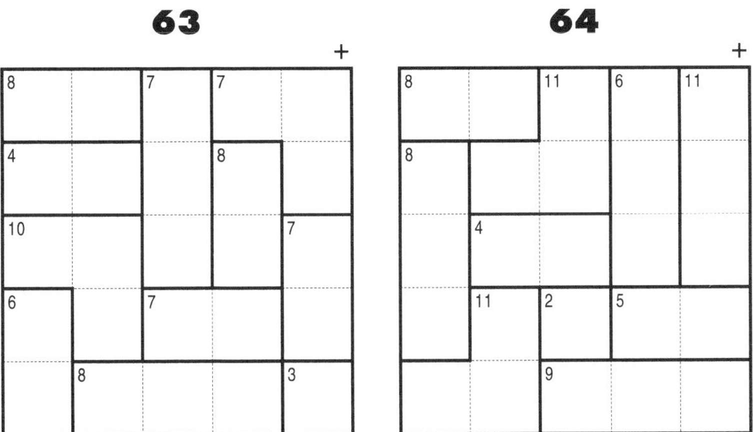

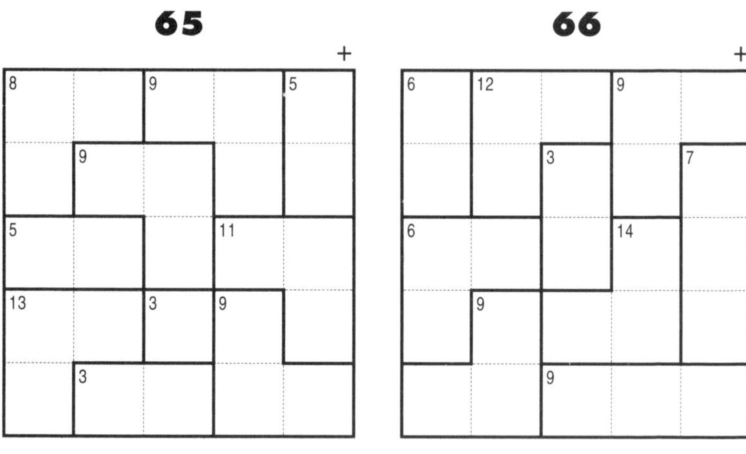

67

+

4		14	6	
7	11			8
			6	
	4			
8			7	

68

+

8			6	4
12		10		
7				11
	4	12		
			1	

69

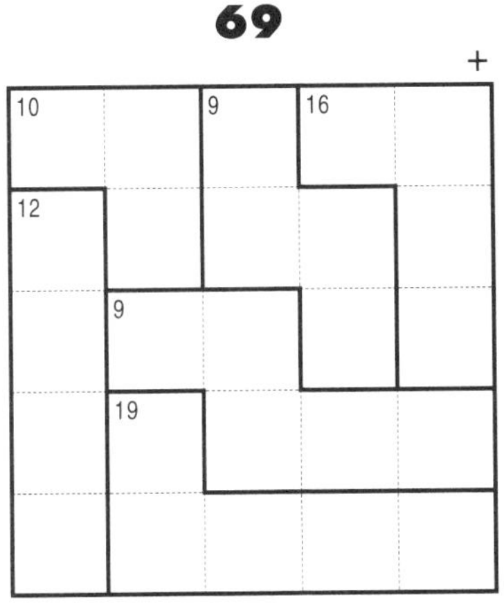

70

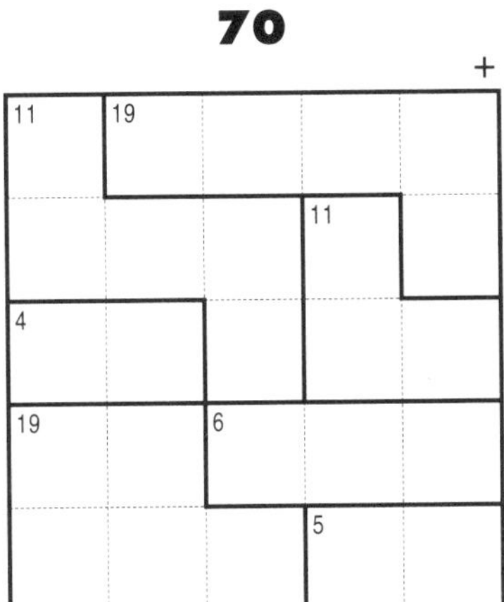

71

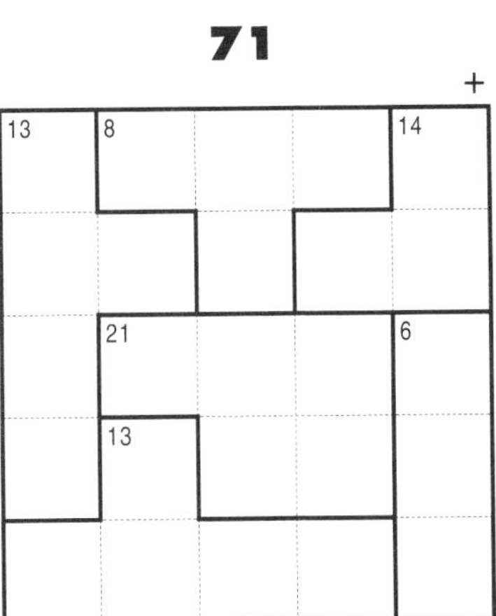

72

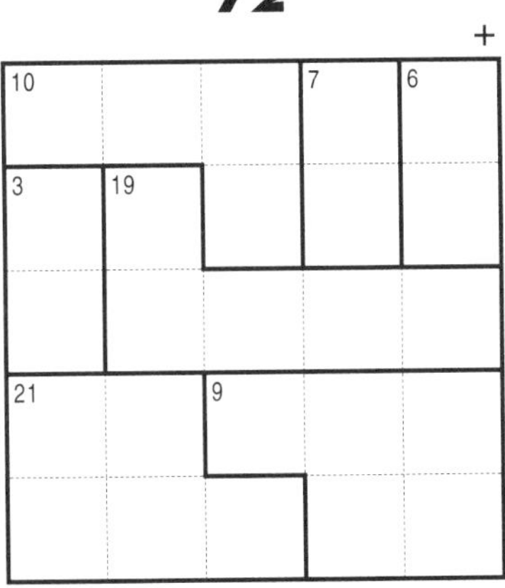

73

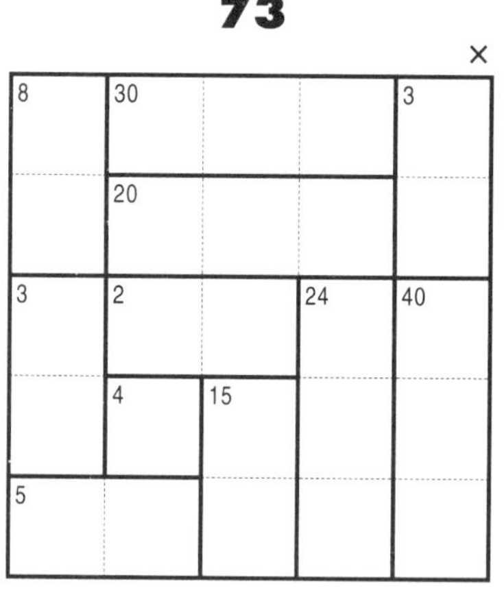

74

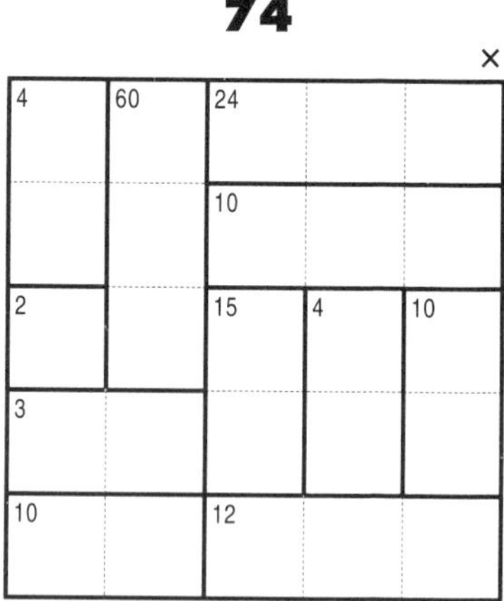

75

×

5	12		1	6
	10	8		
12		5		20
	6			
6		20		

76

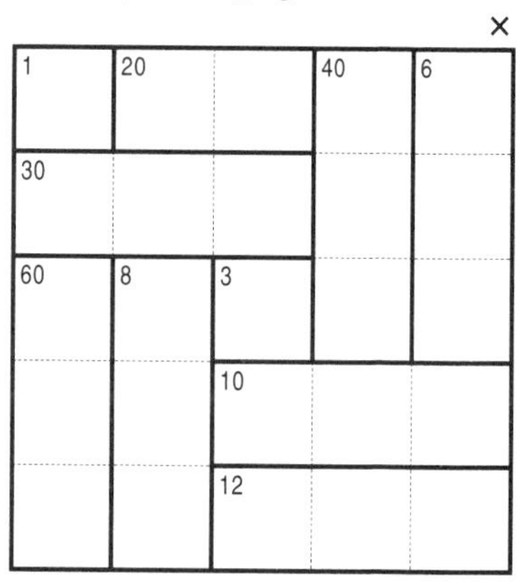

77

×

10		12		
	6	5	24	
60				15
	32		10	

78

×

10		60		6
12				
		10		8
5	12			
6			20	

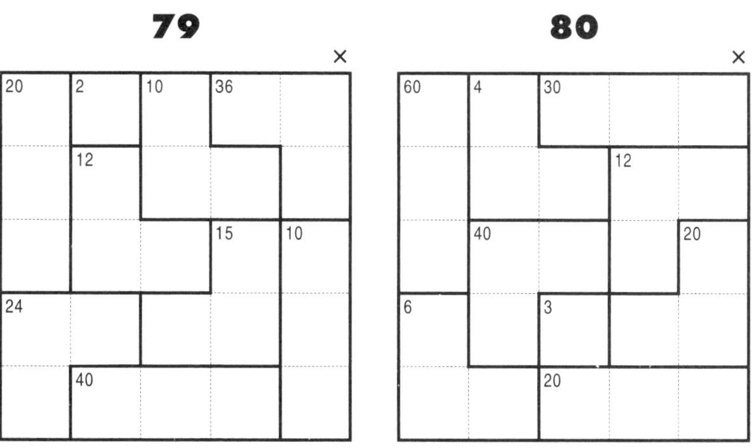

81

82

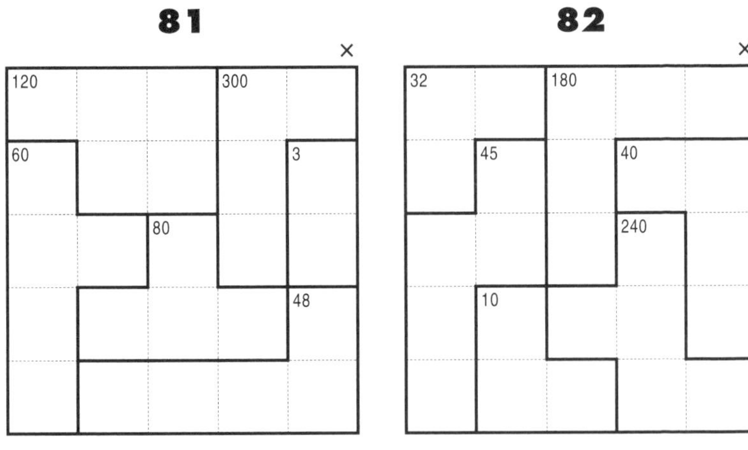
×
120
300
60
3
80
48
×
32
180
45
40
240
10

83

84

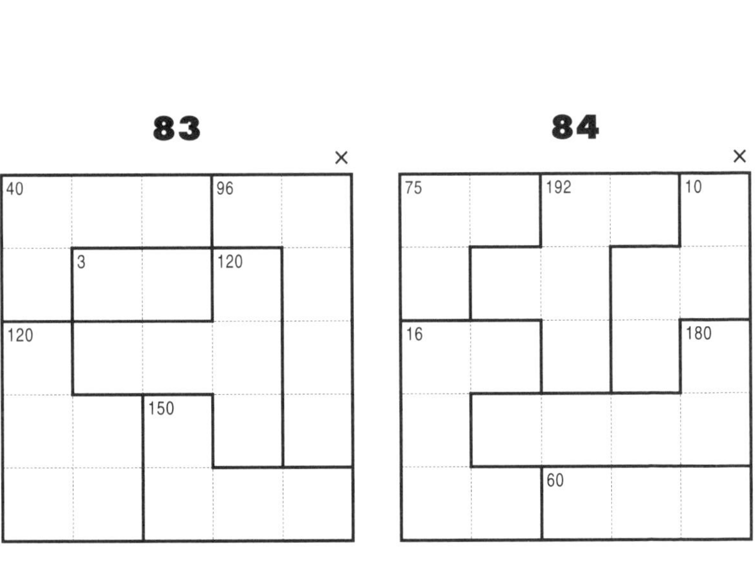
×
40
96
3
120
120
150
×
75
192
10
16
180
60

85

+ −

4−	8+			2
	6+		8+	
11+			4+	
3−		1−		9+
8+		1−		

86

+ −

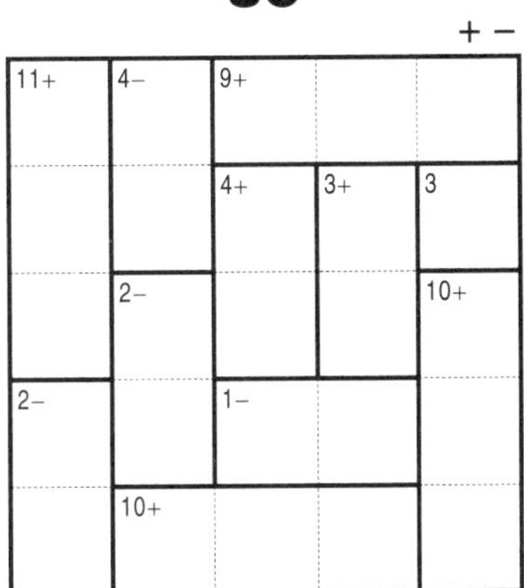

87

+ −

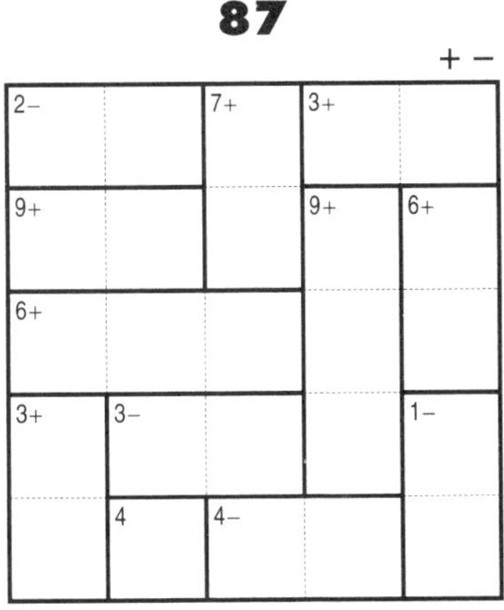

88

+ −

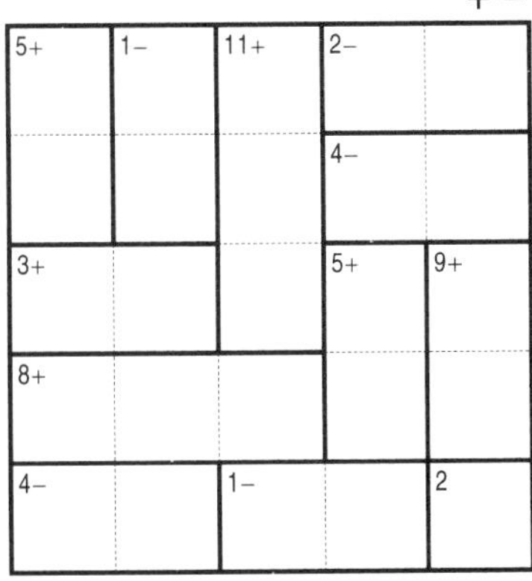

89

+ −

4	13+		3−	9+
8+				
	2−		8+	
9+		7+		
			2−	

90

+ −

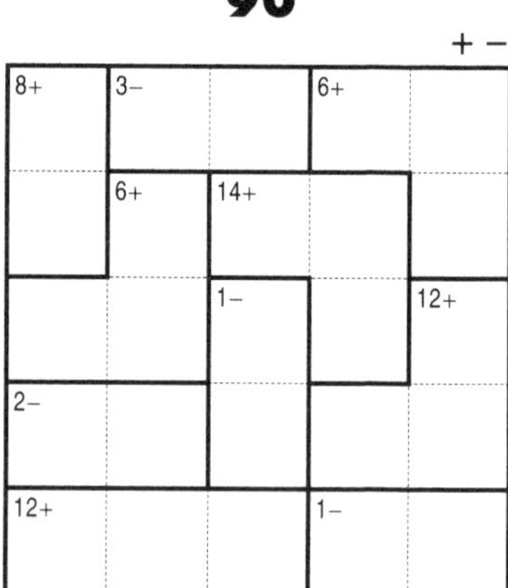

91

+ −

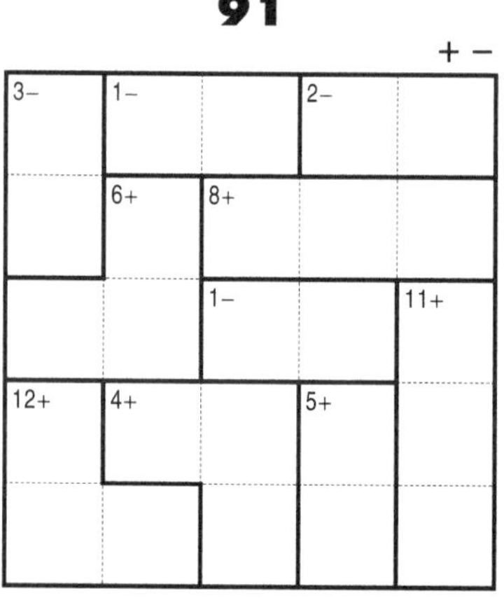

92

+ −

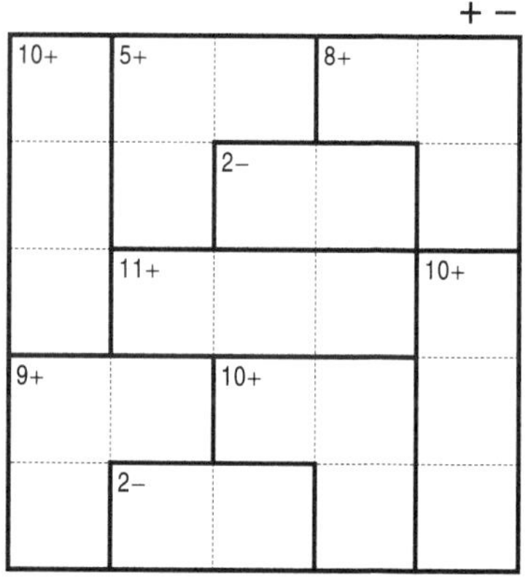

93

+ −

11+			20+	3−
8+		8+		
	17+	3+		
			1−	

94

+ −

11+			9+	
21+		3−	1−	14+
6+				
		6+		

95

+ −

1−		12+	21+	
1−				
	5+			
14+		12+		
			1−	

96

+ −

7+		8+	1−	21+
1−				
	6+			
14+			8+	1−

97

× ÷

6×			24×	40×
15×	5	40×		
	4÷			
			3÷	
2÷		15×		

98

× ÷

10×			4÷	30×
4×	20×	6×		
			3	
3	5÷		10×	4÷
24×				

99

× ÷

3×	8×			60×
	10×	20×	3÷	
2÷				
	3÷	15×		2
5		8×		

100

× ÷

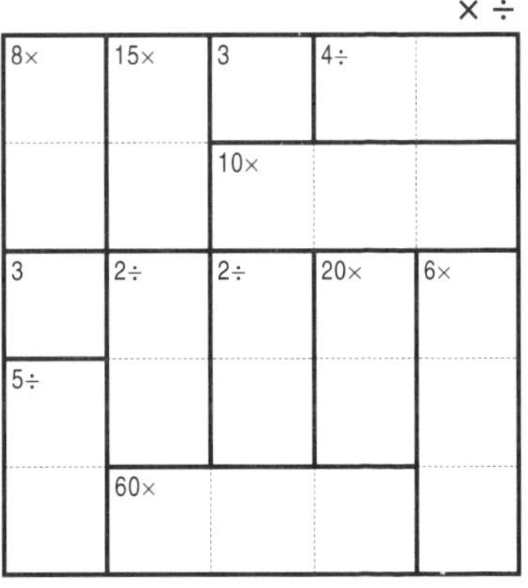

8×	15×	3	4÷	
		10×		
3	2÷	2÷	20×	6×
5÷				
	60×			

101

× ÷

20×	3	20×		12×
		5÷		
2÷			15×	
15×	24×			
			2÷	

102

× ÷

15×			16×	
2÷	60×			15×
		2÷		
5÷			12×	
2÷		15×		

103

× ÷

5÷		12×	12×	
2÷				15×
	20×			
45×		20×		2
			2÷	

104

× ÷

3÷	60×		20×	2
		20×		3÷
20×				
		6×		60×
2÷				

105

× ÷

75×			2÷	
5÷		24×		
	2÷			30×
24×		60×		

106

× ÷

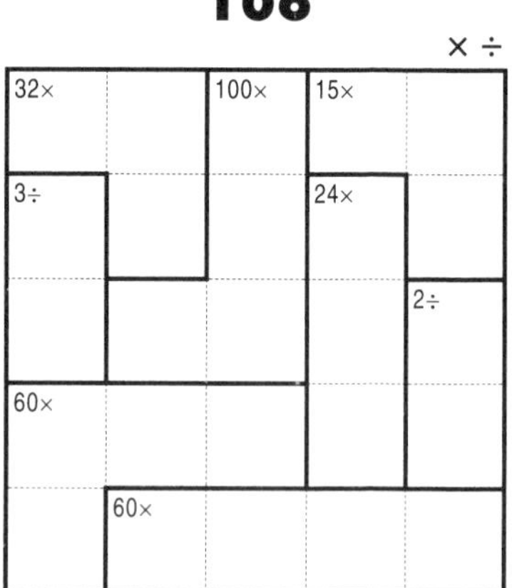

107

× ÷

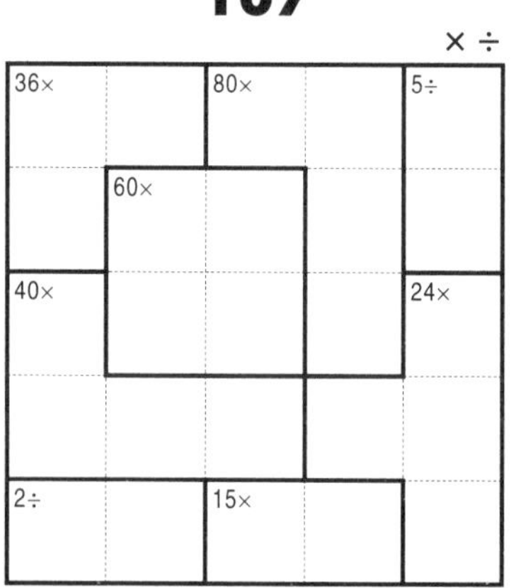

108

× ÷

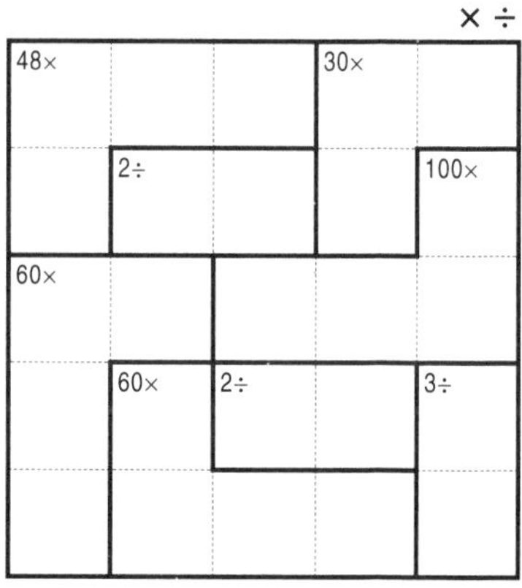

109

+ − × ÷

5÷	10+			7+
	4+	8×	2−	
2÷				
	4	9+		
6+			20×	

110

+ − × ÷

6+	11+	2−		4÷
		12×		
		4−		10+
1−	6×		1	
	7+			

111

+ − × ÷

8×	5	5+		5÷
	8+			
2×		8+		9+
1−		1−	9+	
5÷				

112

+ − × ÷

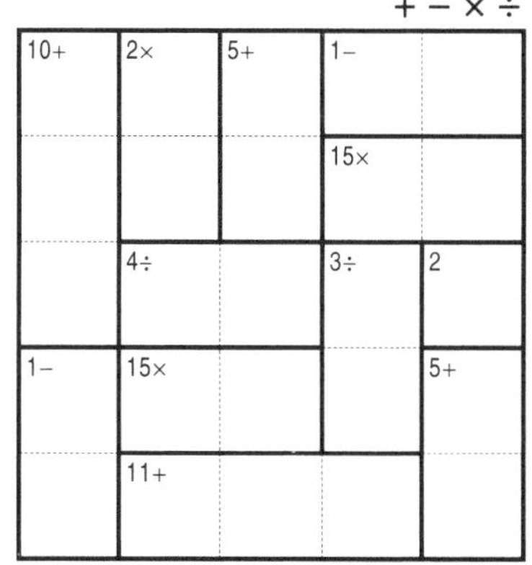

10+	2×	5+	1−	
			15×	
	4÷		3÷	2
1−	15×			5+
	11+			

113

+ − × ÷

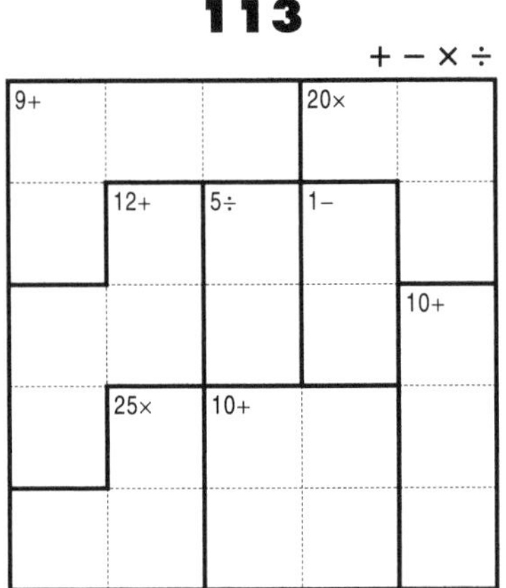

114

+ − × ÷

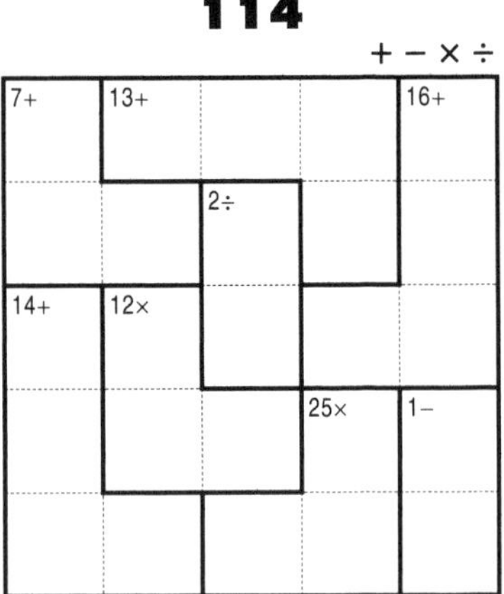

115

+ − × ÷

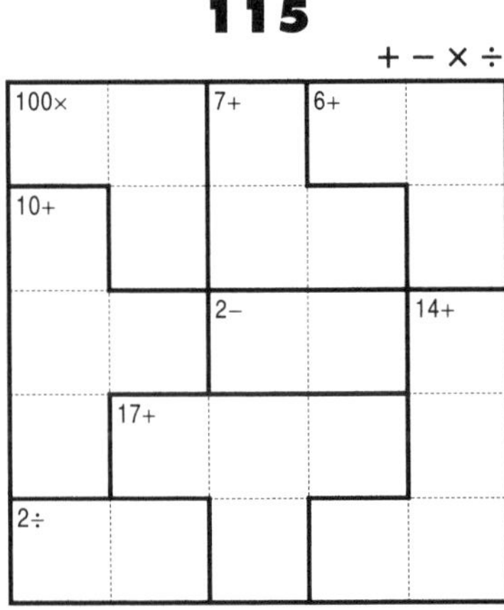

116

+ − × ÷

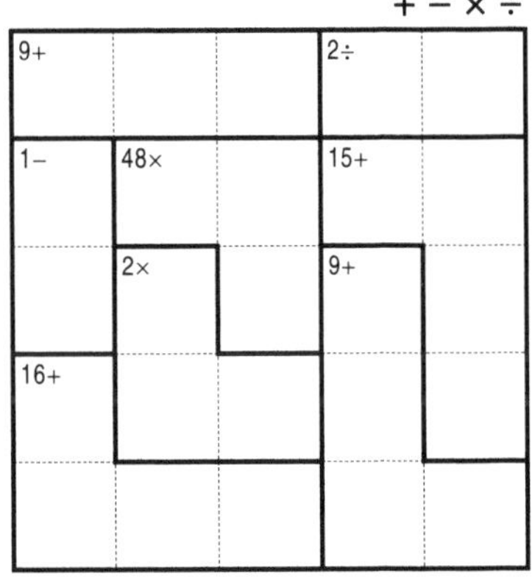

117

+ − × ÷

2− 12+
60×
32× 21+ 3÷
2−
2÷

118

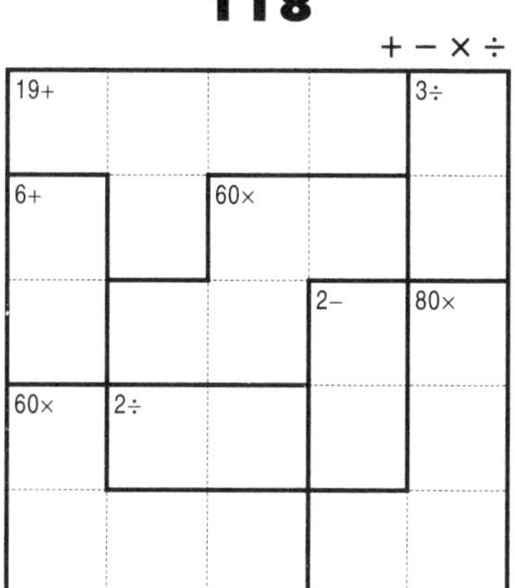

119

+ − × ÷

3÷ 40×
9+ 12×
21+ 2− 60×
4÷

120

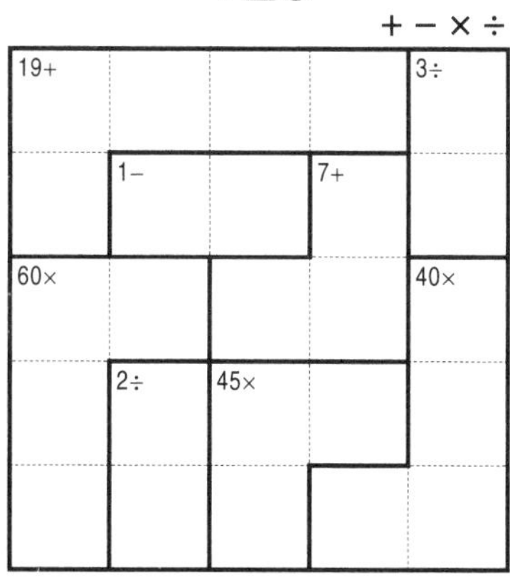

121

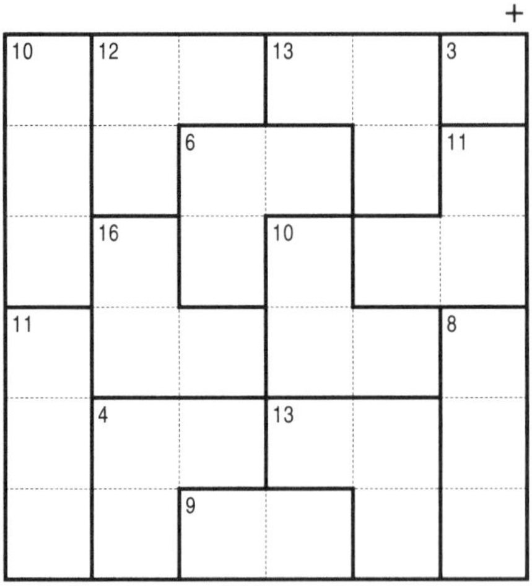

+

122

+

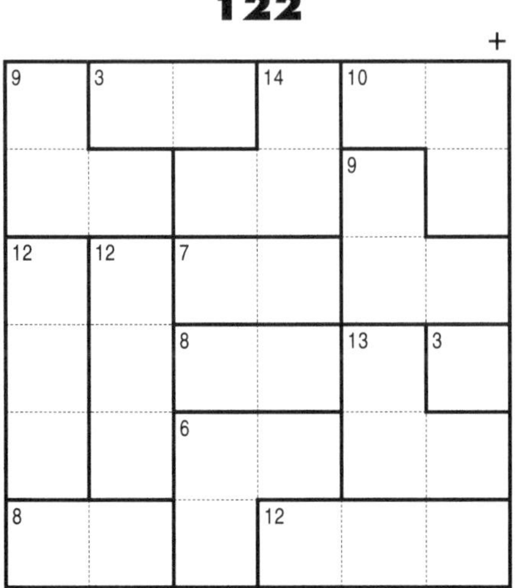

123

+

10		12			12
11		8			
		6	9		
9	5		13		5
	12			14	

124

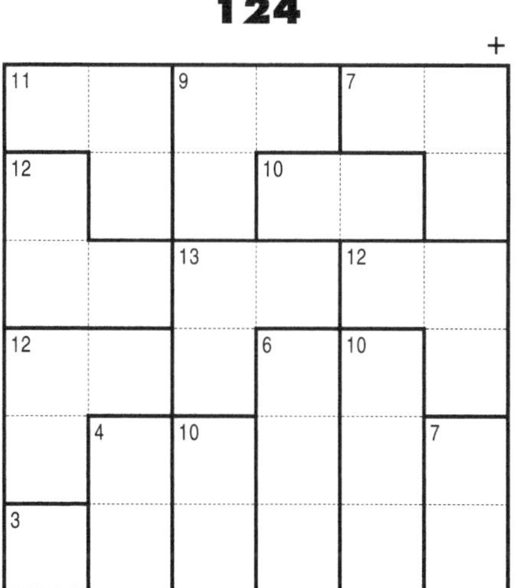

125

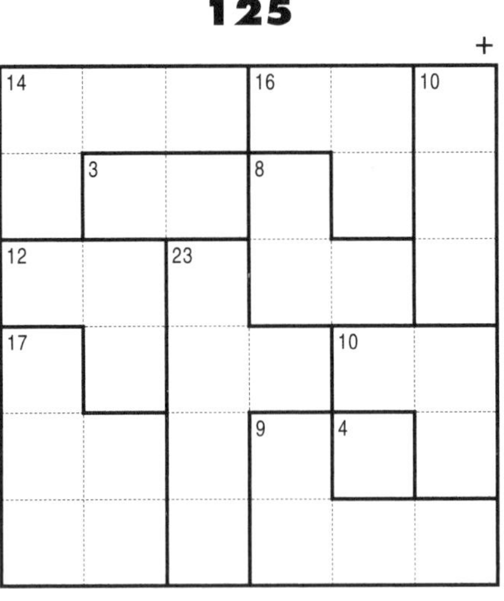

126

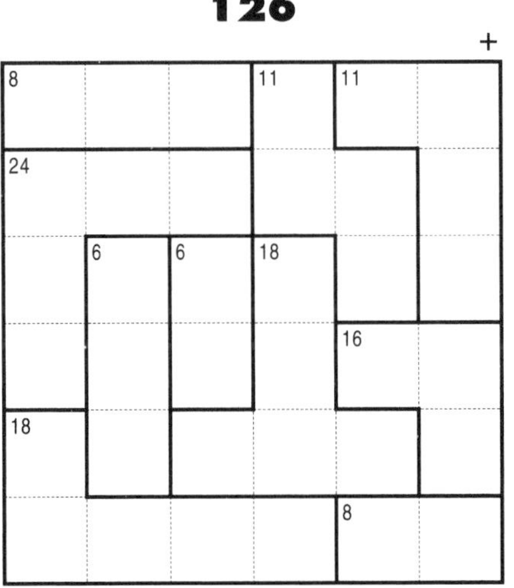

127

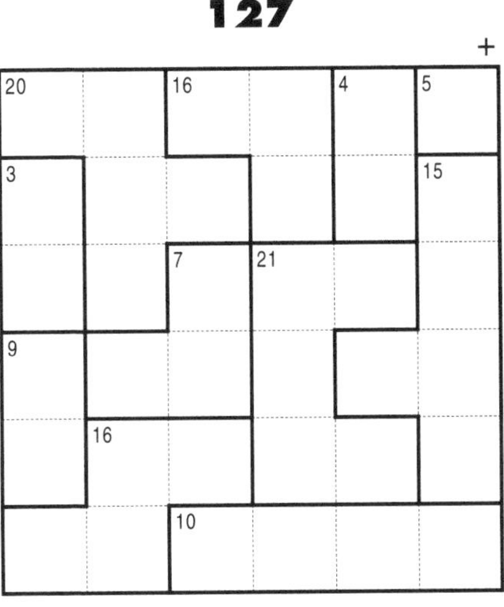

128

+

10			5		10
22	8	21			
		7			
			12	22	
4	5				

129

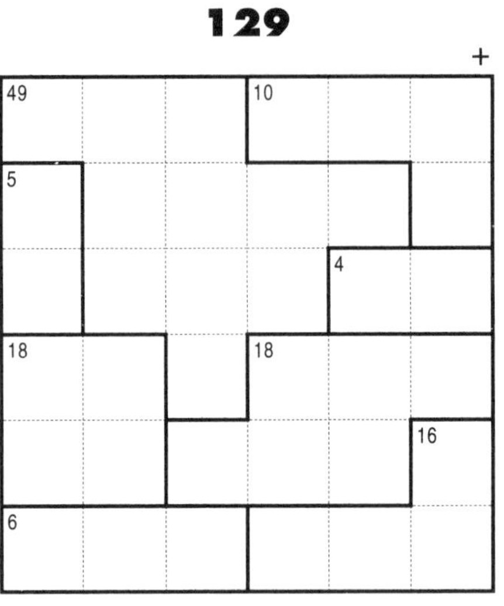

130

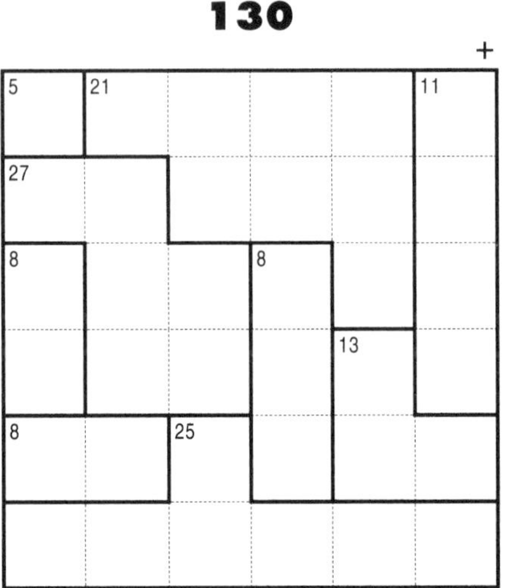

131

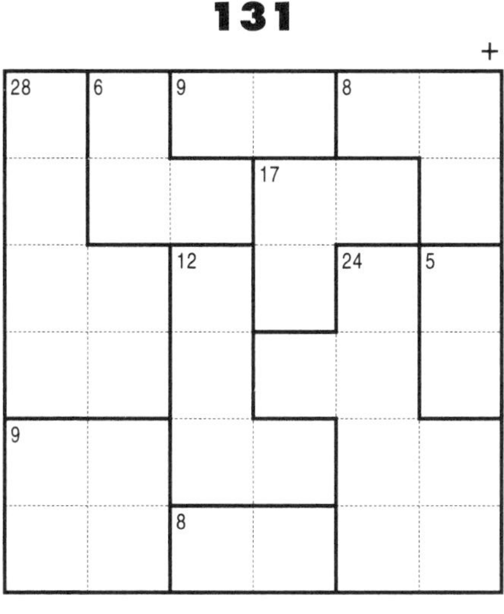

132

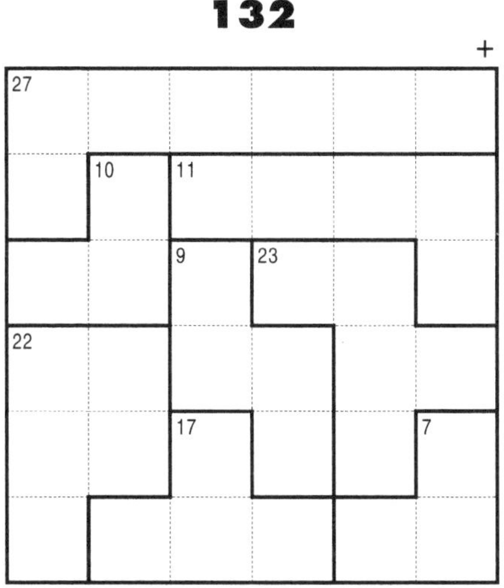

133

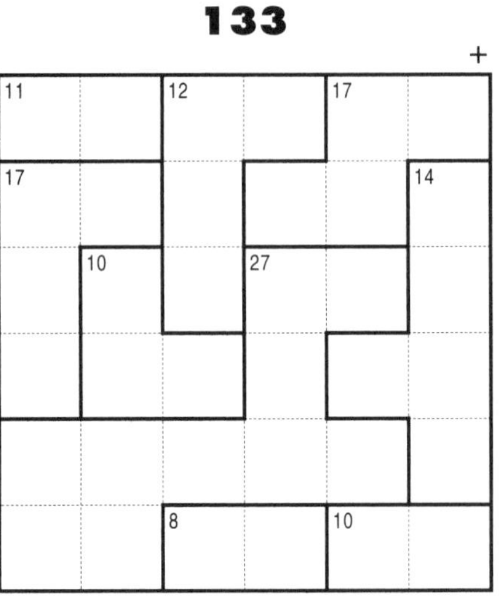

134

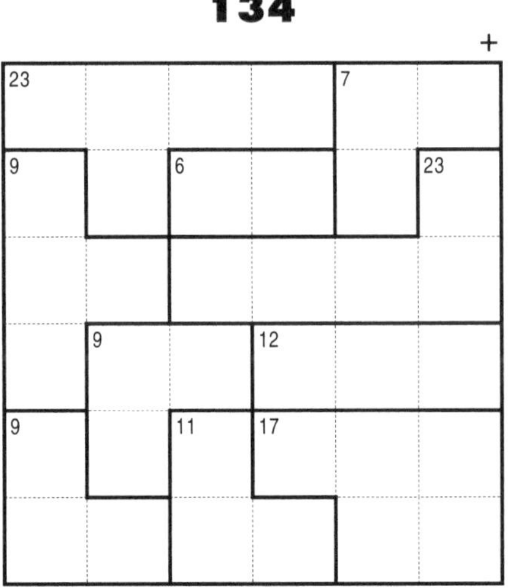

135

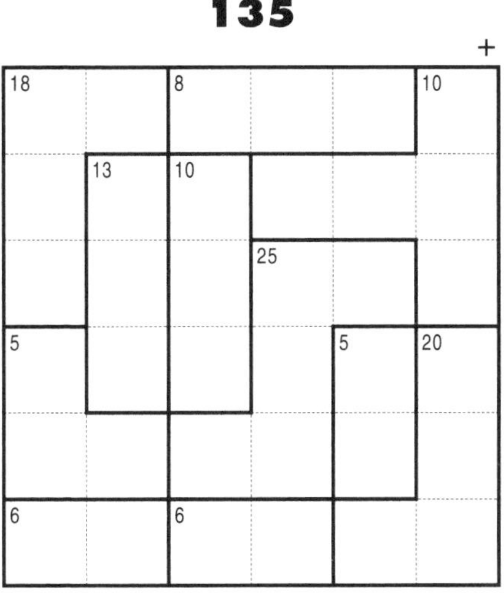

136

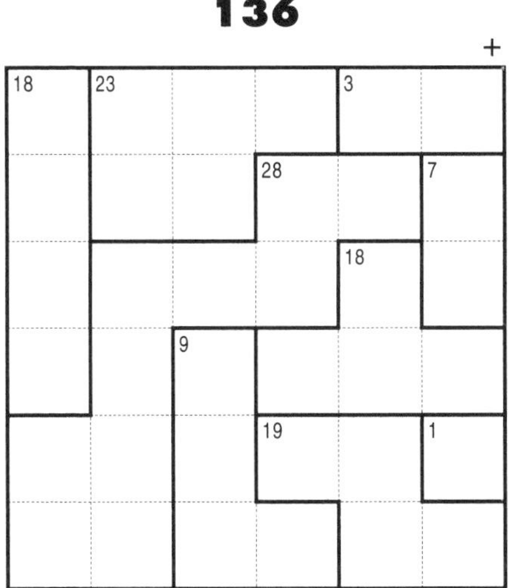

137

×

96 3 50
10 36
12 10 108
12
36 5 120 8

138

×

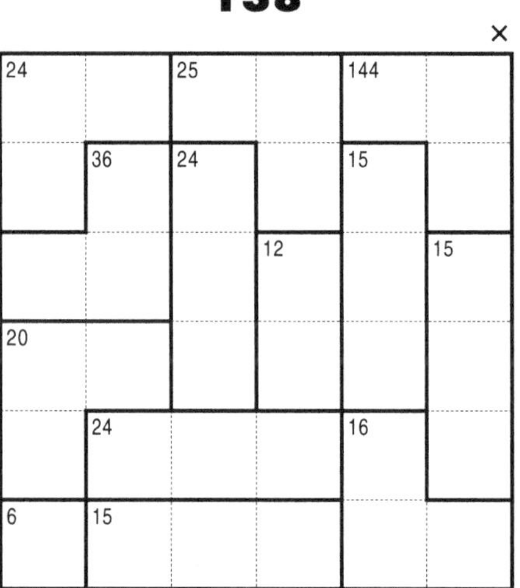

139

×

12			60		
36	30		24		30
	80				
			2	3	24
15				60	
24					

140

×

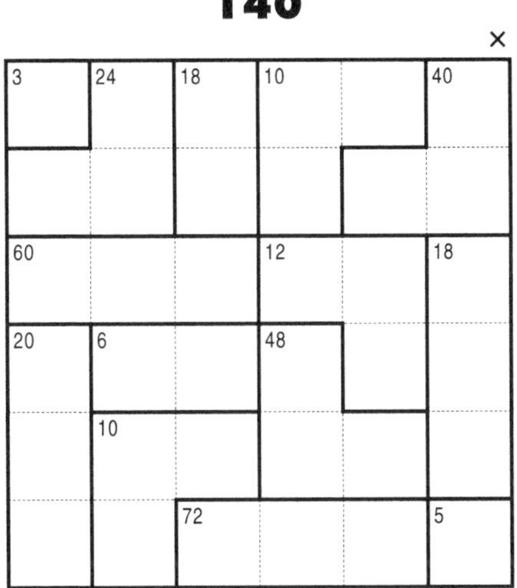

141

×

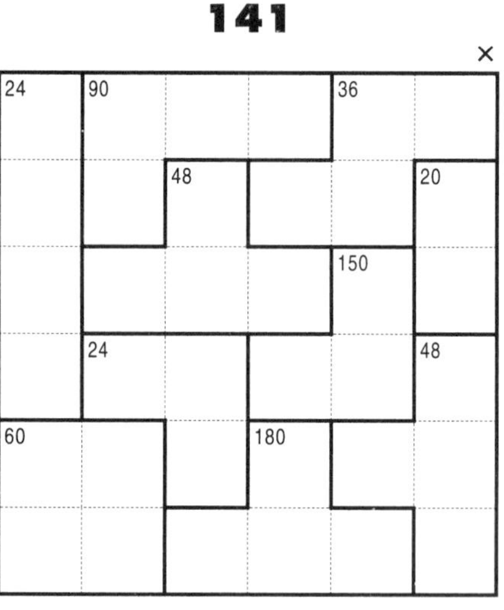

142

×

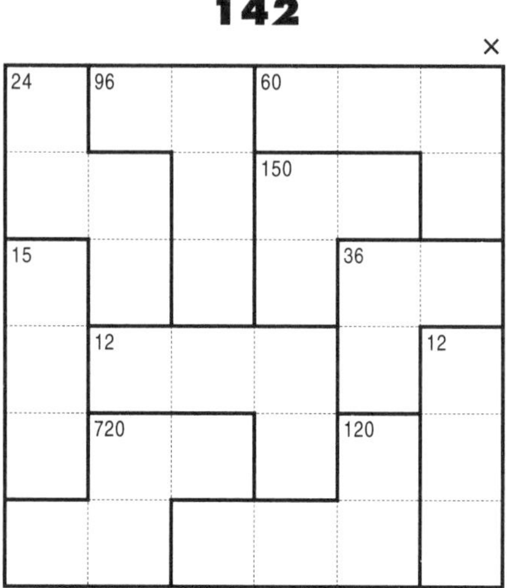

143

×

120 180 120 20

2 12 72

72

120 180

144

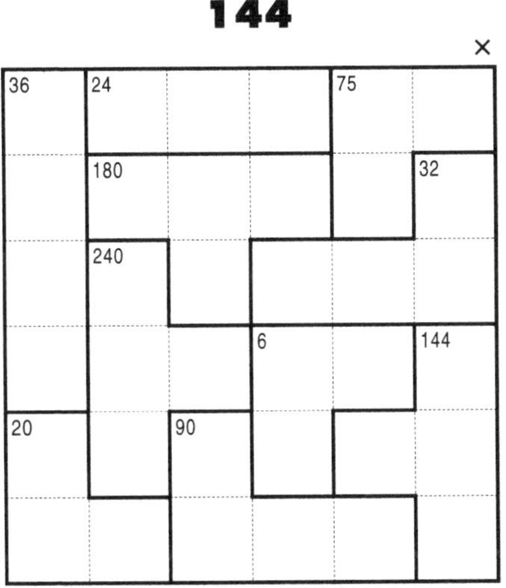

145

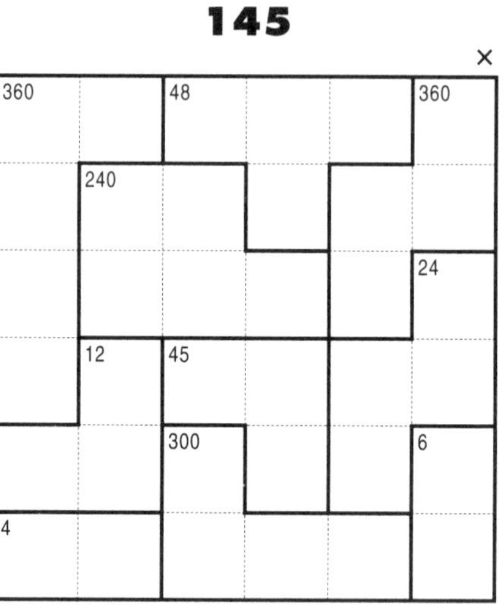

146

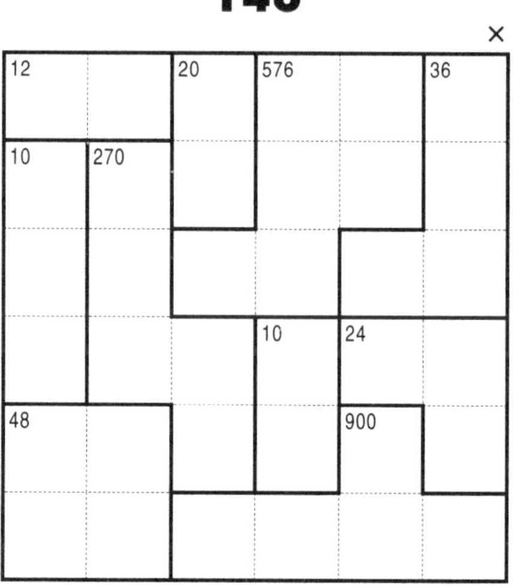

147

×

960 | 60 | 12 | 4320 | 9 | 16 | 15 | 180 | 15 | 8

148

×

1200 | 48 | 216 | 6 | 14400 | 72 | 40 | 45

149

×

36 9000

192

8640 120

72

30

150

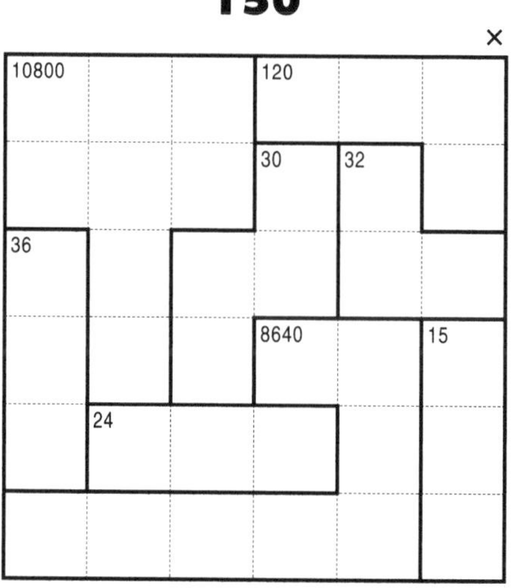

151

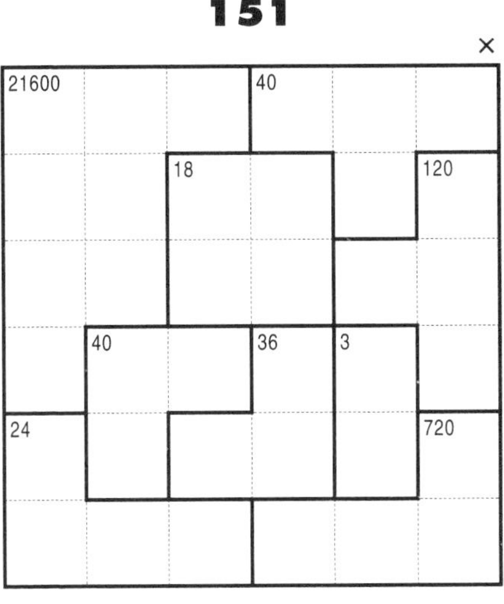

152

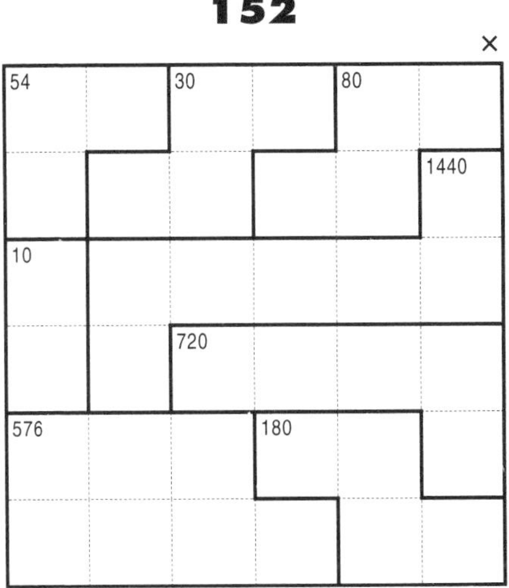

153

+ −

3−		13+			9+
14+		5−			
	11+	1−		9+	1−
		6+			
3+	14+		2−		5+
				2	

154

+ −

1−	7+		3−	4−	
	9+			2	1−
		3−	8+	1−	
13+					5+
	12+	2−			
			13+		

155

+ −

9+		9+	1−		6
2−				10+	
	13+			4+	
8+	3−	1−			14+
			5		
9+			12+		

156

+ −

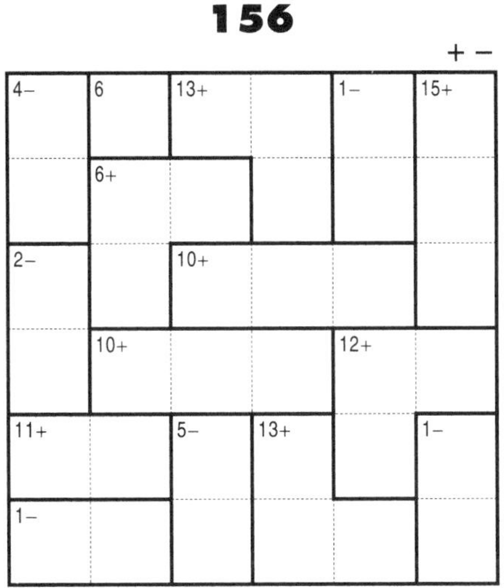

157

\+ −

2−		19+	4−		10+
2−			11+		
	13+				
11+			21+		5−
				12+	

158

\+ −

22+			15+		
	12+			2−	
			21+		15+
1−					
13+			17+		
	2−				

159

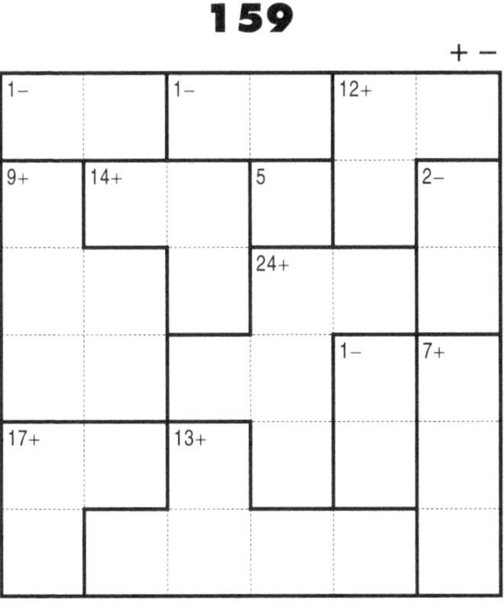

160

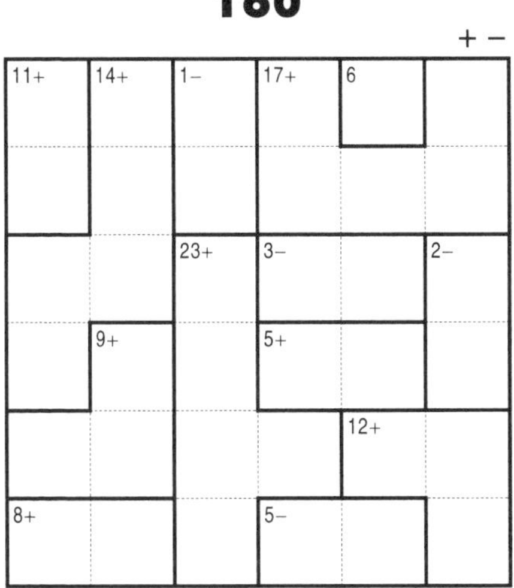

161

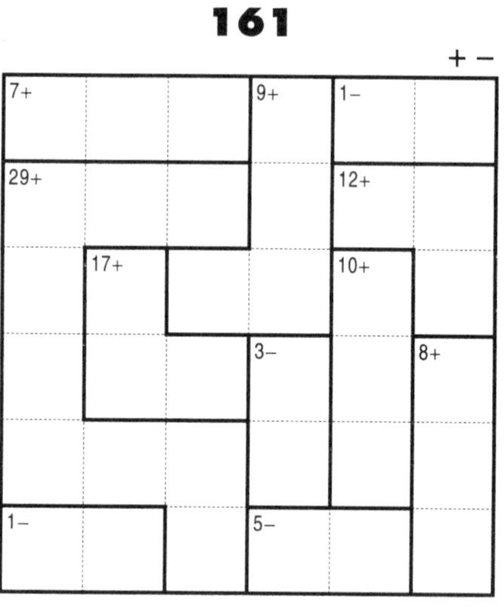

162

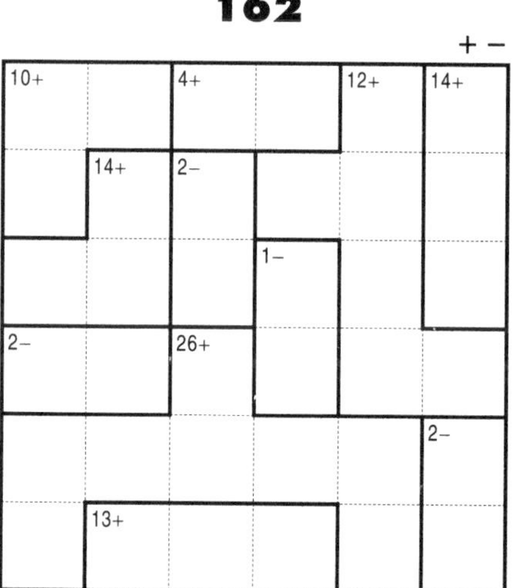

163

+ −

8+	21+	1−	5+		21+
					6+
1−		2−			
	22+				4−
		5−			

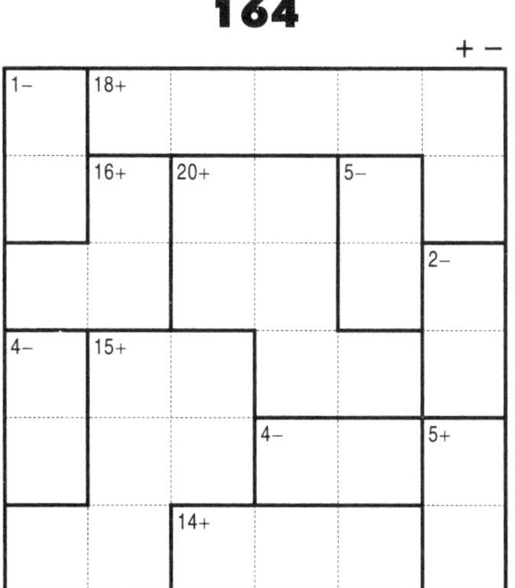

165

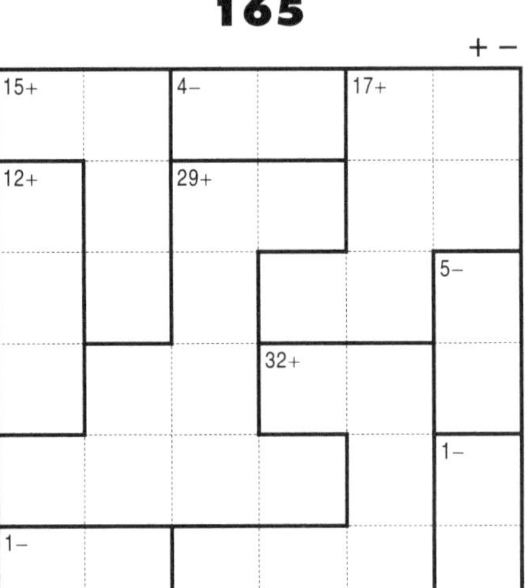

166

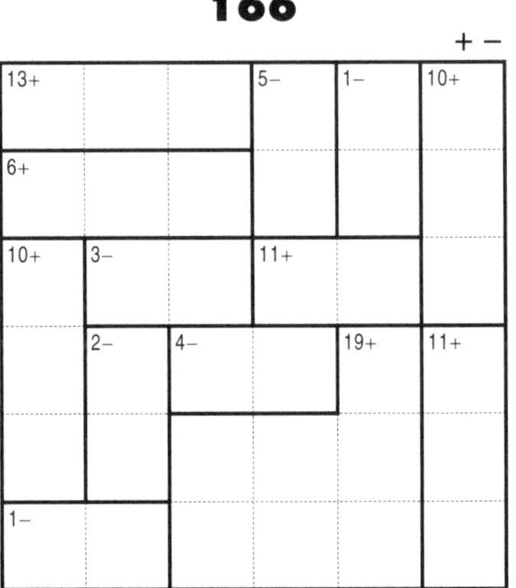

167

+ –

29+ 4– 13+ 2–

5+ 13+

10+ 1– 28+

7+

168

+ –

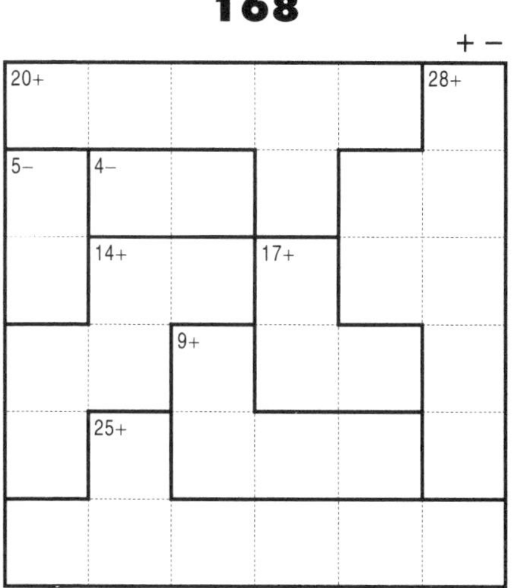

169

× ÷

24×		5÷		48×	12×
2÷	30×				
		2÷	6÷	5	
60×				2÷	
	30×	16×	3×		90×

170

× ÷

12×	60×			48×	
	60×				5÷
	24×	12×		1	
60×				15×	72×
		2÷			
5÷			2÷		

171

× ÷

48×			6×	72×	5
30×					
2÷		60×			30×
	4×		120×		
2÷				12×	
30×			4÷		

172

× ÷

30×		2÷		6÷	
3		24×			60×
24×		60×		5÷	
2÷		15×			
			30×		36×
24×					

173

× ÷

120×		72×	360×		
				3÷	
288×	30×		40×		2÷
				180×	
5÷		6×			4

174

× ÷

2÷	50×		2÷	24×	
		432×			
5×					360×
	144×	6÷		10×	
		120×			

175

× ÷

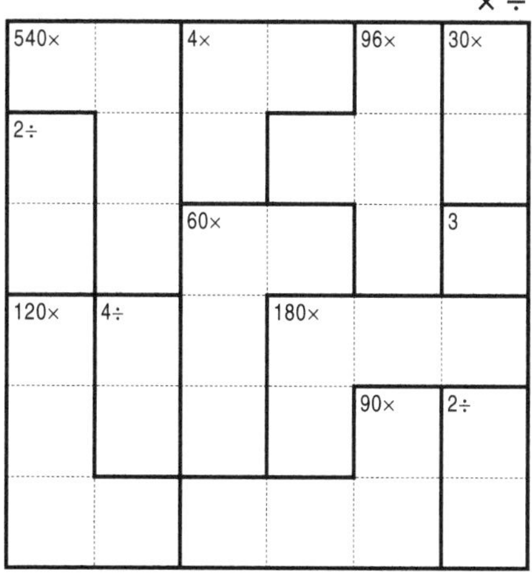

176

× ÷

3÷		40×		3÷	
40×		216×			120×
120×		2×	3÷		
	216×		150×		
				4	

177

× ÷

12×	60×		10×	30×	
				48×	
3÷			3÷		
120×	5÷	2÷		72×	
		1080×			

178

× ÷

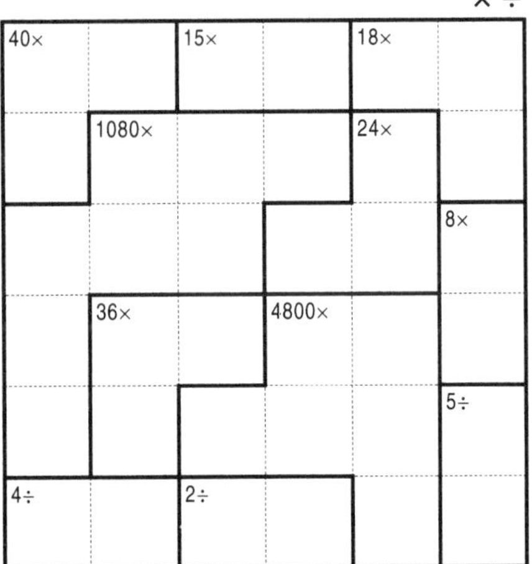

179

× ÷

120×		12960×	3×		19200×
	3÷				
			6÷	15×	
					36×
20×		2÷			

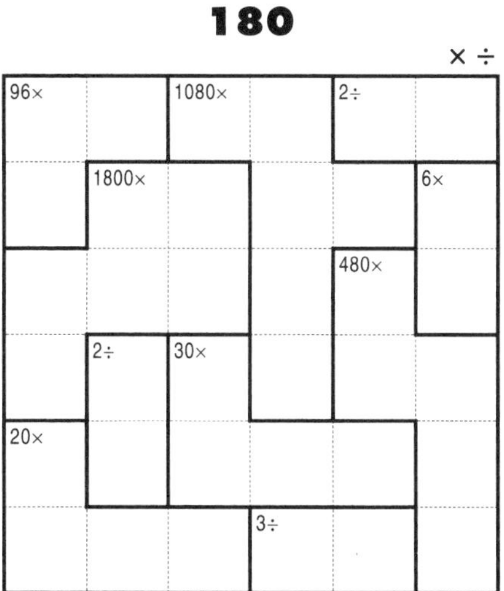

181

× ÷

36×		3840×		10×	
30×					6480×
	15×				
		30×			
2÷		2÷			2÷
4×					

182

× ÷

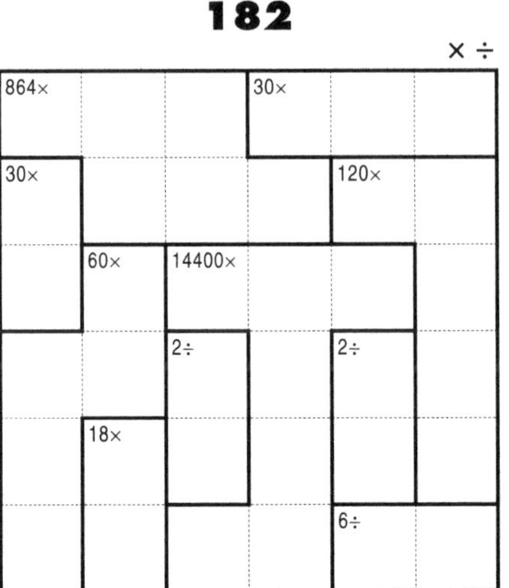

183

× ÷

20×	9720×		2÷		6×
		20×	2÷		
				600×	3÷
24×					60×
	4÷				

184

× ÷

30×		43200×	6×		12×
3÷				1440×	
96×			5÷		
10×			2÷		
		4÷			

185

+ − × ÷

14+	36×			3−	
	1−		2÷		30×
	9+				
6×		14+		3	2÷
8+		18×		90×	

186

+ − × ÷

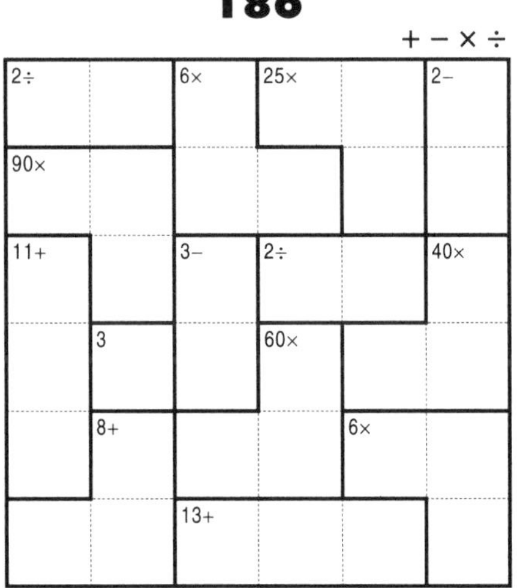

187

+ − × ÷

4	1−	12×		9×	
12×		60×			5÷
			9+	120×	
	7+				
2−		60×			2÷
		10+			

188

+ − × ÷

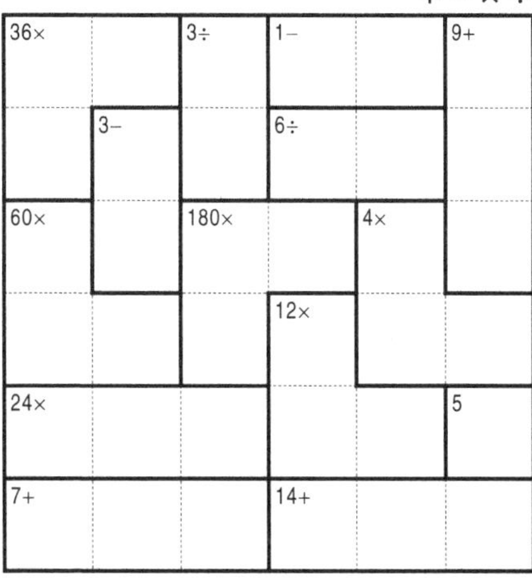

189

+ − × ÷

4÷		14+			144×
2−		120×	8×		
18+		2−		14+	
	1−		3÷		
		72×			

190

+ − × ÷

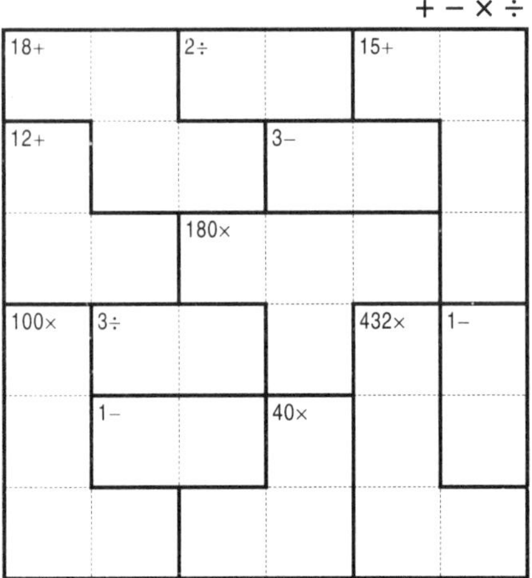

191

+ − × ÷

13+	1−		2÷	5×	
	150×			180×	
	3÷		144×		
		1−			
13+			60×		6
				8+	

192

+ − × ÷

3−	12+		6+	6÷	
				75×	
120×		13+	144×		
			2−		2÷
90×				120×	

193

+ − × ÷

1−		80×	17+		24×
2÷					
	12+			8+	
		240×			
5÷				360×	
2÷		1−			

194

+ − × ÷

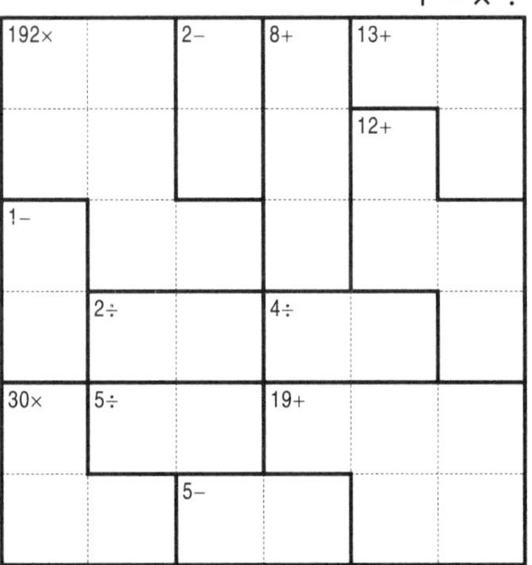

195

+ − × ÷

15+		1200×	108×		
		36×	180×		5÷
			30+		
3÷					2−

196

+ − × ÷

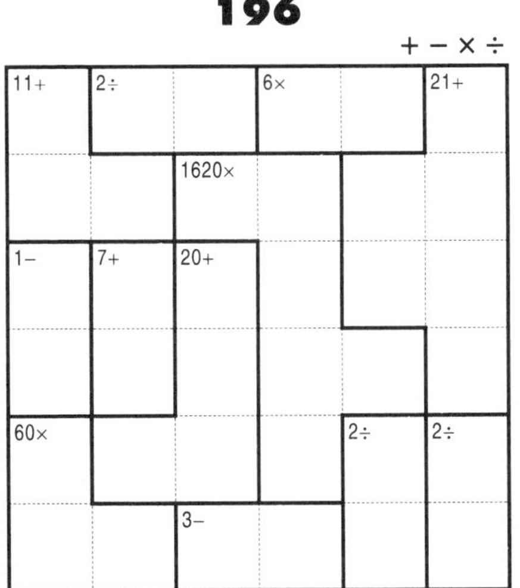

197

+ − × ÷

2÷		2÷		23+	2÷
20×	1440×	9+			
			3−		2−
15+			20×	30×	

198

+ − × ÷

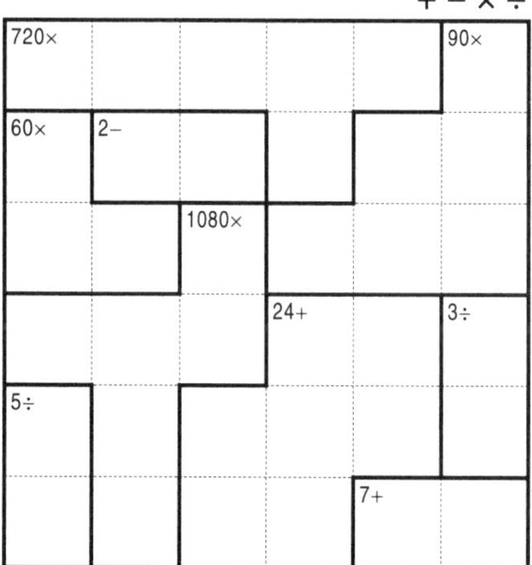

199

+ − × ÷

6÷		27+			
3600×		3÷		120×	
	300×				
	72×				
				1−	
		12+			

200

+ − × ÷

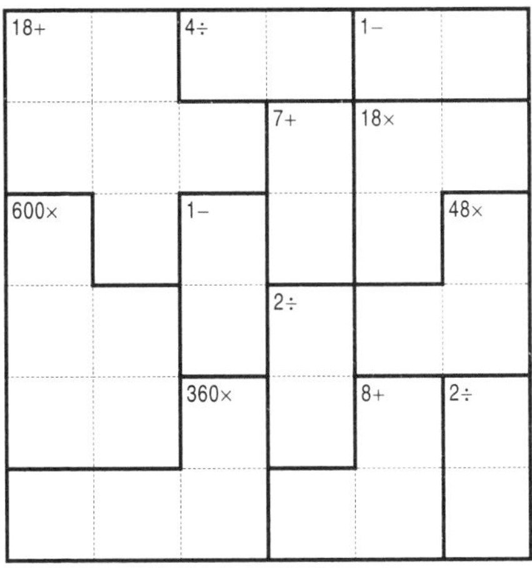

201

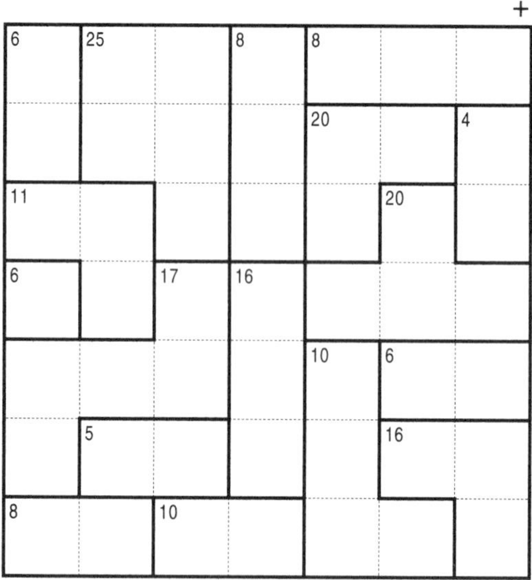

202

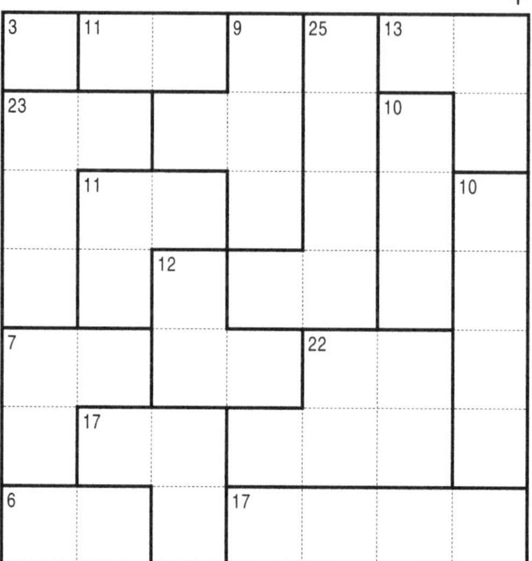

203

+

7		12		4	6	
12		14			25	
				15		
13	24		18			
				20		8
18						

204

+

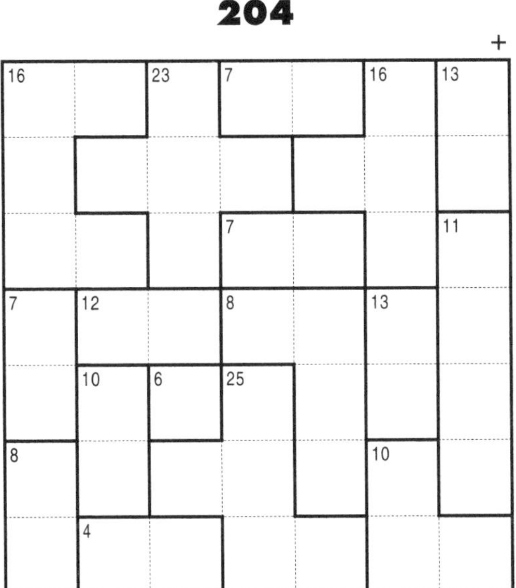

205

+

11		14		10		
4			10	13		
16				9		
15		5		37	18	
						13
8				9	4	

206

+

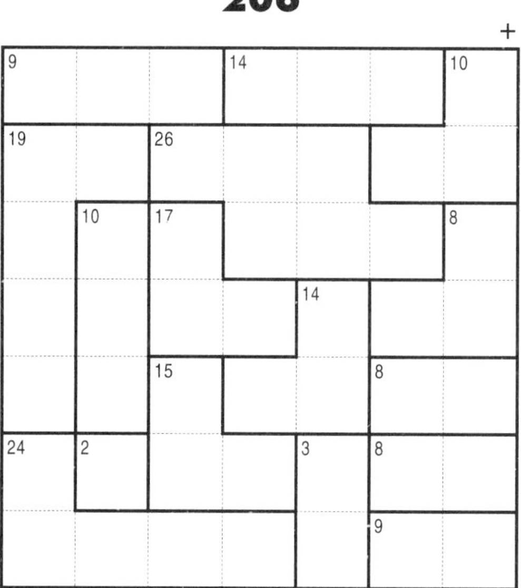

207

+

17 39 8 13
8 16 16
14
19
7 9
14 9
7

208

+

8 28 3 21
12 6
18
9 21 16
8 11
14
13 8

209

+

210

+

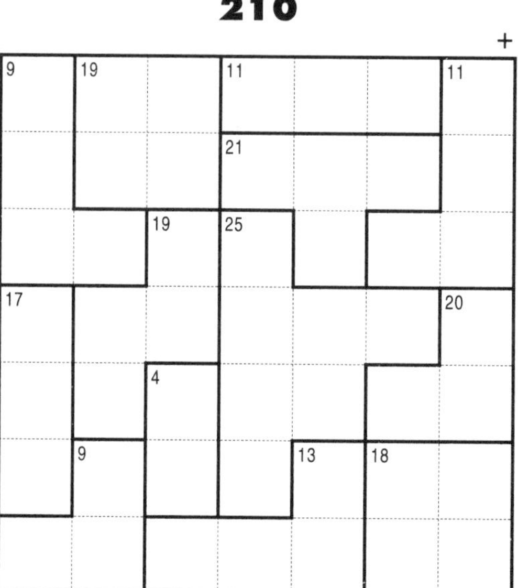

211

+

12	16		7			11
		25	31			
			4			
						19
11		33	16			
					11	

212

+

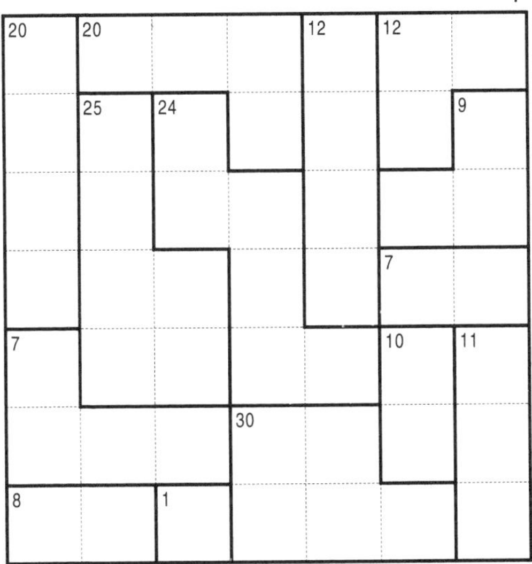

213

×

540	20		56		6	
			7			210
12	14		120			
		180				
35				12		84
42		24				
			30		4	

214

×

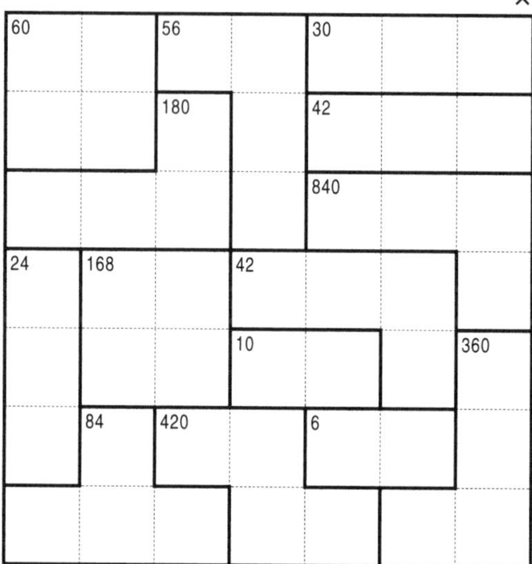

215

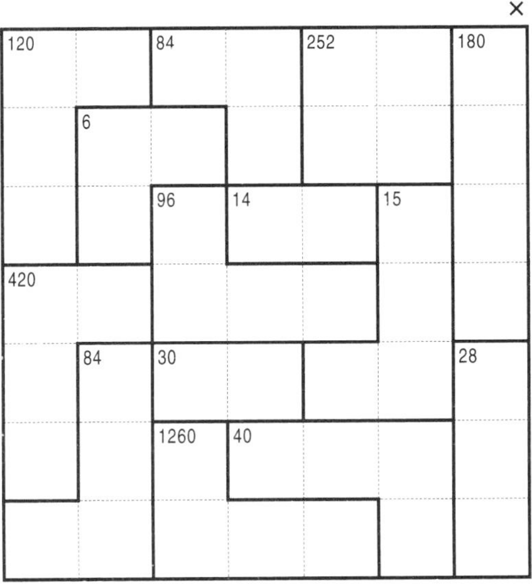
×
120
84
252
180
6
96
14
15
420
84
30
28
1260
40

216

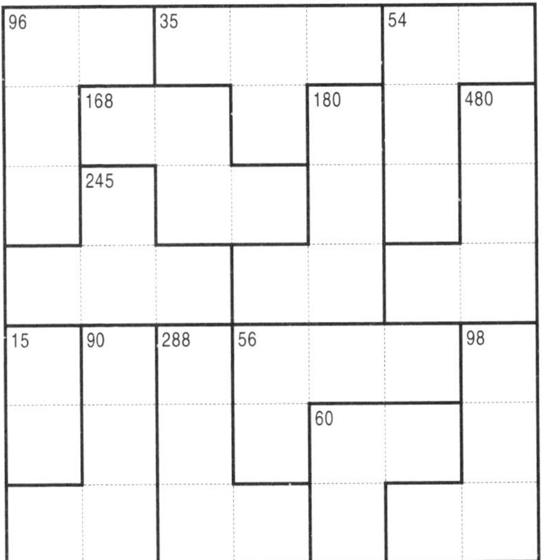
×
96
35
54
168
180
480
245
15
90
288
56
98
60

217

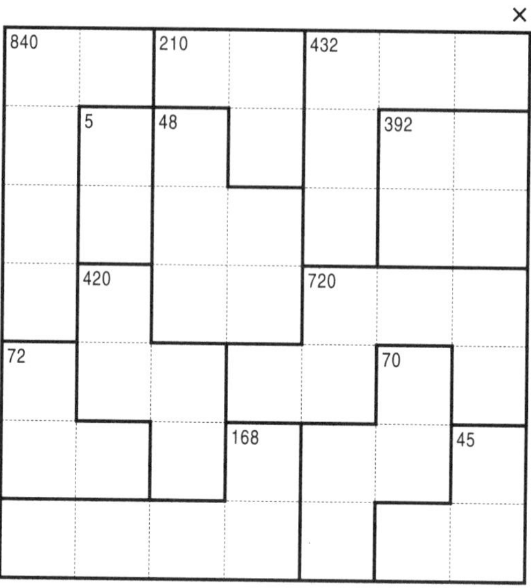
×
840
210
432
5
48
392
420
720
72
70
168
45

218

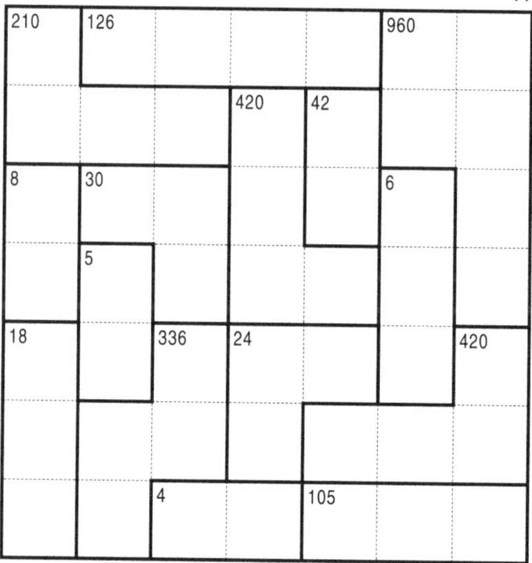
×
210
126
960
420
42
8
30
6
5
18
336
24
420
4
105

219

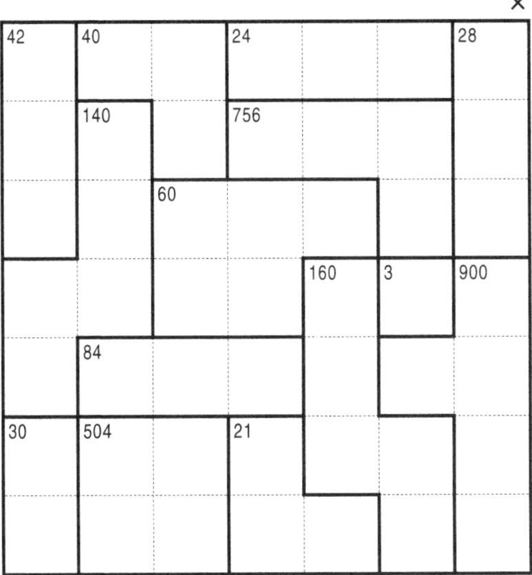
×
42
40
24
28
140
756
60
160
3
900
84
30
504
21

220

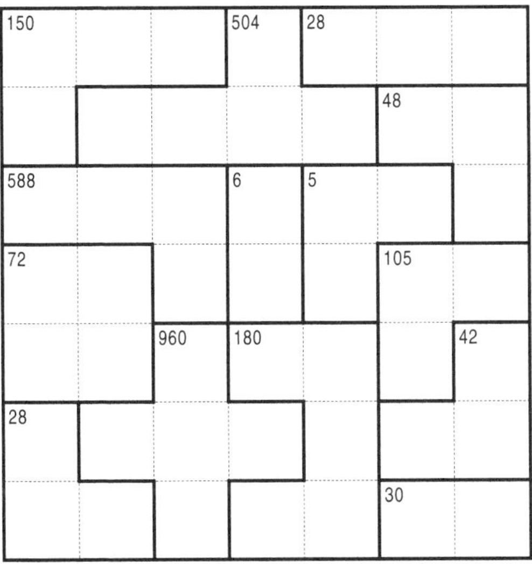
×
150
504
28
48
588
6
5
72
105
960
180
42
28
30

221

×

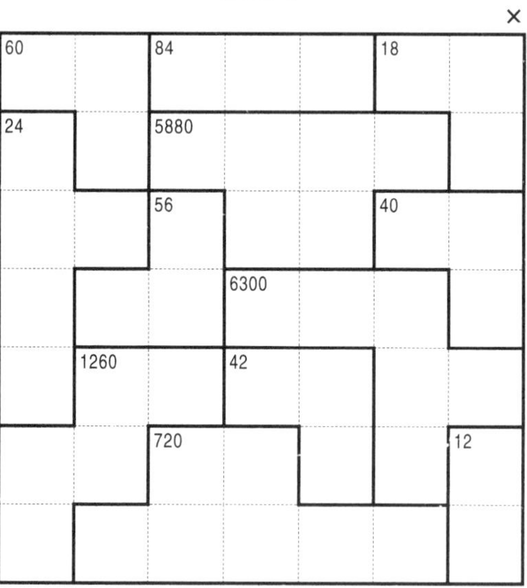

222

×

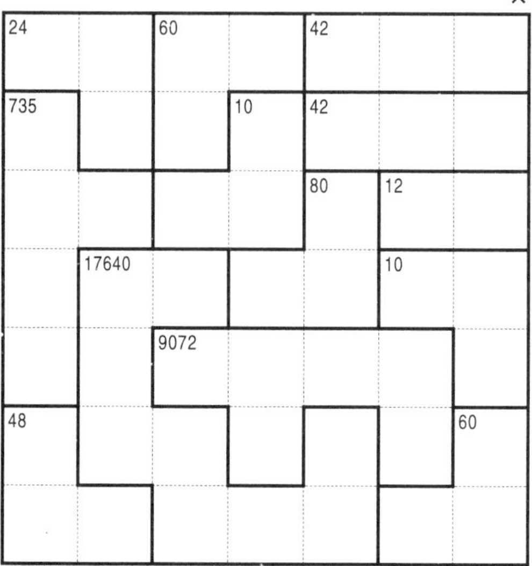

223

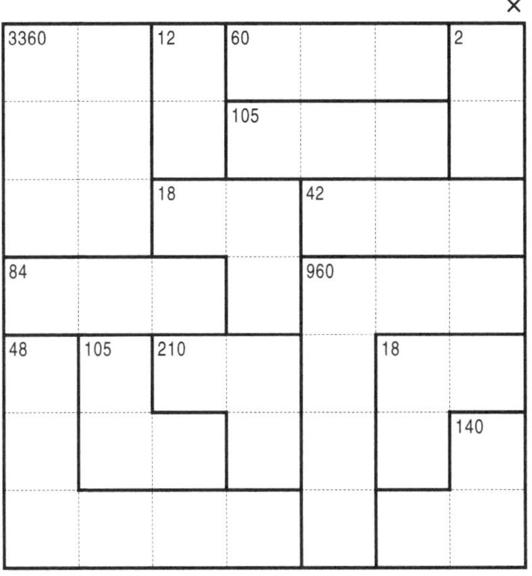
×
3360
12
60
2
105
18
42
84
960
48
105
210
18
140

224

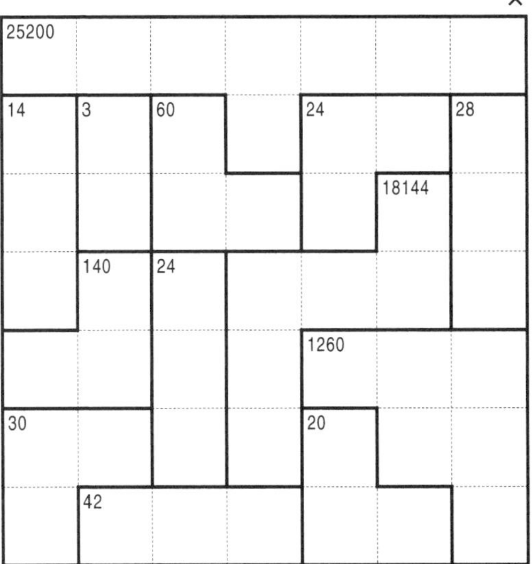
×
25200
14
3
60
24
28
18144
140
24
1260
30
20
42

225

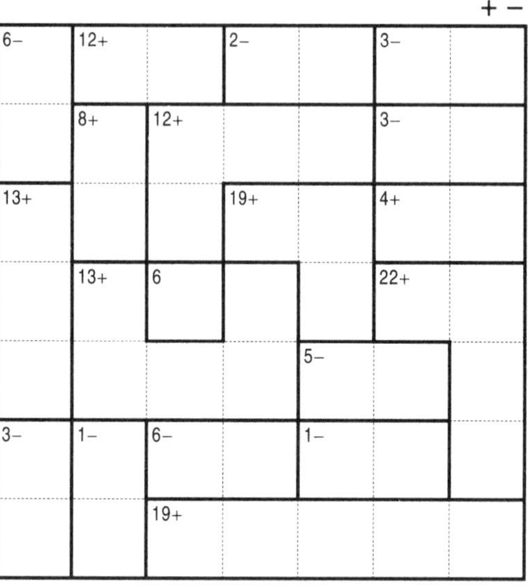

226

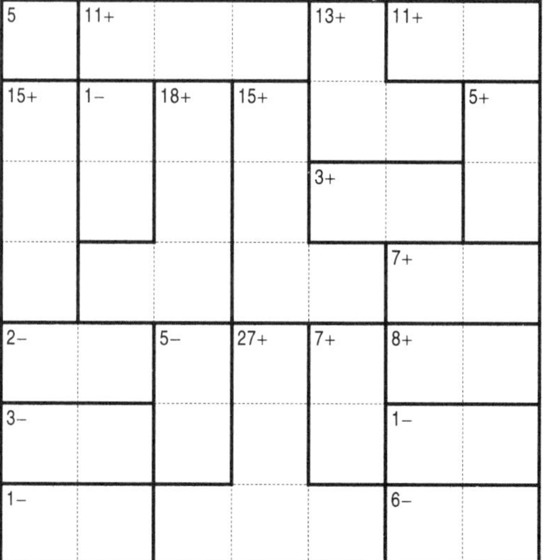

227

+ –

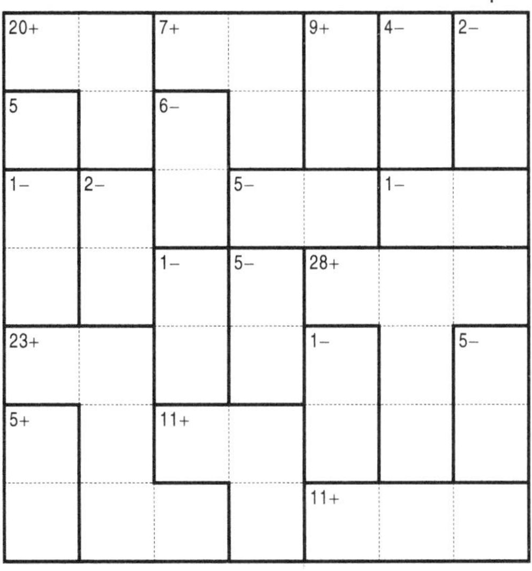

228

+ –

7+	11+		24+	1–	11+	
						25+
6–	16+	8+		1–		
				1		
8+			6–	24+	5–	
	6+					2–
14+						

229

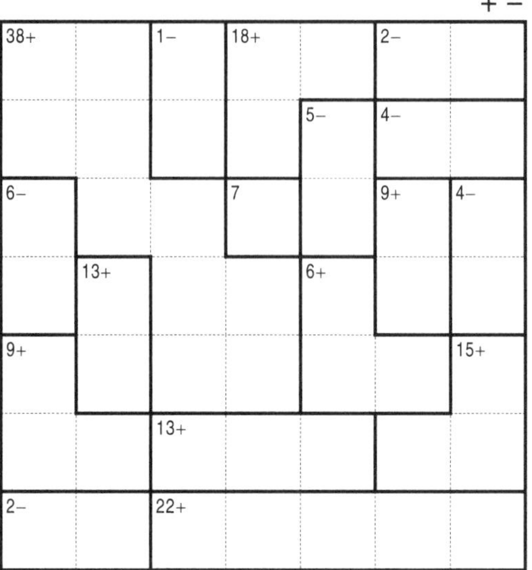

230

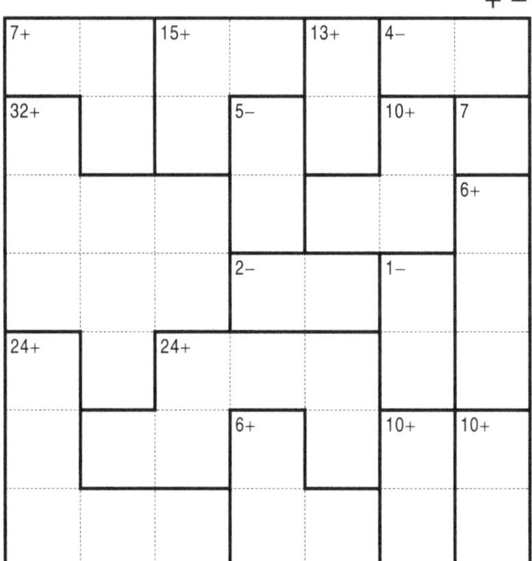

231

+ −

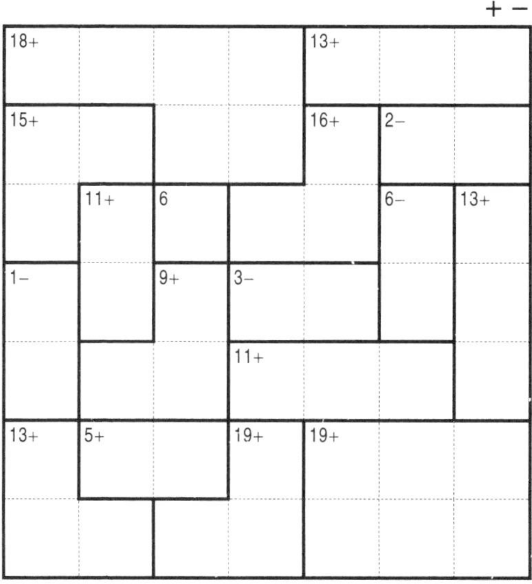

232

+ −

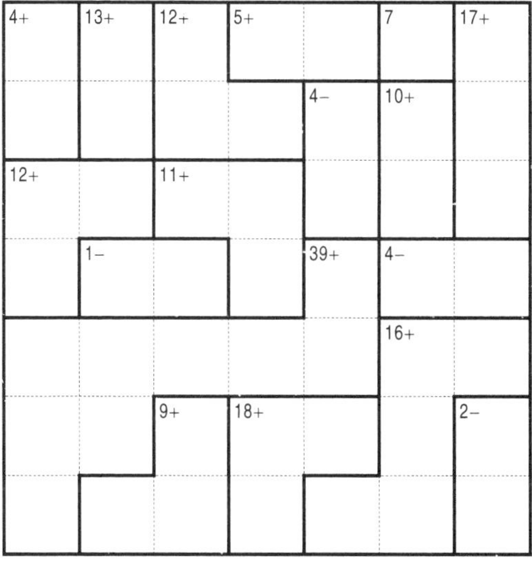

233

+ −

13+			2−		9+	7+
6−	3−	2−		17+		
		3+			9+	
14+		2−				
	2−		25+	10+		
22+				14+		

234

+ −

1−	18+			33+	8+	4−
	10+	5+				
11+						14+
		12+				
10+				3−		
13+		6−		2−		12+
	14+					

235

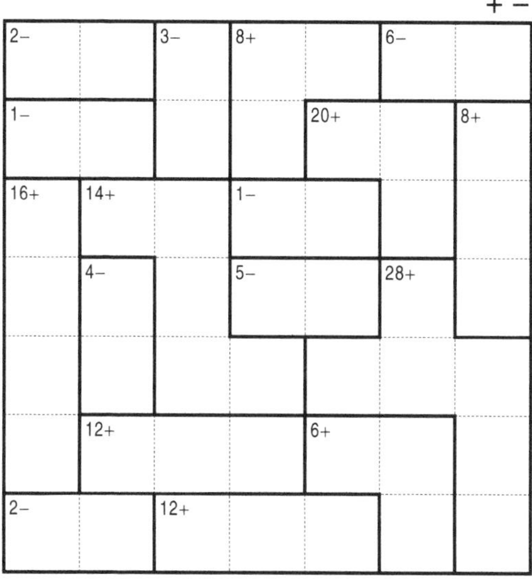

236

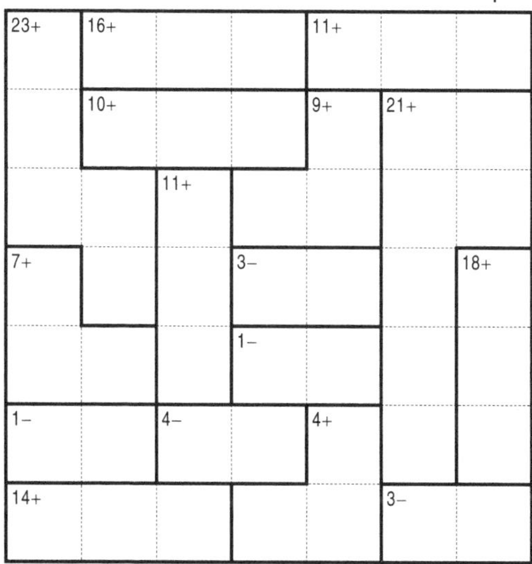

237

× ÷

21×	120×		3÷		7÷	
	24×		168×		280×	5
						432×
140×	3÷		15×			
24×	105×	84×		5×	3×	
					2÷	

238

× ÷

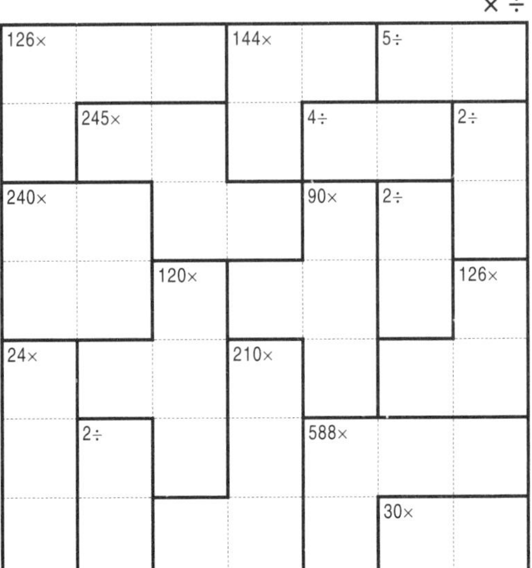

239

× ÷

15× 168× 210× 96×
12×
35× 90×
24× 4 196× 210×
168× 3÷ 150×
3÷ 3÷

240

× ÷

140× 2÷ 2÷ 252×
180× 175×
112× 3÷
252× 30×
60× 96× 84×
3÷ 140×

241

× ÷

24×	50400×	72×	21×		2÷	
			6300×			
			2÷		84×	
				35×		
42×					3÷	
			2÷	16×	120×	
	35×					

242

× ÷

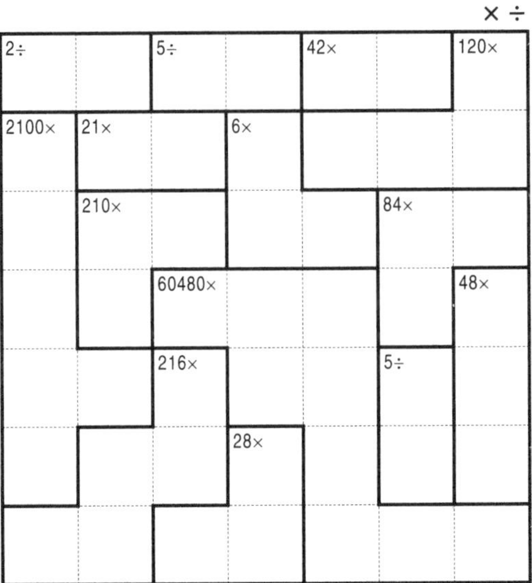

243

× ÷

60×
3528×
15×
72×
7÷
2÷
20160×
15750×
4÷
2÷
2×
84×
1680×

244

× ÷

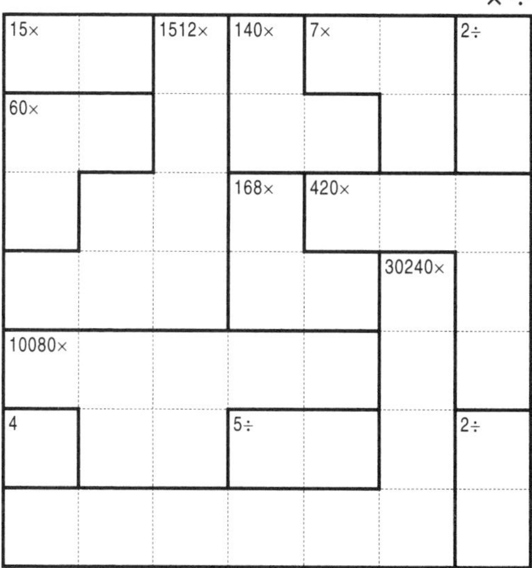

245

× ÷

1260× 5÷ 252× 4÷
35280× 2÷
36×
480× 210× 5÷
84×
12× 210×
12×

246

× ÷

5040× 90×
28× 14×
30× 3× 24× 28×
90× 448× 4÷
2÷ 5÷
29400× 2÷

247

× ÷

7×		100×		42×	24×	
15×		2÷			37800×	
	3÷		21×	420×		
3360×						
		3÷				
		7÷	144×			
6×						

248

× ÷

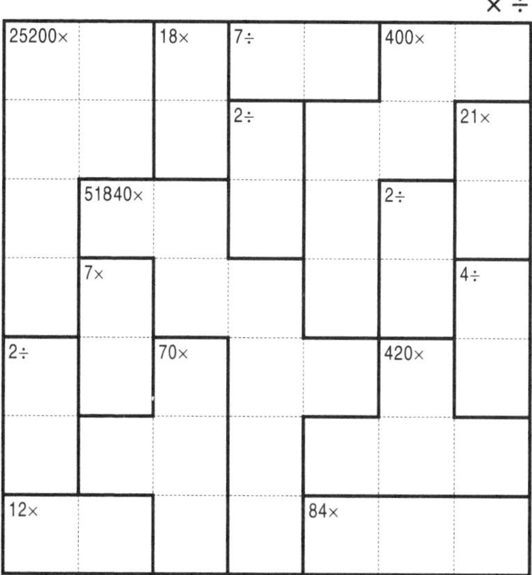

249

+ − × ÷

294×			80×			2÷
	2−			2−	3×	
3−		21+	7÷			
3÷				14×	2−	
	8×		17+		700×	
		7			42×	
9+						

250

+ − × ÷

19+			6×		168×	
4−		432×				
	21+	2−			20×	
				672×	7÷	
	1−		21+			3÷
1−						
12+			3÷		2−	

251

+ − × ÷

4−		20+		70×	1−	
42×					2÷	
		120×		144×		4−
80×		1−				
	2÷		15+	7÷		300×
630×				4÷		

252

+ − × ÷

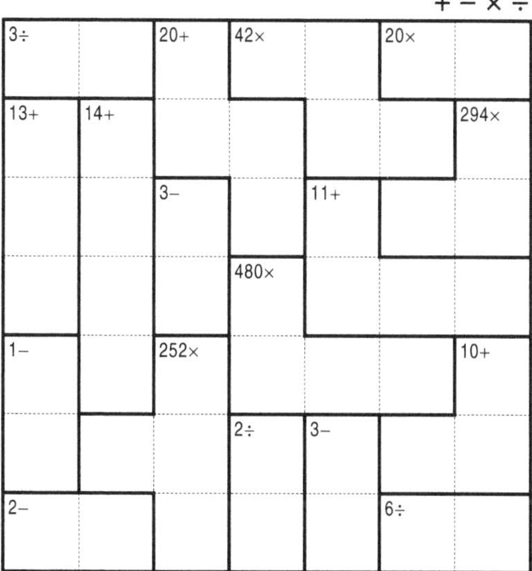

253

+ − × ÷

3− | 20× | 10+ | 3÷
4200× | 2÷ | 21× | 24+
42× | 19+
360×
1800×
2÷ | 3− | 1−

254

+ − × ÷

21+ | 3240× | 19+
2÷
2− | 4480× | 2÷
144× | 5− | 13+
21×
4− | 48× | 2÷
12+

255

+ − × ÷

5÷ 4032× 98× 3÷ 60× 10+ 2− 4− 4÷ 3− 630× 26+ 84× 17+ 2−

256

+ − × ÷

12+ 3÷ 2− 14112× 4− 1− 4÷ 15× 13+ 6× 144× 17+ 12+ 245× 6× 4÷ 14+

257

+ − × ÷

12+			2520×			35+
4÷						
28×		150×		1−		
	4−					
1−		3−	28×			840×
2÷	6×					
				5÷		

258

+ − × ÷

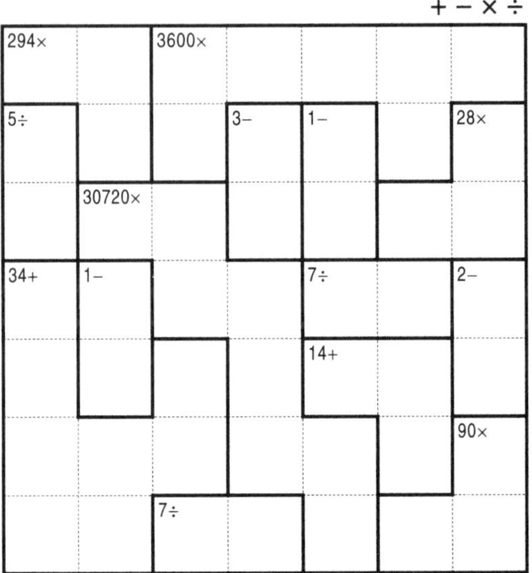

259

+ − × ÷

1−
240×
32+
3÷
7+
30×
49×
84×
11+
2÷
30240×
2−
3−
4÷
10+

260

+ − × ÷

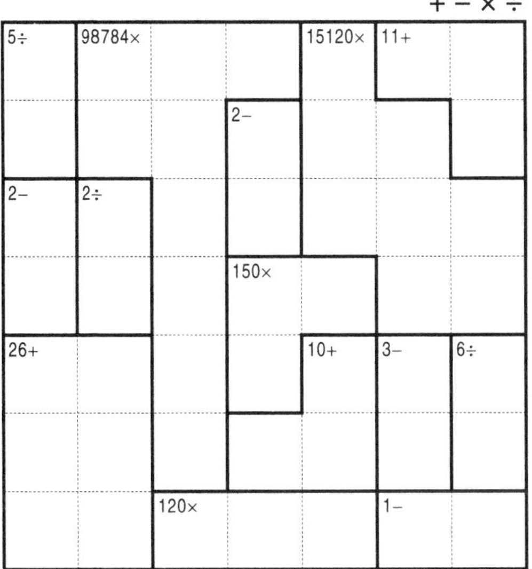

261

+

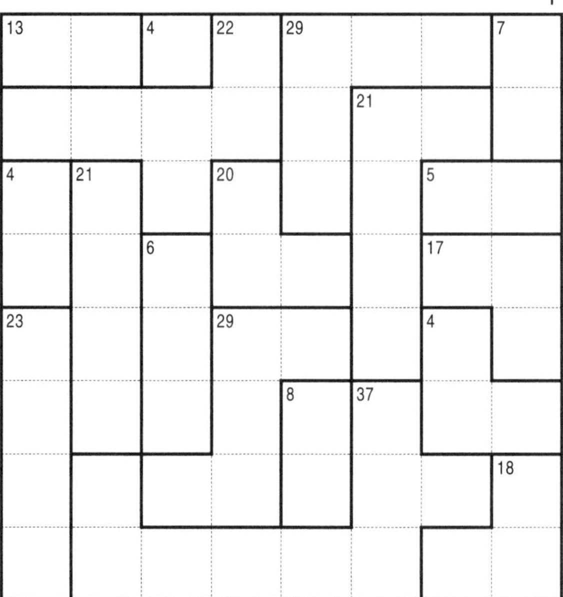

262

+

12	19			15	8	10	
						9	11
10	15		17				
		12	31			11	
13							10
				6		16	
3	17			13			10
	14		6				

263

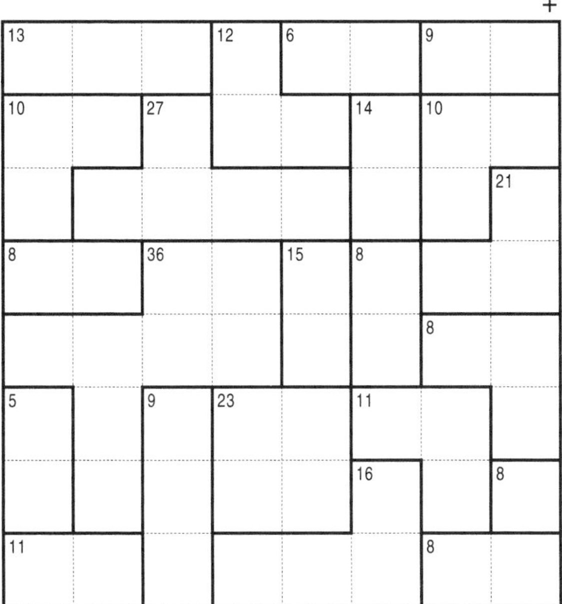

264

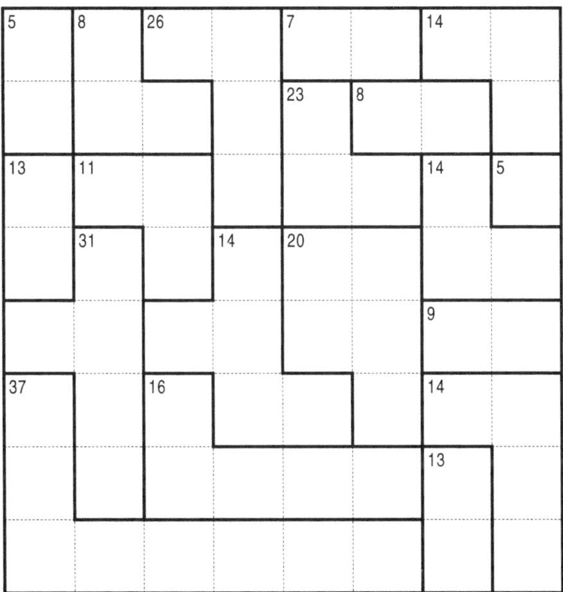

265

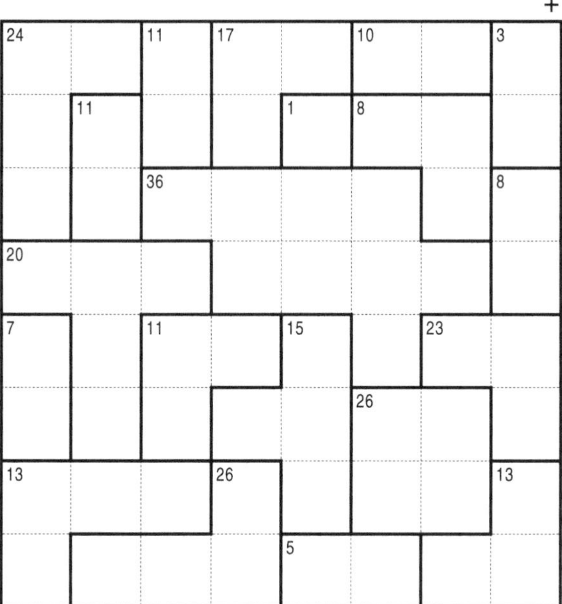

266

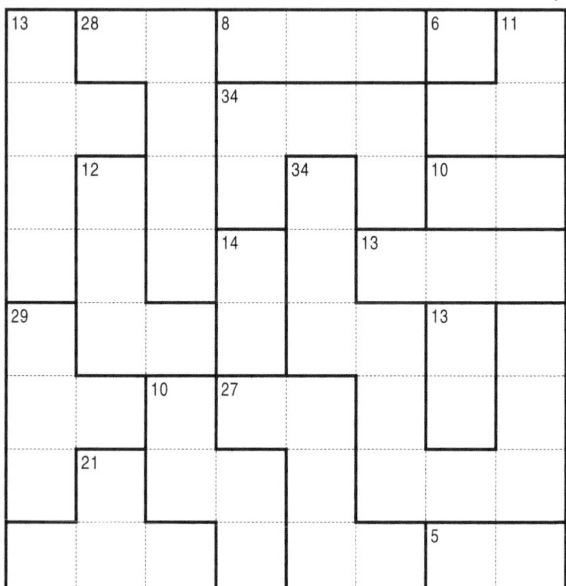

267

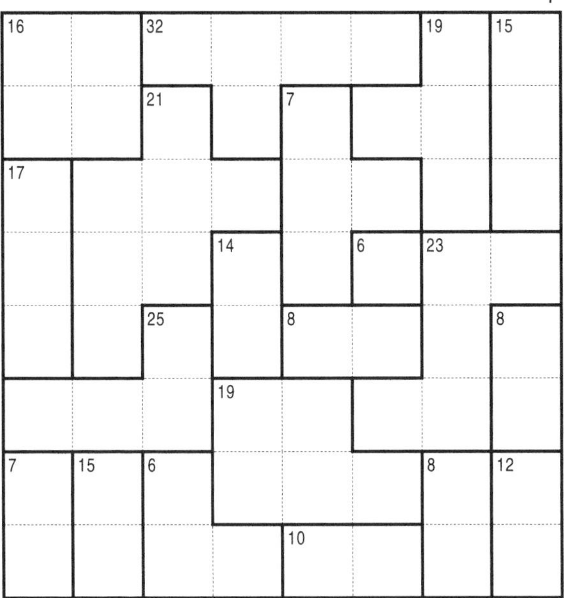

268

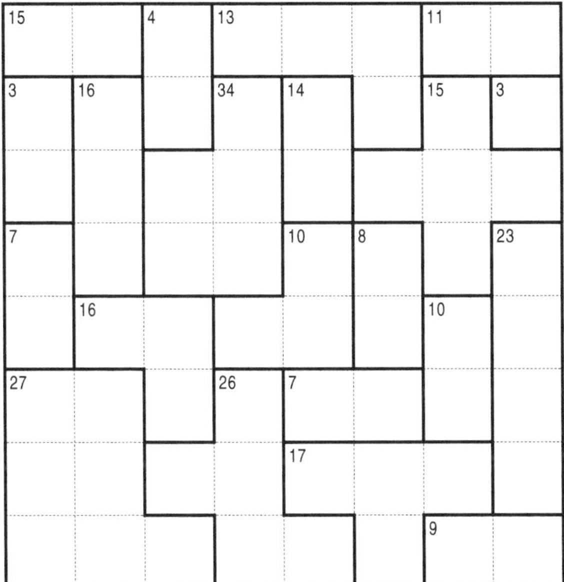

269

×

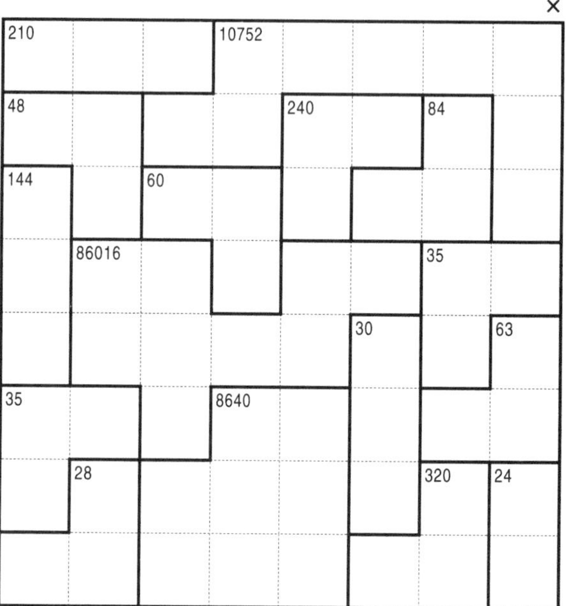

270

×

40 46080 42 280 6 72

42 36 16128 20

24

160 56

3136 6300

30 12

271

×

42		12			6720		
72		34560		14			
						16	33600
		12		35			
5			192				
39200		28	96			72	18
				2			

272

×

224	32			2016			35
	96				90		
			24		30		
30	140					48	
			56			48	
18		69120	175				4
					21		
					224		

273

×

25, 60480, 24, 224, 224, 35280, 48, 54, 5, 24, 8, 80, 8960, 288, 35, 24, 21, 12

274

×

60480, 336, 7680, 6, 1260, 112, 6720, 24, 240, 60, 5, 36, 28, 35, 96, 24, 56

275

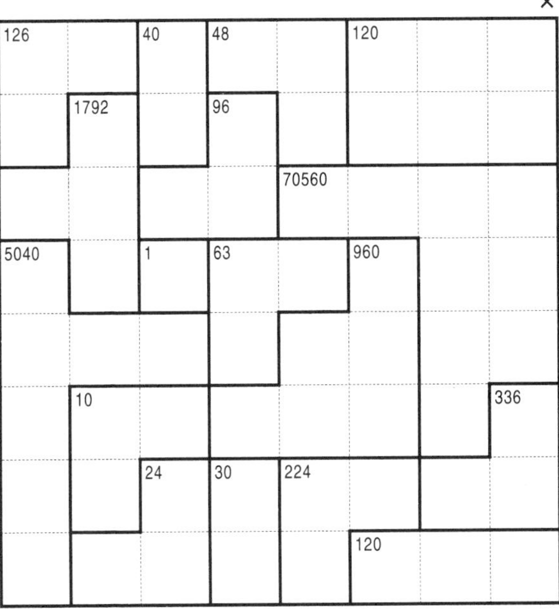

×
126
40
48
120
1792
96
70560
5040
1
63
960
10
336
24
30
224
120

276

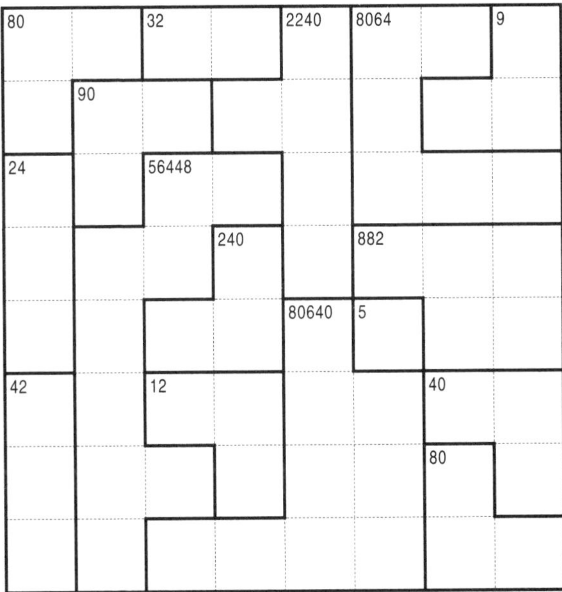

×
80
32
2240
8064
9
90
24
56448
240
882
80640
5
42
12
40
80

277

+ −

9+			15+		1−		12+
5−	19+		8+	6−		2−	
		2		14+	4+		
14+							17+
1−		11+	3−	11+			
17+					45+		
3−		20+			11+		

278

+ −

7+		6+		12+	35+		
11+			8+			21+	
11+		15+					
6−	7+			19+			8+
		14+				8	
23+					1−	14+	
1−		15+					3−
	3−		1−		9+		

279

+ −

15+			6−		3−		3−
10+		21+		14+		15+	
	16+			4−			
1−			12+	13+			4−
		14+		17+			
15+				7−	17+		
	16+	6−	5−			7	9+
				4+			

280

+ −

15+		17+		38+		8+	
1−			14+				
	11+			1−			4−
2−							
3+	6+	8+		21+			1
			16+	15+		12+	19+
2−					7+		
17+							

281

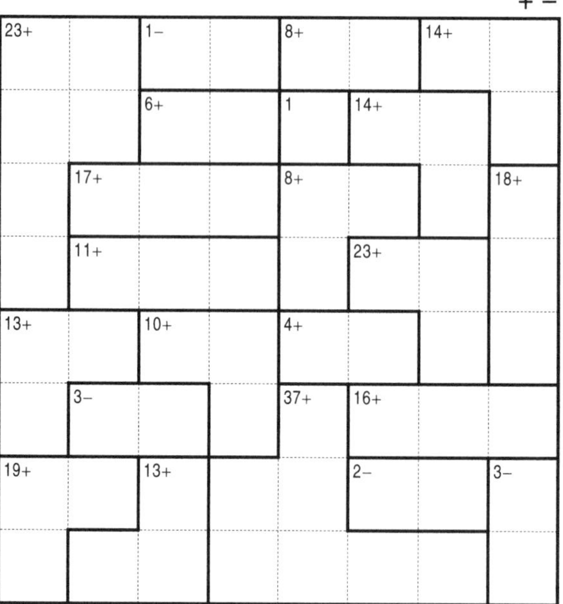

+ −
23+
1−
8+
14+
6+
1
14+
17+
8+
18+
11+
23+
13+
10+
4+
3−
37+
16+
19+
13+
2−
3−

282

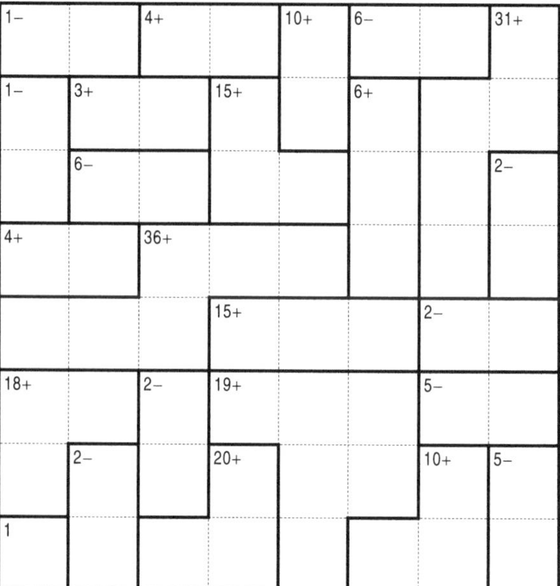

+ −
1−
4+
10+
6−
31+
1−
3+
15+
6+
6−
2−
4+
36+
15+
2−
18+
2−
19+
5−
2−
20+
10+
5−
1

283

+ −

8+	10+			7+		14+	
	2−		19+			8+	
1−	1−		4−	8+		15+	
	17+	7−		20+		9+	
13+			1−				
		1−		15+			
1−		14+		13+	11+		7+
1−		3+					

284

+ −

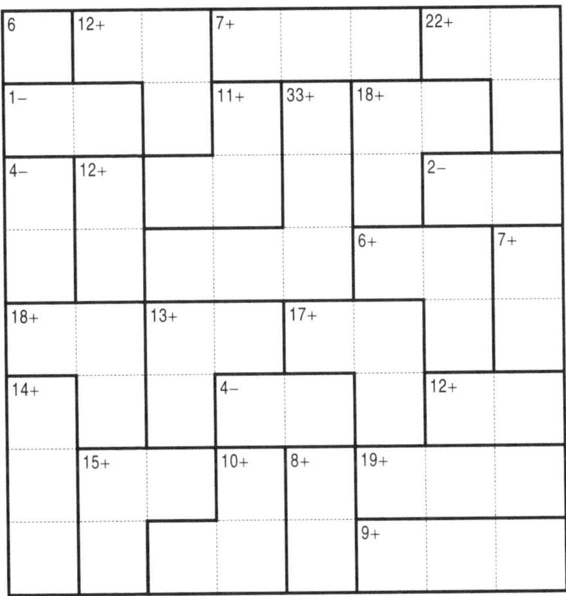

285

× ÷

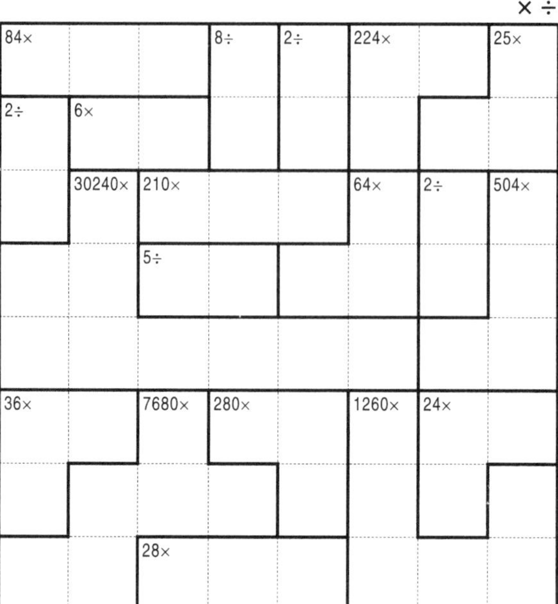

286

× ÷

30× 224× 64× 2÷ 2940×

84× 4÷

2÷ 1280× 90× 12×

90×

14×

3024× 7÷ 80× 240×

14× 48× 48×

5÷

287

× ÷

24×
10368×
8000×
21×
1120×
252×
40320×
70×
10×
16128×
4÷
4÷
210×
448×
3÷
2÷
36×

288

× ÷

288×
35×
2÷
36×
10×
61440×
336×
21×
21600×
98×
2÷
40×
336×
8×
18×
40×
420×
3÷
7÷
12×

289

× ÷

48×	53760×			8×		1260×	
		3÷		60×	2÷		
84×			84×				
				40×	180×		
	7×					112×	
10×	20×	2÷		2÷			
		30×	2÷	378×			
					112×		

290

× ÷

24×	30×		2÷		84×		4÷
	2÷		75×			37632×	
14×		10080×			3÷		
5040×				40×			
						2÷	
		32×		4×			60×
24×			3×	84×	40×		
	56×						

291

× ÷

672×			10080×			40×	
4÷			30×				
	126×					16×	
30×			9408×	8064×		40×	
40×	6÷						24×
		2÷					
280×				30×			42×
	2÷						

292

× ÷

120×	588×		3÷		224×		
			30×		2520×	32×	
		1120×		8×			108×
28800×							
			336×				10×
56×					2÷		
		6×		336×	90×		8÷
		4÷					

293

+ − × ÷

4−		19+	11+			13+	20+
252×							
	9408×				9+		
		2÷				96×	
	38400×		16×		49×		
						1−	
	24×	17+	175×		5−		4÷
					3÷		

294

+ − × ÷

30+	168×			14×	48×		
					120×		
	288×		72000×		7÷		36×
2−		12+				19+	
2−			19+		8÷	60×	
5÷				180×			
2−					10+		

295

+ − × ÷

30×		4480×	18+			13+	
8+				36×			
		2÷				1−	
14×			1−		6×	2160×	64×
7560×		16+					
					7÷		
1536×			147×				
					20×		

296

+ − × ÷

4−	48×	42×			5÷		37+
			31+	40×		144×	
28×		3×					
	28×			22+	2÷		
13+		3−			29+		2÷
33+							

297

+ − × ÷

30×	5−	28+		392×		6+	
			2÷		3×		15+
20×						17+	
			960×				
1680×					1120×		3÷
		210×			24+		
2÷		12+					
3−						14+	

298

+ − × ÷

40×	42×	28×		36+			3÷
		35×					
9+			20160×	2÷			
	1−						
28×	192×	2÷		4+		14×	120×
		3−			3−		
		8×		18+		16+	
60×							

299

+ − × ÷

8960× 9+ 11+ 8× 11+ 4− 8+ 80× 27+ 24× 6÷ 128× 2÷ 108× 20+ 2÷ 16+ 4− 16+ 2− 256× 48×

300

+ − × ÷

11+ 28× 28+ 21600× 9+ 17280× 320× 8820× 56× 6÷ 4÷ 3− 3÷ 24× 8× 4− 7+ 15+ 7× 2−

Sudoku

301

9				4		2	7	
					7	8		
7		4	8	6	3	9		
2		3		1	8			
5								8
			5	2		4		6
		2	4	7	1	6		9
		8	3					
	7	1		8				5

302

			3		7			
9			8	6	2			1
	2	7				6	3	
		4	9		1	8		
	8						9	
		3	6		5	1		
	4	1				9	8	
5			7	9	4			2
			2		8			

303

		2		6		9		4
			1		2	6	5	
6							1	3
	4				9		2	
3				2				6
	6		7				8	
8	1							9
	3	7	5		6			
4		6		7		1		

304

	7			1		3		9
1		9						
	3		5	7		4		8
		8			6			
5		1		2		8		3
			1			7		
6		3		5	7		2	
						6		1
9		4		3			8	

305

9			4		8			7
1	3						8	6
		5	6	1	7	3		
			7	4	5			
		4				7		
			2	8	1			
		1	9	6	3	2		
6	4						1	3
7			1		4			9

306

7	8		5		3		1	9
		6				4		
	5		1	6	4		7	
5								6
2			6	5	7			4
4								3
	2		8	4	5		3	
		9				5		
3	1		7		6		4	2

307

2		3	4	7				5
					9			
		5			1	2		8
	7	2		1				9
8								3
9				5		1	7	
5		6	2			3		
			9					
4				6	3	7		2

308

2	9	5				1	3	4
			4		9			
7								8
	5		2		3		4	
		9		1		6		
	3		9		7		1	
5								2
			6		5			
6	2	1				9	5	7

309

5			9		4	7		
	3	9				5		
		8	5		1		3	
	8				3			
	5		8	9	2		6	
			1				8	
	9		2		6	8		
		4				2	7	
		6	7		8			4

310

	1	6					9	
5			7	1	4			8
4		3		9				
	2			5			4	
	4	8	6		1	2	7	
	3			4			1	
				8		7		4
7			3	6	2			1
	8					5	2	

311

		3	9	7	8		4	6
			4				2	9
4						8		
7	4				3			5
9				2				1
6			7				9	3
		2						4
8	5				7			
3	6		2	4	1	7		

312

	1	6	9		8	7	2	
				3				
		4	1		5	9		
6		9				5		7
	8			9			3	
7		2				1		4
		7	3		9	8		
				6				
	9	1	4		2	3	5	

313

1			9	3		2		6
		2			1	4		
9	4						8	
	3		8		9			4
7				2				1
4			5		7		9	
	2						1	5
		4	1			6		
3		1		7	6			8

314

4		3	5		2			6
		2				7		
	5			1			3	2
8			4	9	6			3
		9				8		
3			1	2	8			9
9	1			6			2	
		4				5		
5			2		7	9		8

315

7		9		3		4		2
				6				
5	3		7		8		9	1
		6				9		
9	8			5			1	6
		4				5		
6	9		5		2		7	4
				1				
2		8		9		3		5

316

		3	7		9	8		
	2		1		8		9	
8								2
4	3			6			1	9
			4	7	3			
6	7			8			5	4
2								5
	9		8		2		6	
		1	5		4	2		

317

	5	6						
			5		9	7		1
	9	8	4		1	6		5
	4	7				2	9	
				7				
	6	2				1	7	
8		4	6		7	9	1	
6		5	9		2			
						3	5	

318

			8	7	3			
	5	3				8	9	
	8			4			6	
1				2				8
8		7	3		4	9		2
4				9				5
	1			6			8	
	7	9				5	2	
			9	3	7			

319

	5	7				3	9	
6		4				2		5
2			1		5			7
9			8		6			2
		1		5		4		
7			3		9			8
5			2		3			4
3		8				5		1
	9	2				6	7	

320

9	8			5	2		4	
2	6				8			9
			6		3	2		
		4				6	2	7
7				1				3
3	9	8				1		
		9	5		4			
1			9				7	5
	4		3	7			9	2

321

1								5
		9	6		1	7		
	3		7		2		4	
	5	3		7		4	9	
			9		6			
	8	6		4		1	2	
	2		8		4		6	
		8	5		9	2		
5								3

322

5				6				2
	8		7		5		3	
3	7						8	5
	2	8	1		6	5	4	
				8				
	5	6	3		2	9	7	
7	4						2	9
	9		4		1		6	
8				2				1

323

	7		2		3		5	
1		2		5		3		8
	5						9	
5				9				2
	6		5		4		3	
4				6				5
	1						8	
3		7		4		5		1
	8		7		5		6	

324

1				5				8
3			2	8	1			5
		4				9		
	7			1			8	
2	1		9		8		6	7
	8			4			3	
		9				8		
5			3	2	7			6
6				9				4

325

1		3					7	9
				3	2			5
2		9						
				7			1	
	8		6		5		9	
	9			1				
						6		3
8			2	6				
9	4					5		1

326

			5	1			3	
		2					6	1
	7				6			
1				5		7		
2			9	8	3			4
		9		2				3
			4				9	
3	2					5		
	9			3	1			

327

				2				
	4	2	8		7	6	5	
	5			1			3	
	7		9		8		6	
8		4				2		7
	9		2		4		1	
	6			8			4	
	1	8	3		9	7	2	
				5				

328

9		4	2	5		8		
	6		7		4	5		
1								
		8			5			
			6	7	2			
			3			9		
								3
		9	4		8		6	
		7		3	9	4		2

329

	9		8		7		3	
4		1				2		6
	6						9	
5				1				2
			7		2			
6				3				8
	2						8	
7		6				9		4
	3		5		4		6	

330

				3	8			
7			4	9				1
	1						2	
2			7		1		9	
6	4			2			1	5
	7		3		5			6
	5						4	
9				1	4			3
			9	8				

331

				5	6	4	1	
		5		9				3
	4				2			7
			6			1		5
8	5			4			2	6
1		9			3			
7			2				3	
5				7		9		
	9	3	4	6				

332

	5			1		9		
6		1						
	7			3	6			2
			3			2		
4		3		6		8		9
		9			1			
3			4	7			9	
						7		4
		8		2			6	

333

		3			8			
		4	3	2		6		
	5						4	8
8				4			3	
	6		2		7		1	
	9			5				7
1	4						5	
		7		6	3	1		
			9			2		

334

			2		8			
		8		4		7		
	1			7			2	
9			3		2			8
	5	2				3	1	
7			9		5			2
	8			3			6	
		7		5		2		
			1		4			

335

1	2	3	6	7				
				5			3	
7								8
			5			9		
	9	8	1	2	6	5	7	
		2			7			
4								7
	1			9				
				4	3	1	6	5

336

4			5				7	
		7	1				8	9
	1		8		3			
5	2	6	3			8		
		1			2	7	3	5
			4		8		1	
9	6				1	5		
	3				9			8

337

6			7			5		
	8			1			4	
		2			6			7
7			6			1		
	9			2			6	
		3			5			4
3			1			2		
	7			3			9	
		4			2			5

338

				4				
2	7		8		9		1	5
8		1						4
					8		2	
		6				5		
	4		6					
7						2		1
9	8		1		5		7	6
				3				

339

		2				9		
			3					
7	1			9	8		4	6
		6	8		9		2	
		9				5		
	2		7		4	8		
5	3		6	8			9	1
					1			
		4				3		

340

	8				1	5	3	
9		5						6
	3	6		9				4
			3					7
		1				2		
4					8			
6				2		9	7	
7						8		1
	9	8	6				4	

341

5						1		9
	6		5		8	2		3
6			9				2	
	3	1		4		8	7	
	2				7			1
7		9	2		4		6	
4		2						7

342

5				3				4
8			2	7	1			9
3		6	7		2	5		1
		9				4		
4		1	9		3	6		7
7			4	6	5			8
9				1				6

343

3					1			8
		5	2		7	1		
				4				
2	5			9			1	
		7		3		8		
	8			1			3	4
				8				
		6	5		4	7		
4			1					9

344

		4		2		6		
			5	6	8			
8								7
	5		3		2		6	
1	3			5			2	8
	6		7		1		3	
3								6
			8	4	9			
		7		3		5		

345

5		1		3				7
			7		8			
		2				6		3
	6			8			5	
7			2		9			6
	2			4			7	
6		4				1		
			4		5			
8				6		3		9

346

	4		6			5		
9	2			8	1			
					3			8
4						7	9	
	5			3			6	
	7	1						2
1			3					
			5	2			8	1
		8			6		4	

347

			4					
		8				9		5
1	5			3				4
2	8						4	9
		7		5		3		
3	1						6	8
4				6			1	7
5		3				2		
					9			

348

3								6
	1		5		3		2	
7			2		8			1
	9	3				2	5	
	6	8				7	4	
8			6		2			7
	5		8		1		6	
9								5

349

8		9				2		1
2			7		6			4
	6		4		5		7	
	3		6		2		4	
5			3		9			6
9		3				1		7

350

	8	3	1	2		4	9	
7			6					5
				4		7	8	
	6						3	
	2	4		8				
6					5			8
	1	5		9	4	6	7	

351

	9		7					8
	5			3				
	3					6		
					9	7		
4	2						5	3
		5	6					
		7					8	
				9			2	
8					6		1	

352

	4	3		9	5			
				2		6		8
	2							4
9								
8	3			7			1	9
								6
1							8	
3		5		1				
			9	5		7	4	

353

		9	4		3	6		
8								2
	7						1	
6			9		8			4
9			2		4			5
	2						6	
4								3
		7	1		9	4		

354

				4		8	9	
7	5						2	
2				1				
			9		5			
9		2				4		5
			3		4			
				9				1
	8						4	6
	3	5		8				

355

	8		2	7		6	4	
1				3			7	
		5						2
			7					
		6		8		2		
					5			
6						8		
	4			9				1
	7	2		5	3		9	

356

6	4					3		
1			8		2			
					9			7
	5					6	4	
	1	2					8	
3			1					
			4		8			6
		9					2	5

357

3		6			2			8
	4			5			1	
					7			2
9		1						
	8			6			4	
						8		5
6			1					
	5			4			9	
2			9			3		6

358

9			8		1			3
				7				
	3						6	
8		5	1		2	4		7
		6				5		
7		1	4		3	8		6
	7						8	
				2				
4			9		8			2

359

			2				1	
	3	7		8				5
	6			9		2		
3								
	4	6		5		8	7	
								6
		9		7			2	
8				4		6	3	
	5				6			

360

	2		7		8			
					6			9
		5			3	2		
2	9	6						7
3						4	9	6
		7	5			6		
1			4					
			9		1		5	

361

		9				5		
	5						2	
		2	8		4	9		
		1		8		3		
	6		5		3		7	
		7		6		8		
		5	7		9	4		
	1						3	
		8				2		

362

				2				
1								6
8	5			4			2	7
	9		4		7		1	
		5		6		3		
	8		3		5		4	
6	4			9			8	3
2								9
				7				

363

	2		3	7	8			
							9	
5					4		2	8
		3				5		
8				1				4
		4				6		
2	6		7					9
	7							
			5	9	3		6	

364

				9			3	
8	4		7		1		5	
		2				4		
	7						9	
3				1				5
	8						6	
		9				3		
	6		4		3		1	2
	1			7				

365

		8				4		
	9			8			3	
1			2		5			7
		7				9		
	5			2			6	
		1				8		
4			6		1			5
	6			3			4	
		5				3		

366

4		1		8		5		9
			7		6			
9								6
	2						1	
7				3				2
	3						6	
2								1
			8		5			
5		9		4		8		7

367

		8	5		7	3		
			1		3			
1				8				6
8	2						3	4
		6				9		
5	9						7	1
6				1				2
			8		5			
		7	6		4	8		

368

	1						5	
	7						8	
9			2		5			3
		7		6		4		
			1		4			
		8		9		2		
6			8		7			9
	9						7	
	4						3	

369

			6		3			
	3			9			6	
	8		5		2		3	
7		4				8		6
			7		6			
2		3				7		4
	9		8		5		7	
	7			3			1	
			2		1			

370

	9		8			6		
5			2		3			
								8
9	6		1				5	
	8				7		1	4
2								
			3		1			5
		5			9		3	

371

		9						
	5			7			1	
		7	8		1	4		3
		4				8		
	7			6			2	
		2				9		
8		6	4		5	2		
	1			2			9	
						1		

372

7			5					4
		8		3		9		
	4			9			8	
								2
	8	4				6	3	
1								
	1			6			2	
		6		8		7		
5					9			3

373

			4					
		1				2		
	5		9	6			4	
8		2			6			
		3				9		
			5			3		6
	1			9	5		3	
		4				7		
					2			

374

	8	3	2			9		
					5			6
5					1			7
	6	2						9
4						2	8	
3			8					5
1			5					
		7			2	3	6	

375

4			6			1		
	6				3			
					7	8		
2		8						9
	4		1		8		7	
3						2		5
		5	3					
			8				6	
		2			4			1

376

	2					4		
				4			8	5
9		1		7				
					2	6		
8								3
		5	9					
				6		8		1
2	9			5				
		3					6	

377

			1			8		
		4			2			
	6		3					7
3		9		6			4	
			4		8			
	2			1		7		3
8					1		5	
			7			6		
		1			6			

378

	6							
3			1		4	2		
		8			6		4	
	1					8	7	
				3				
	4	7					6	
	2		9			3		
		9	2		1			7
							1	

379

2						4		
			3	8			9	
3								8
6	1		8					9
		8		6		7		
5					7		8	3
4								5
	6			1	2			
		9						1

380

	1	9				3	8	
	3		5		1		6	
		3		5		8		
			2		4			
		4		6		5		
	6		1		8		3	
	5	2				4	7	

381

7		6				4	3	
				4	2	6		
	2					5		
			9					
	8		6		7		9	
					3			
		1					2	
		2	7	5				
	9	5				1		8

382

4				6				9
							3	
		2		3		6	7	
	7		8					
	3			2			8	
					4		5	
	4	6		7		9		
	8							
2				5				1

383

3		2				4		9
1			5		6			7
		5		6		2		
			7		3			
		4		8		3		
8			9		4			6
7		1				9		5

384

4		7		5			9	
			3				7	8
8		6						
3							4	
			9		4			
	1							2
						8		1
2	4				6			
	7			1		4		9

385

			5	3		4	8	
3	6						9	
1								
			7		3			6
6								3
2			6		5			
								2
	9						7	8
	3	7		8	4			

386

		2			9		4	
				7				1
3					1			
			1		7	8		4
	5						6	
7		9	6		3			
			4					6
6				1				
	3		8			7		

387

		8	4			3	5	
				5	7			
2								
7					2			6
		6		4		1		
9			1					7
								4
			2	6				
	1	5			3	9		

388

5	7						4	9
			1		6			
	8						1	
	9		5		4		8	
				8				
	6		9		2		3	
	3						5	
			7		1			
8	4						9	3

389

			9		1			
		7				2		
1	9						8	5
5				1				4
			6	3	5			
6				8				2
3	8						2	1
		2				7		
			4		8			

390

								1
			9	1			4	
		2		6		9		
	5		8					
	7	3				2	5	
					4		7	
		1		2		3		
	4			7	8			
8								

391

		5			1	2		
	4						9	
				4	7			
2		7		6				
		6				3		
				3		9		4
			6	1				
	7						8	
		8	2			1		

392

7		4				3		2
		9	2		1	4		
				8				
	4						2	
		8				5		
	3						1	
				5				
		1	4		3	8		
2		6				9		4

393

					1		9	
		7					8	2
	6		5					
		8		2				3
			3		4			
2				7		1		
					8		5	
1	4					6		
	9		7					

394

	8		3				1	
9		7						4
				7			8	
			9		2			6
		4		5		9		
8			4		3			
	2			1				
7						1		2
	1				6		3	

395

		4					9	
		7		5				6
5			2		8		1	
			1	9				
	9						8	
				6	5			
	5		6		2			7
3				1		4		
	7					6		

396

	3	8						
			9		7	2		4
	4				6			7
	5	3					6	
	9					3	8	
8			1				2	
9		5	6		2			
						7	5	

397

4					6			
	7					3		
3				2			9	
			8					6
		2				7		
9					3			
	6			9				4
		8					5	
			4					8

398

9	8				5			
7					3			
				4		1		
			4				2	7
		5				4		
1	6				7			
		6		2				
			1					2
			8				1	9

399

						1		
			3			5	6	
		6		8				
			1				4	8
3								7
1	7				9			
				3		2		
	5	8			4			
		1						

400

				5			9	
9	7			6				
3		5	2					
			3					8
	4			8			1	
6					7			
					6	9		3
				3			7	5
	1			4				

401

		7	5					
					8	6		2
4	8							
			6	2		1	7	
	1	6		4	9			
							3	4
1		2	7					
					4	9		

402

6	2							
		1	7					
				9	5	8		
		8	4					
4	6						5	8
					7	2		
		7	8	4				
					2	3		
							9	6

403

		9		6		3		
		1	7		3	2		
				5				
	1						7	
6		3				4		5
	4						3	
				9				
		7	5		2	1		
		2		3		6		

404

			6				1	4
			8			6		
		1			9			
8	9				7			
		6				4		
			2				3	5
			9			8		
		3			5			
4	5				2			

405

9								
		4		6	2		9	
	7		3					
		6			9		4	
	3			1			8	
	5		4			7		
					7		6	
	2		8	3		9		
								7

406

		5				7		
			7		4			
1		7				8		4
	6			3			9	
			2		8			
	4			1			5	
8		2				9		1
			1		5			
		3				2		

407

	4		2		8	7		
3				7				
					6			1
5						4		6
	3			4			5	
4		9						8
1			9					
				2				5
		7	8		1		2	

408

	5	8		9				
		3	6			8		
			1					
3			2					8
		4	5		3	2		
2					7			6
					1			
		2			9	7		
				4		5	1	

409

		5	4		7	6		
	3			8			4	
	2		8		5		6	
		4				9		
	1		7		9		3	
	4			2			1	
		2	5		6	7		

410

					3		9	
		3					1	2
	8		5					
		2		8				1
			1		2			
1				9		3		
					9		4	
7	4					8		
	6		7					

411

		6						
		8	9	4				
					6		7	2
		9		3			2	
	6		1		7		3	
	4			8		9		
1	3		8					
				1	4	7		
						1		

412

7					8			4
	6			9			5	
		2	7			8		
9						3		
	5			1			6	
		4						1
		3			2	1		
	8			5			7	
6			3					9

413

				7				2
				1				3
		1			8		6	
		3			1		8	
		2				4		
	7		9			6		
	9		5			2		
4				8				
6				3				

414

			1	6		9		
	2				8		6	
			2					1
9		6					3	
4								9
	7					1		5
6					7			
	1		9				4	
		3		8	4			

415

1		7	6	2				8
5					7		4	6
		5		3				
	6		8		1		3	
				6		9		
9	7		4					1
2				9	3	5		4

416

	1				5			
		7						4
			6		8		3	
6		3				8		
			4		2			
		5				9		1
	2		1		3			
8						5		
			2				6	

417

2			3				7	
		4	9			1		2
	8					6	4	
7	4							
				9				
							8	3
	1	3					6	
8		2			5	4		
	9				4			8

418

4	9			6				7
		7				2		4
	5						9	
			9		7			
3								5
			1		8			
	4						6	
6		8				1		
1				4			8	9

419

	7							
				6		4		9
	1	5	2			3		
				8		7		
	3						6	
		6		2				
		2			4	8	1	
8		4		9				
							5	

420

	5	2	6					
	9			8				
	1		2					
1			3					
	8	3				1	7	
					4			9
					9		3	
				5			2	
					3	5	1	

421

		3	2	4				
	9		5		7		3	
								1
	2						5	9
4								2
8	6						7	
6								
	7		4		8		2	
				1	3	8		

422

	7	2	5			4	9	
				2				
4					6			5
		8						9
	2						1	
5						3		
6			9					4
				8				
	3	4			1	7	8	

423

7					6			4
			5			2		
	5	4	8			1		
1						3	9	
	7	9						2
		2			5	4	6	
		8			7			
3			9					5

424

			8		3			
3		7				1		8
		4				2		
7			1		6			9
4			7		9			5
		1				5		
8		2				6		3
			5		4			

425

	7		4	9				
		4			2	5		
3				5				
9				6				3
	4						7	
6				3				4
				8				9
		2	5			6		
				1	6		2	

426

			2					7
	5	4						
	3			7	9	1		
1						9		
		3		5		2		
		8						4
		9	5	4			1	
						8	6	
6					7			

427

2							1	
			5		6	9		7
			1				2	
	6	5	8				4	
	9				2	7	6	
	2				5			
1		8	4		7			
	5							8

428

		8						
	2	3		1			4	
				2	6		3	9
		4						
	3	2		9		8	1	
						5		
2	7		9	4				
	8			7		4	2	
						7		

429

1		8		6				4
				5				
			9		1			3
		4				5		
6	8			2			9	1
		9				2		
3			7		2			
				9				
4				8		3		6

430

	9			2			3	
		5	4		6	1		
		7		3		9		
	4		9		7		8	
		9		8		6		
		4	6		1	8		
	2			9			7	

431

						9		
			7		2			
3		8		1		5		
	2						7	
		3		9		1		
	7						4	
		5		4		3		6
			8		5			
		9						

432

6						2		5
	9			4			3	
4					7			
		7		8				
	6		1		3		9	
				5		1		
			8					6
	4			9			5	
5		8						7

433

6			4		5			8
				9				
		7				2		
5			2		9			4
	6			3			2	
8			1		6			7
		9				3		
				7				
4			9		3			1

434

	4				8		3	
6		5		7		4		9
				1				
2								
	1	6				2	8	
								7
				9				
3		4		5		6		1
	9		4				2	

435

	1	9	4			3		
					8			6
5					7			1
	8	7						9
2						1	5	
1			7					3
7			2					
		6			5	8	9	

436

				1			9	
	2		6		4			5
		5						
	3		1				4	
8				3				9
	7				6		8	
						6		
3			5		2		1	
	8			9				

437

						8		
	1		3		6		5	
3				4				
	7		8		4		3	
		2		3		4		
	9		7		5		1	
				5				9
	5		6		1		4	
		8						

438

			6	7			3	
5	3		2			4	8	
	7							
							6	2
9								8
4	5							
							1	
	1	7			5		2	9
	9			1	7			

439

			9	6		5		
			5			4		
				1	3		7	2
4	3					9		
9		2				7		1
		5					6	4
5	7		6	2				
		8			4			
		1		3	9			

440

	5			1		8		
				4				7
7		2				9		
			4		7			
6	7						3	5
			3		8			
		6				1		4
1				8				
		4		2			5	

441

5								
	7			8				
9		3	6		7		8	
7	2					6		3
				9				
3		1					5	2
	6		8		9	7		1
				7			9	
								8

442

9		2			8			6
			1			3		
	5				3			9
3		5					7	
				2				
	7					9		5
8			9				6	
		1			6			
4			2			5		8

443

	1						4	
4					8			3
			1		2			
		3		9		6	1	
			5		6			
	9	6		7		8		
			7		9			
5			8					2
	8						7	

444

				2	5			
		3				7		
	9				1		2	
				3		4		6
4			1		6			7
7		2		8				
	5		2				3	
		8				9		
			5	1				

Answers

1

[4] 3	1	[5] 2	[5] 4
[3] 2	[7] 4	3	1
1	3	[6] 4	2
[7] 4	2	1	[3] 3

2

[8] 3	4	1	[5] 2
[3] 1	2	[6] 4	3
[6] 4	[4] 3	2	[1] 1
2	1	[7] 3	4

3

[3] 1	[6] 2	4	[4] 3
2	[7] 4	3	1
[7] 3	[1] 1	[6] 2	4
4	[6] 3	1	2

4

[3] 2	1	[6] 4	[6] 3
[7] 3	4	2	1
[5] 4	[4] 3	1	2
1	[2] 2	[7] 3	4

5

[6] 3	[7] 4	1	2
2	1	[6] 4	[4] 3
[8] 4	3	2	1
1	[5] 2	3	[4] 4

6

[3] 3	[7] 4	[3] 2	1
2	1	[4] 3	[6] 4
[8] 4	3	1	2
1	[9] 2	4	3

7

1	2	3	4
4	1	2	3
2	3	4	1
3	4	1	2

8

1	3	2	4
2	4	3	1
3	1	4	2
4	2	1	3

9

4	1	2	3
1	4	3	2
2	3	4	1
3	2	1	4

10

4	1	3	2
1	2	4	3
3	4	2	1
2	3	1	4

11

1	3	2	4
3	4	1	2
2	1	4	3
4	2	3	1

12

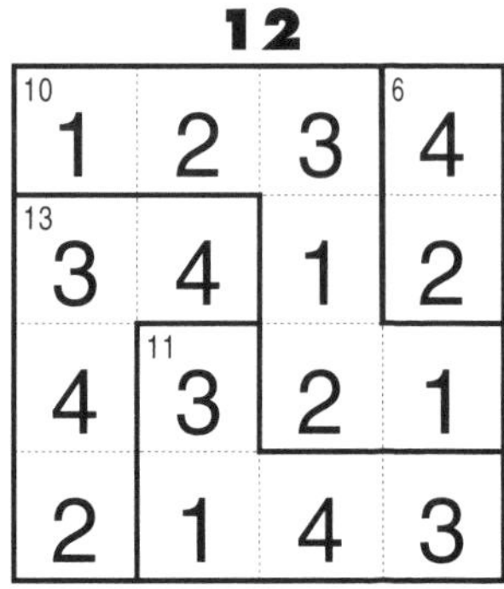

1	2	3	4
3	4	1	2
4	3	2	1
2	1	4	3

13

24 2	3 1	6 3	4 4
4	3	2	6 1
3	4 4	1	2
8 1	2	4	3

14

8 4	2	3 3	8 1
3 3	12 4	1	2
1	3	2 2	4
8 2	1	4	3 3

15

12 1	6 2	3	8 4
3	4 4	1 1	2
4	1	6 2	3
2 2	12 3	4	1

16

3 3	1	4 4	6 2
8 1	4	2	3
8 4	6 2	3	4 1
2	3 3	1	4

17

24 3	8 1	4	2
2	4 4	3 1	3
4	12 2	3	4 1
3 1	3	2	4

18

8 1	4	2	24 3
12 4	3	1	2
12 2	1 1	12 3	4
3	2	4	1

19

(4) 4	(12) 3	(6) 2	1
(6) 2	1	3	(4) 4
3	4	(8) 1	(6) 2
1	2	4	3

20

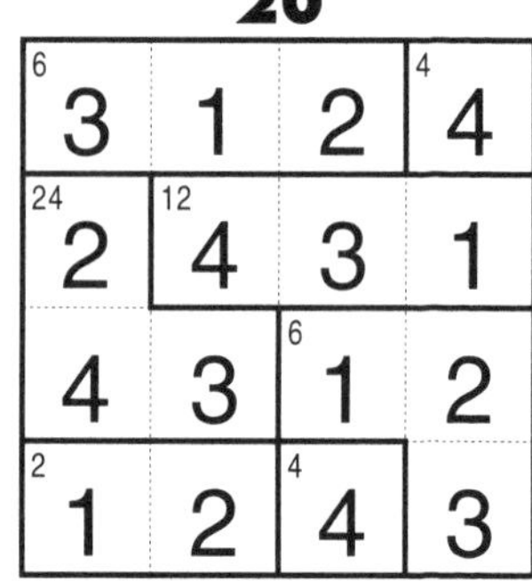

(6) 3	1	2	(4) 4
(24) 2	(12) 4	3	1
4	3	(6) 1	2
(2) 1	2	(4) 4	3

21

(12) 1	4	3	(32) 2
(12) 2	3	1	4
(12) 3	2	4	1
4	(6) 1	2	3

22

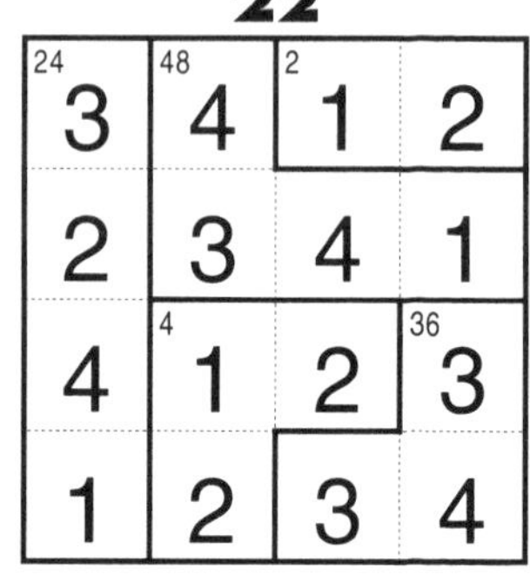

(24) 3	(48) 4	(2) 1	2
2	3	4	1
4	(4) 1	2	(36) 3
1	2	3	4

23

(12) 3	(8) 2	4	1
4	(12) 1	(48) 2	3
(6) 1	4	3	2
2	3	1	4

24

(24) 4	1	3	2
(36) 3	4	(2) 2	(48) 1
(4) 2	3	1	4
1	2	4	3

25

5+ 1	2 2	1− 4	3
4	4+ 3	1	7+ 2
7+ 3	4	5+ 2	1
1− 2	1	3	4

26

4+ 1	3	4 4	6+ 2
9+ 3	1− 1	2	4
2	3− 4	1	4+ 3
4	1− 2	3	1

27

6+ 3	3− 1	4	6+ 2
1	1− 3	1− 2	4
2	4	3	1 1
6+ 4	2	4+ 1	3

28

3 3	7+ 2	1	4
3− 4	1	9+ 2	6+ 3
4+ 1	3	4	2
2− 2	4	3	1

29

1− 3	7+ 2	4	1
2	3 3	8+ 1	2− 4
6+ 1	4	3	2
4	1	5+ 2	3

30

1− 2	4 4	8+ 3	1
3	1− 1	2	4
5+ 4	4+ 3	1	5+ 2
1	2− 2	4	3

31

7+ 4	1	2	1− 3
7+ 3	2	6+ 1	4
2	1− 3	4	1
1 1	4	1− 3	2

32

1− 3	6+ 1	6+ 4	2
2	4	1	8+ 3
4 4	7+ 2	3	1
2− 1	3	2	4

33

13+ 2	4	2− 1	3
3	1− 1	9+ 2	4
4	2	11+ 3	1
1	3	4	2

34

3− 1	16+ 2	3	4
4	3	13+ 2	2− 1
2 2	4	1	3
3	1	4	2

35

15+ 4	3	1− 2	1
2	4	1	16+ 3
3 3	1	4	2
1− 1	2	3	4

36

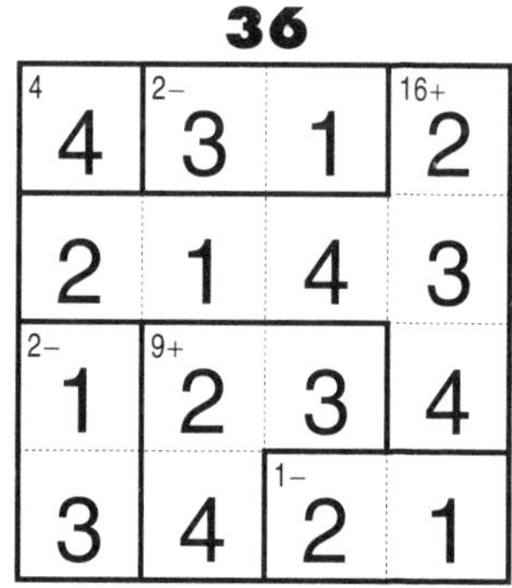

37

8× 2	12× 3	4	1
1	2÷ 4	6× 3	2
4	2	3÷ 1	3
6× 3	1	2	4 4

38

2× 2	3 3	6× 1	8× 4
1	4× 4	3	2
12× 4	1	2	3÷ 3
3	2÷ 2	4	1

39

12× 3	4÷ 4	1	2÷ 2
1	6× 3	2 2	4
4	2	12× 3	3× 1
2× 2	1	4	3

40

8× 4	6× 3	2	1
1	24× 2	4	3
2	4× 1	3÷ 3	2÷ 4
3 3	4	1	2

41

4÷ 1	4	6× 2	3
24× 3	2÷ 2	1	16× 4
2	9× 3	4	1
4	1	3	2 2

42

24× 4	3	2	3÷ 1
2÷ 2	1	16× 4	3
3÷ 3	4	1	24× 2
1	2 2	3	4

43

2÷ 1	2	24× 4	3
3 3	4÷ 4	2	6× 1
2÷ 4	1	3	2
2	12× 3	1	4

44

2÷ 4	6× 2	3	12× 1
2	1	2÷ 4	3
1 1	36× 3	2	4
3	4	2÷ 1	2

45

24× 1	3	24× 2	4
2	2÷ 1	4 4	3
4	2	36× 3	2÷ 1
3	4	1	2

46

3 3	96× 2	1	4 4
4÷ 4	1	2	3
72× 1	3	4	2
2	4	3	1

47

18× 3	2	96× 4	2÷ 1
4	3	1	2
2	1	3	96× 4
1	4	2	3

48

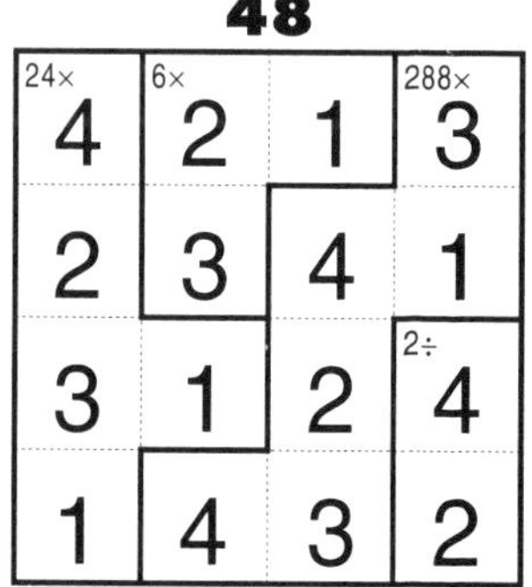

49

1– 1	2	12× 3	4
6× 2	7+ 3	4÷ 4	1 1
3	4	1	5+ 2
5+ 4	1	2 2	3

50

1– 2	12× 3	4	5+ 1
1	3+ 2	3 3	4
7+ 4	1	5+ 2	3
3	4÷ 4	1	2 2

51

4+ 1	3 3	2÷ 2	4
3	5+ 1	12× 4	2 2
2– 2	4	3	3× 1
4	1– 2	1	3

52

3– 4	1	2÷ 2	1– 3
2 2	7+ 3	1	4
4+ 1	4	6× 3	2
3	6+ 2	4	1 1

53

2– 4	2	7+ 3	1
2÷ 2	1– 4	1 1	3
1	3	8+ 2	4
3 3	4× 1	4	2

54

7+ 4	2	3× 3	1
1	1– 3	4	2÷ 2
1– 3	4÷ 1	2÷ 2	4
2	4	1	3 3

55

1− 3	8+ 4	1− 2	1
4	1	6× 3	2
2÷ 2	3	8+ 1	4
1	2÷ 2	4	3

56

6+ 1	9+ 4	3	2
2	3	4× 1	4
8+ 3	2÷ 2	4	2− 1
4	1	2 2	3

57

9+ 1	2	2÷ 4	12× 3
4	9× 3	2	1
2	1	3	4
1− 3	4	1− 1	2

58

3÷ 1	1− 3	32× 4	2
3	2	6× 1	4
7+ 4	1	2	3
2	12× 4	3	1

59

3+ 1	2	24× 3	4
13+ 3	12× 1	4	2
4	3	2÷ 2	1
2	4	2− 1	3

60

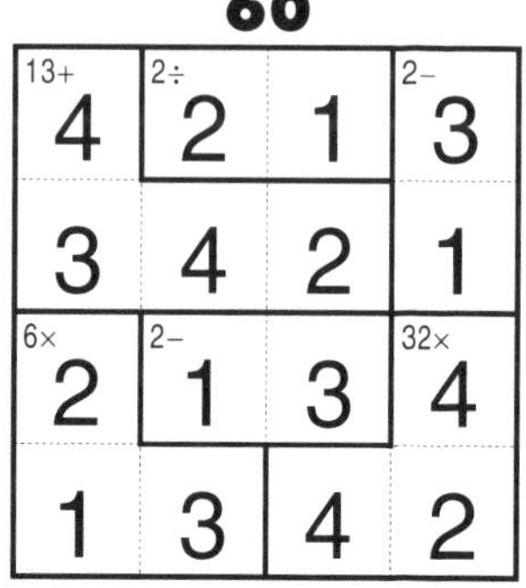

13+ 4	2÷ 2	1	2− 3
3	4	2	1
6× 2	2− 1	3	32× 4
1	3	4	2

61

[5] 1	4	[5] 3	2	[9] 5
[6] 2	[6] 3	[6] 5	1	4
4	2	1	[12] 5	[6] 3
[13] 5	[1] 1	[6] 4	3	2
3	5	2	4	1

62

[7] 4	[7] 5	[3] 1	2	[8] 3
3	2	[10] 4	1	5
[6] 1	3	2	5	[10] 4
[5] 5	[4] 1	3	4	2
[11] 2	4	5	[4] 3	1

63

[8] 3	5	[7] 4	[7] 2	1
[4] 1	3	2	[8] 5	4
[10] 5	4	1	3	[7] 2
[6] 2	1	[7] 3	4	5
4	[8] 2	5	1	[3] 3

64

[8] 5	3	[11] 4	[6] 1	[11] 2
[8] 1	2	5	3	4
4	[4] 1	3	2	5
3	[11] 5	[2] 2	[5] 4	1
2	4	[9] 1	5	3

65

(8) 2	5	(9) 4	3	(5) 1
1	(9) 3	5	2	4
(5) 3	2	1	(11) 4	5
(13) 5	4	(3) 3	(9) 1	2
4	(3) 1	2	5	3

66

(6) 2	(12) 4	3	(9) 1	5
4	5	(3) 2	3	(7) 1
(6) 3	2	1	(14) 5	4
1	(9) 3	5	4	2
5	1	(9) 4	2	3

67

(4) 3	1	(14) 5	(6) 2	4
(7) 2	(11) 3	4	5	(8) 1
4	5	3	(6) 1	2
1	(4) 4	2	3	5
(8) 5	2	1	(7) 4	3

68

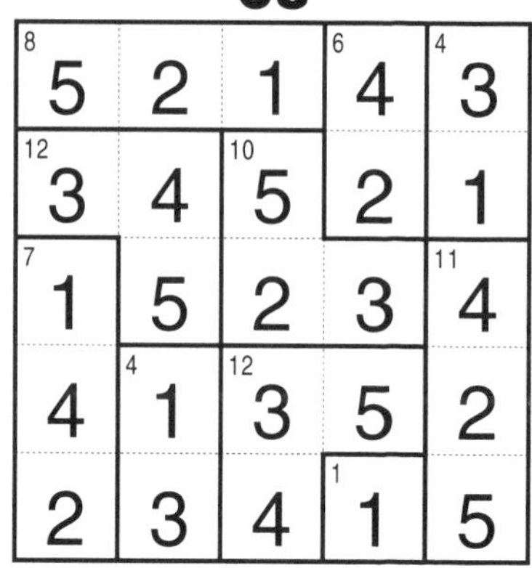

(8) 5	2	1	(6) 4	(4) 3
(12) 3	4	(10) 5	2	1
(7) 1	5	2	3	(11) 4
4	(4) 1	(12) 3	5	2
2	3	4	(1) 1	5

69

[10] 3	4	[9] 1	[16] 5	2
[12] 2	3	4	1	5
5	[9] 1	2	3	4
4	[19] 5	3	2	1
1	2	5	4	3

70

[11] 1	[19] 4	5	2	3
2	3	1	[11] 4	5
[4] 3	1	4	5	2
[19] 4	5	[6] 2	3	1
5	2	3	[5] 1	4

71

[13] 4	[8] 2	3	1	[14] 5
1	3	2	5	4
2	[21] 5	4	3	[6] 1
3	[13] 1	5	4	2
5	4	1	2	3

72

[10] 3	1	2	[7] 4	[6] 5
[3] 2	[19] 5	4	3	1
1	2	3	5	4
[21] 5	4	[9] 1	2	3
4	3	5	1	2

73

[8] 4	[30] 3	2	5	[3] 1
2	[20] 5	4	1	3
[3] 3	[2] 2	1	[24] 4	[40] 5
1	[4] 4	[15] 5	3	2
[5] 5	1	3	2	4

74

[4] 1	[60] 5	[24] 4	2	3
4	3	[10] 2	5	1
[2] 2	4	[15] 3	[4] 1	[10] 5
[3] 3	1	5	4	2
[10] 5	2	[12] 1	3	4

75

[5] 5	[12] 4	3	[1] 1	[6] 2
1	[10] 5	[8] 4	2	3
[12] 3	2	[5] 1	5	[20] 4
4	[6] 1	2	3	5
[6] 2	3	[20] 5	4	1

76

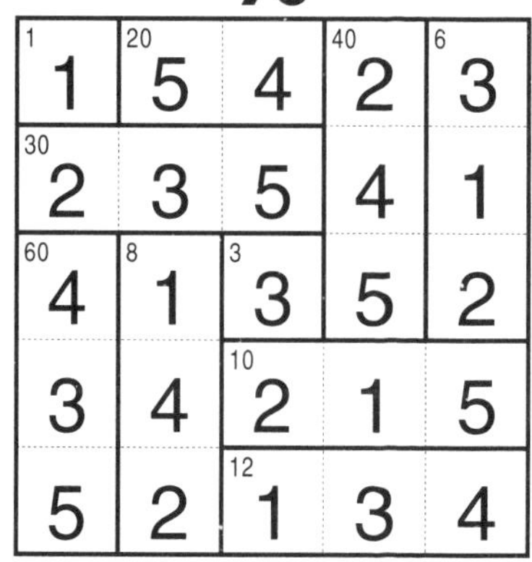

[1] 1	[20] 5	4	[40] 2	[6] 3
[30] 2	3	5	4	1
[60] 4	[8] 1	[3] 3	5	2
3	4	[10] 2	1	5
5	2	[12] 1	3	4

77

(10) 2	5	(12) 3	1	4
1	(6) 3	(5) 5	(24) 4	2
(60) 4	1	2	3	(15) 5
3	(32) 2	4	(10) 5	1
5	4	1	2	3

78

(10) 2	5	(60) 4	3	(6) 1
(12) 4	1	5	2	3
1	3	(10) 2	5	(8) 4
(5) 5	(12) 4	3	1	2
(6) 3	2	1	(20) 4	5

79

(20) 5	(2) 2	(10) 1	(36) 3	4
4	(12) 1	5	2	3
1	3	4	(15) 5	(10) 2
(24) 2	4	3	1	5
3	(40) 5	2	4	1

80

(60) 4	(4) 1	(30) 2	5	3
5	4	1	(12) 3	2
3	(40) 5	4	2	(20) 1
(6) 1	2	(3) 3	4	5
2	3	(20) 5	1	4

81

120 4	1	2	300 3	5
60 2	5	3	4	3 1
1	2	80 4	5	3
3	4	5	1	48 2
5	3	1	2	4

82

32 2	4	180 5	1	3
4	45 1	3	40 5	2
5	3	4	240 2	1
1	10 5	2	3	4
3	2	1	4	5

83

40 2	5	1	96 4	3
4	3 1	3	120 5	2
120 5	3	4	2	1
3	2	150 5	1	4
1	4	2	3	5

84

75 3	5	192 4	2	10 1
5	4	3	1	2
16 4	1	2	5	180 3
2	3	1	4	5
1	2	60 5	3	4

85

4− 5	8+ 3	1	4	2 2
1	6+ 2	4	8+ 5	3
11+ 2	4	5	4+ 3	1
3− 4	1	1− 3	2	9+ 5
8+ 3	5	1− 2	1	4

86

11+ 5	4− 1	9+ 4	3	2
4	5	4+ 1	3+ 2	3 3
2	2− 4	3	1	10+ 5
2− 3	2	1− 5	4	1
1	10+ 3	2	5	4

87

2− 5	3	7+ 4	3+ 1	2
9+ 4	5	3	9+ 2	6+ 1
6+ 3	1	2	4	5
3+ 1	3− 2	5	3	1− 4
2	4 4	4− 1	5	3

88

5+ 2	1− 5	11+ 4	2− 1	3
3	4	2	4− 5	1
3+ 1	2	5	5+ 3	9+ 4
8+ 4	3	1	2	5
4− 5	1	1− 3	4	2 2

89

4 4	13+ 5	3	3− 1	9+ 2
8+ 1	2	5	4	3
5	2− 3	1	8+ 2	4
9+ 3	4	7+ 2	5	1
2	1	4	2− 3	5

90

8+ 5	3− 1	4	6+ 2	3
3	6+ 2	14+ 5	4	1
1	3	1− 2	5	12+ 4
2− 2	4	1	3	5
12+ 4	5	3	1− 1	2

91

3− 2	1− 4	5	2− 1	3
5	6+ 2	8+ 3	4	1
1	3	1− 4	5	11+ 2
12+ 4	4+ 1	2	5+ 3	5
3	5	1	2	4

92

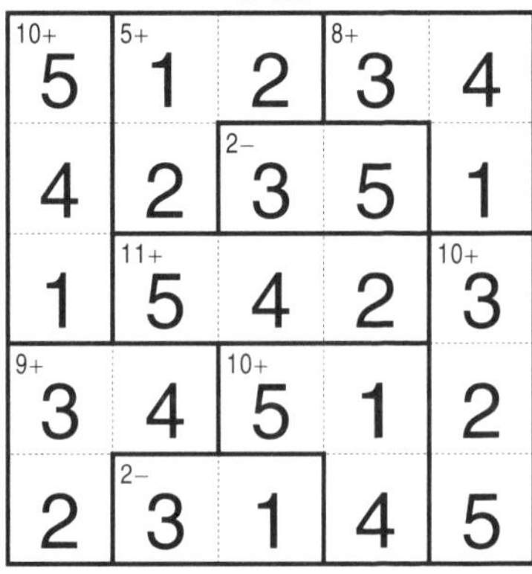

10+ 5	5+ 1	2	8+ 3	4
4	2	2− 3	5	1
1	11+ 5	4	2	10+ 3
9+ 3	4	10+ 5	1	2
2	2− 3	1	4	5

93

11+ 3	4	2	20+ 5	3− 1
8+ 1	2	8+ 5	3	4
2	1	3	4	5
4	17+ 5	3+ 1	2	3
5	3	4	1− 1	2

94

11+ 1	2	3	9+ 5	4
21+ 4	5	3− 1	1− 2	14+ 3
5	3	4	1	2
6+ 2	4	5	3	1
3	1	6+ 2	4	5

95

1− 3	2	12+ 1	21+ 4	5
1− 2	3	5	1	4
1	5+ 4	2	5	3
14+ 5	1	12+ 4	3	2
4	5	3	1− 2	1

96

7+ 3	4	8+ 1	1− 2	21+ 5
1− 1	2	5	3	4
2	6+ 1	4	5	3
14+ 5	3	2	8+ 4	1− 1
4	5	3	1	2

97

6× 2	3	1	24× 4	40× 5
15× 1	5 5	40× 4	3	2
3	4÷ 1	5	2	4
5	4	2	3÷ 1	3
2÷ 4	2	15× 3	5	1

98

10× 5	2	1	4÷ 4	30× 3
4× 4	20× 5	6× 3	1	2
1	4	2	3 3	5
3 3	5÷ 1	5	10× 2	4÷ 4
24× 2	3	4	5	1

99

3× 3	8× 4	1	2	60× 5
1	10× 2	20× 5	3÷ 3	4
2÷ 2	5	4	1	3
4	3÷ 1	15× 3	5	2 2
5 5	3	8× 2	4	1

100

8× 2	15× 5	3 3	4÷ 1	4
4	3	10× 1	2	5
3 3	2÷ 2	2÷ 4	20× 5	6× 1
5÷ 5	1	2	4	3
1	60× 4	5	3	2

101

20× 1	3 3	20× 2	5	12× 4
4	5	5÷ 1	2	3
2÷ 2	4	5	15× 3	1
15× 3	24× 2	4	1	5
5	1	3	2÷ 4	2

102

15× 3	5	1	16× 4	2
2÷ 1	60× 4	5	2	15× 3
2	3	2÷ 4	1	5
5÷ 5	1	2	12× 3	4
2÷ 4	2	15× 3	5	1

103

5÷ 1	5	12× 2	12× 4	3
2÷ 4	2	3	1	15× 5
2	20× 4	5	3	1
45× 3	1	20× 4	5	2 2
5	3	1	2÷ 2	4

104

3÷ 1	60× 3	4	20× 5	2 2
3	5	20× 2	4	3÷ 1
20× 4	2	5	1	3
5	1	6× 3	2	60× 4
2÷ 2	4	1	3	5

105

75× 3	1	5	2÷ 4	2
5÷ 1	5	24× 2	3	4
5	2÷ 2	4	1	30× 3
24× 4	3	60× 1	2	5
2	4	3	5	1

106

32× 4	2	100× 5	15× 1	3
3÷ 3	4	1	24× 2	5
1	5	4	3	2÷ 2
60× 5	3	2	4	1
2	60× 1	3	5	4

107

36× 4	3	80× 2	5	5÷ 1
3	60× 4	1	2	5
40× 1	5	3	4	24× 2
5	2	4	1	3
2÷ 2	1	15× 5	3	4

108

48× 1	4	3	30× 5	2
4	2÷ 1	2	3	100× 5
60× 3	2	5	1	4
5	60× 3	2÷ 4	2	3÷ 1
2	5	1	4	3

109

5÷ 1	10+ 5	3	2	7+ 4
5	4+ 1	8× 4	2− 3	2
2÷ 4	3	2	5	1
2	4 4	9+ 5	1	3
6+ 3	2	1	20× 4	5

110

6+ 1	11+ 2	2− 5	3	4÷ 4
2	5	12× 3	4	1
3	4	4− 1	5	10+ 2
1− 4	6× 3	2	1 1	5
5	7+ 1	4	2	3

111

8× 4	5 5	5+ 3	2	5÷ 1
2	8+ 3	4	1	5
2× 1	2	8+ 5	3	9+ 4
1− 3	4	1− 1	9+ 5	2
5÷ 5	1	2	4	3

112

10+ 1	2× 2	5+ 3	1− 4	5
4	1	2	15× 5	3
5	4÷ 4	1	3÷ 3	2 2
1− 2	15× 3	5	1	5+ 4
3	11+ 5	4	2	1

113

9+ 1	3	2	20× 5	4
3	12+ 2	5÷ 5	1− 4	1
2	4	1	3	10+ 5
4	25× 5	10+ 3	1	2
5	1	4	2	3

114

7+ 1	13+ 5	3	2	16+ 4
4	2	2÷ 1	3	5
14+ 5	12× 1	2	4	3
2	3	4	25× 5	1− 1
3	4	5	1	2

115

100× 5	4	7+ 1	6+ 2	3
10+ 3	5	2	4	1
4	2	2− 3	1	14+ 5
1	17+ 3	4	5	2
2÷ 2	1	5	3	4

116

9+ 1	3	5	2÷ 4	2
1− 2	48× 4	3	15+ 5	1
3	2× 1	4	9+ 2	5
16+ 5	2	1	3	4
4	5	2	1	3

117

[2−] 3	5	[12+] 2	1	4
[60×] 5	1	4	3	2
[32×] 4	3	[21+] 5	2	[3÷] 1
2	4	[2−] 1	5	3
[2÷] 1	2	3	4	5

118

[19+] 3	2	4	5	[3÷] 1
[6+] 2	5	[60×] 1	4	3
4	3	5	[2−] 1	[80×] 2
[60×] 5	[2÷] 1	2	3	4
1	4	3	2	5

119

[3÷] 3	1	[40×] 2	5	4
[9+] 5	2	[12×] 4	3	1
2	[21+] 4	[2−] 3	1	[60×] 5
[4÷] 4	5	1	2	3
1	3	5	4	2

120

[19+] 2	3	4	5	[3÷] 1
5	[1−] 1	2	[7+] 4	3
[60×] 3	5	1	2	[40×] 4
1	[2÷] 4	[45×] 5	3	2
4	2	3	1	5

121

1	5	4	6	2	3
4	3	2	1	5	6
5	6	3	2	1	4
2	4	6	5	3	1
6	2	1	3	4	5
3	1	5	4	6	2

122

3	1	2	6	4	5
4	2	5	3	6	1
6	5	3	4	1	2
1	4	6	2	5	3
5	3	4	1	2	6
2	6	1	5	3	4

123

5	3	6	4	2	1
6	2	4	1	3	5
1	4	2	3	5	6
4	5	3	6	1	2
2	6	1	5	4	3
3	1	5	2	6	4

124

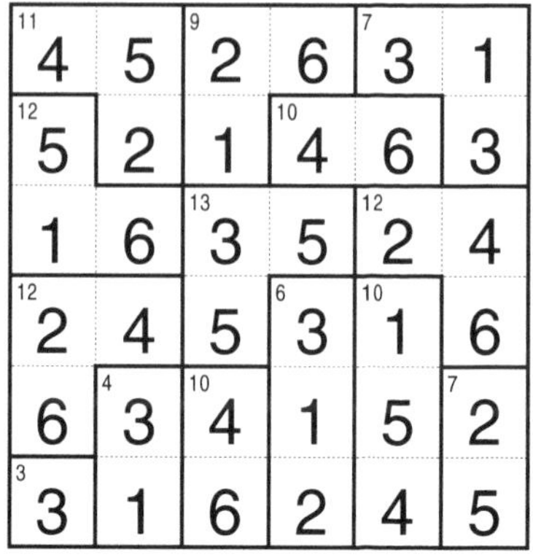

4	5	2	6	3	1
5	2	1	4	6	3
1	6	3	5	2	4
2	4	5	3	1	6
6	3	4	1	5	2
3	1	6	2	4	5

125

4	1	3	5	6	2
6	2	1	4	5	3
2	6	4	3	1	5
5	4	2	6	3	1
1	3	5	2	4	6
3	5	6	1	2	4

126

1	4	3	6	5	2
4	5	6	2	1	3
6	3	5	4	2	1
3	2	1	5	6	4
5	1	2	3	4	6
2	6	4	1	3	5

127

3	2	6	4	1	5
2	4	5	6	3	1
1	6	3	2	5	4
4	3	1	5	2	6
5	1	4	3	6	2
6	5	2	1	4	3

128

1	5	4	3	2	6
5	3	6	4	1	2
3	4	2	6	5	1
6	1	5	2	4	3
2	6	1	5	3	4
4	2	3	1	6	5

129

4	3	6	1	2	5
3	4	1	5	6	2
2	5	4	6	1	3
6	1	5	2	3	4
5	6	2	3	4	1
1	2	3	4	5	6

130

5	1	3	6	4	2
4	6	1	2	3	5
6	2	5	4	1	3
2	4	6	3	5	1
3	5	4	1	2	6
1	3	2	5	6	4

131

6	2	5	4	3	1
2	3	1	5	6	4
4	5	3	6	1	2
5	6	4	1	2	3
1	4	2	3	5	6
3	1	6	2	4	5

132

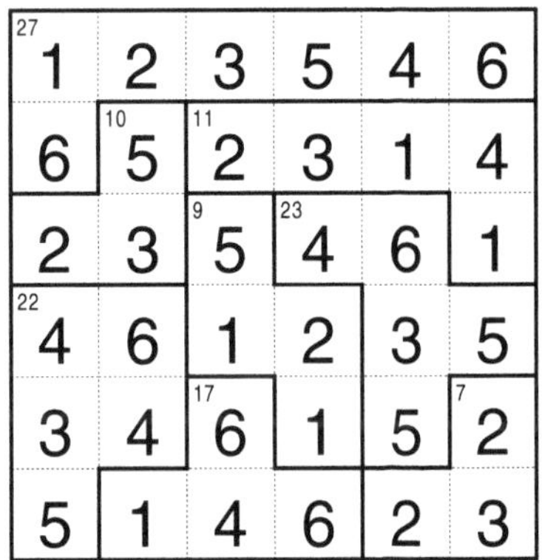

1	2	3	5	4	6
6	5	2	3	1	4
2	3	5	4	6	1
4	6	1	2	3	5
3	4	6	1	5	2
5	1	4	6	2	3

133

5	6	3	1	2	4
3	4	2	6	5	1
4	5	6	2	1	3
6	1	4	5	3	2
2	3	1	4	6	5
1	2	5	3	4	6

134

6	4	5	2	1	3
1	6	2	4	3	5
2	1	3	5	6	4
5	3	1	6	4	2
4	5	6	3	2	1
3	2	4	1	5	6

135

6	5	1	4	3	2
3	6	5	1	2	4
4	3	2	6	5	1
2	4	3	5	1	6
1	2	6	3	4	5
5	1	4	2	6	3

136

3	4	5	6	1	2
5	2	6	1	3	4
6	1	4	2	5	3
4	3	1	5	2	6
2	5	3	4	6	1
1	6	2	3	4	5

137

[96] 4	6	[3] 1	3	[50] 5	2
[10] 1	4	[36] 3	6	2	5
2	[12] 1	4	[10] 5	[108] 3	6
5	3	2	1	6	[12] 4
[36] 3	[5] 5	[120] 6	[8] 2	4	1
6	2	5	4	1	3

138

[24] 2	3	[25] 5	1	[144] 6	4
4	[36] 2	[24] 3	5	[15] 1	6
3	6	4	[12] 2	5	[15] 1
[20] 1	4	2	6	3	5
5	[24] 1	6	4	[16] 2	3
[6] 6	[15] 5	1	3	4	2

139

[12] 1	6	2	[60] 3	4	5
[36] 3	[30] 2	5	[24] 4	1	[30] 6
2	[80] 4	3	6	5	1
6	5	4	[2] 1	[3] 3	[24] 2
[15] 5	3	1	2	[60] 6	4
[24] 4	1	6	5	2	3

140

[3] 3	[24] 1	[18] 6	[10] 5	2	[40] 4
6	4	3	1	5	2
[60] 2	6	5	[12] 3	4	[18] 1
[20] 5	[6] 3	2	[48] 4	1	6
4	[10] 5	1	2	6	3
1	2	[72] 4	6	3	[5] 5

141

24: 4	90: 5	6	1	36: 2	3
2	3	48: 4	6	1	20: 5
3	6	1	2	150: 5	4
1	24: 4	3	5	6	48: 2
60: 5	1	2	180: 3	4	6
6	2	5	4	3	1

142

24: 6	96: 4	2	60: 3	1	5
2	1	3	150: 6	5	4
15: 1	2	4	5	36: 6	3
5	12: 3	1	4	2	12: 6
3	720: 5	6	1	120: 4	2
4	6	5	2	3	1

143

120: 3	180: 6	120: 2	4	5	20: 1
2	1	6	3	4	5
4	5	2: 1	2	12: 6	72: 3
5	72: 3	4	1	2	6
120: 6	2	3	180: 5	1	4
1	4	5	6	3	2

144

36: 2	24: 4	6	1	75: 3	5
1	180: 3	2	6	5	32: 4
3	240: 6	5	4	2	1
6	5	4	6: 2	1	144: 3
20: 5	2	90: 1	3	4	6
4	1	3	5	6	2

145

360 5	3	48 6	1	2	360 4
2	240 6	1	4	3	5
3	5	4	2	6	24 1
4	12 2	45 3	5	1	6
6	1	300 5	3	4	6 2
4 1	4	2	6	5	3

146

12 6	2	20 5	576 1	4	36 3
10 1	270 5	4	6	3	2
5	3	2	4	6	1
2	6	3	10 5	24 1	4
48 3	4	1	2	900 5	6
4	1	6	3	2	5

147

960 4	6	60 5	12 2	3	1
5	4	3	1	4320 6	2
2	9 3	1	4	5	6
3	1	16 2	6	4	15 5
180 6	2	4	15 5	1	3
1	5	6	3	8 2	4

148

1200 4	2	5	3	48 6	1
5	216 3	6	2	1	4
3	4	6 1	6	14400 5	2
1	5	3	4	2	6
72 6	40 1	2	5	4	45 3
2	6	4	1	3	5

149

[36] 2	[9000] 5	4	1	6	3
3	6	1	5	[192] 4	2
[8640] 1	2	5	[120] 4	3	6
5	3	6	2	1	4
4	[72] 1	3	6	2	5
6	4	[30] 2	3	5	1

150

[10800] 1	3	4	[120] 2	5	6
5	1	6	[30] 3	[32] 4	2
[36] 3	6	5	1	2	4
6	5	2	[8640] 4	1	[15] 3
2	[24] 4	1	6	3	5
4	2	3	5	6	1

151

[21600] 6	3	5	[40] 4	2	1
2	4	[18] 6	1	5	[120] 3
5	6	1	3	4	2
1	[40] 2	4	[36] 6	[3] 3	5
[24] 4	5	3	2	1	[720] 6
3	1	2	5	6	4

152

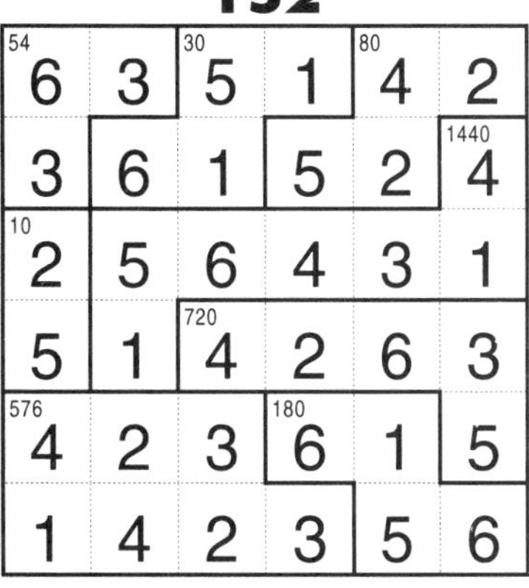

[54] 6	3	[30] 5	1	[80] 4	2
3	6	1	5	2	[1440] 4
[10] 2	5	6	4	3	1
5	1	[720] 4	2	6	3
[576] 4	2	3	[180] 6	1	5
1	4	2	3	5	6

153

3– 4	1	13+ 2	5	6	9+ 3
14+ 3	5	5– 6	1	4	2
6	11+ 2	1– 4	3	9+ 1	1– 5
5	4	6+ 1	2	3	6
3+ 2	14+ 6	3	2– 4	5	5+ 1
1	3	5	6	2 2	4

154

1– 4	7+ 1	5	3– 3	4– 6	2
3	9+ 4	1	6	2 2	1– 5
2	3	3– 6	8+ 1	1– 5	4
13+ 6	2	3	5	4	5+ 1
5	12+ 6	2– 4	2	1	3
1	5	2	13+ 4	3	6

155

9+ 1	2	9+ 5	1– 4	3	6 6
2– 5	6	1	3	10+ 4	2
3	13+ 5	6	2	4+ 1	4
8+ 6	3– 4	1– 3	1	2	14+ 5
2	1	4	5 5	6	3
9+ 4	3	2	12+ 6	5	1

156

4– 1	6 6	13+ 4	3	1– 2	15+ 5
5	6+ 3	2	6	1	4
2– 4	1	10+ 3	2	5	6
2	10+ 4	5	1	12+ 6	3
11+ 6	5	5– 1	13+ 4	3	1– 2
1– 3	2	6	5	4	1

157

2− 3	1	19+ 4	4− 2	6	10+ 5
2− 6	5	2	11+ 3	1	4
4	13+ 6	5	1	3	2
11+ 1	4	3	21+ 5	2	5− 6
2	3	6	4	12+ 5	1
5	2	1	6	4	3

158

22+ 2	6	5	15+ 1	4	3
6	12+ 1	4	2	2− 3	5
3	5	2	21+ 4	1	15+ 6
1− 1	2	6	3	5	4
13+ 5	4	3	17+ 6	2	1
4	2− 3	1	5	6	2

159

1− 4	3	1− 1	2	12+ 5	6
9+ 2	14+ 4	6	5 5	1	2− 3
1	2	4	24+ 3	6	5
3	1	5	6	1− 4	7+ 2
17+ 5	6	13+ 2	4	3	1
6	5	3	1	2	4

160

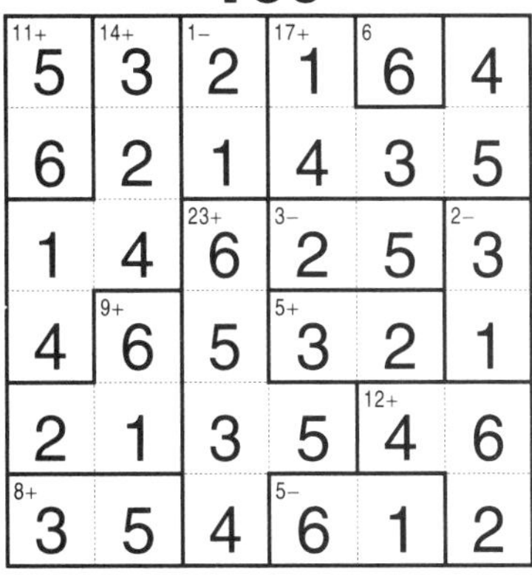

11+ 5	14+ 3	1− 2	17+ 1	6 6	4
6	2	1	4	3	5
1	4	23+ 6	3− 2	5	2− 3
4	9+ 6	5	5+ 3	2	1
2	1	3	5	12+ 4	6
8+ 3	5	4	5− 6	1	2

161

7+ 1	2	4	9+ 3	1− 6	5
29+ 2	3	5	1	12+ 4	6
3	17+ 6	1	4	10+ 5	2
4	5	6	3− 2	3	8+ 1
6	1	3	5	2	4
1− 5	4	2	5− 6	1	3

162

10+ 6	2	4+ 1	3	12+ 4	14+ 5
2	14+ 5	2− 4	1	3	6
5	4	2	1− 6	1	3
2− 4	6	26+ 3	5	2	1
3	1	5	2	6	2− 4
1	13+ 3	6	4	5	2

163

8+ 6	21+ 2	1− 5	5+ 3	1	21+ 4
2	3	6	1	4	5
1	5	4	2	6	6+ 3
1− 4	6	2− 3	5	2	1
5	22+ 1	2	4	3	4− 6
3	4	5− 1	6	5	2

164

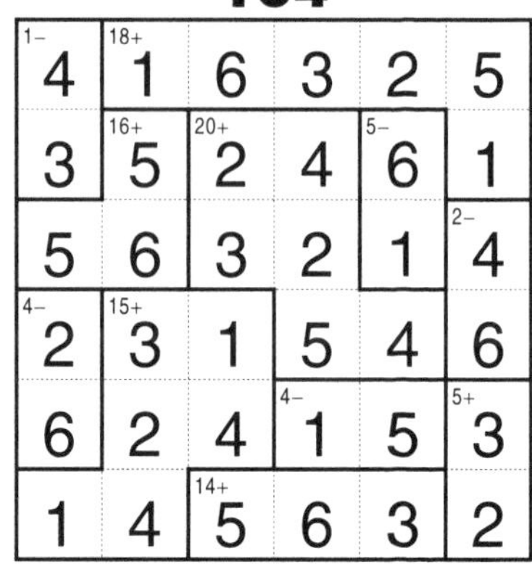

1− 4	18+ 1	6	3	2	5
3	16+ 5	20+ 2	4	5− 6	1
5	6	3	2	1	2− 4
4− 2	15+ 3	1	5	4	6
6	2	4	4− 1	5	5+ 3
1	4	14+ 5	6	3	2

165

15+ 3	6	4− 5	1	17+ 2	4
12+ 6	1	29+ 2	4	3	5
4	5	3	2	1	5− 6
2	3	4	32+ 6	5	1
5	4	1	3	6	1− 2
1− 1	2	6	5	4	3

166

13+ 4	6	3	5− 1	1− 5	10+ 2
6+ 1	3	2	6	4	5
10+ 2	3− 1	4	11+ 5	6	3
5	2− 4	4− 6	2	19+ 3	11+ 1
3	2	5	4	1	6
1− 6	5	1	3	2	4

167

29+ 2	1	4− 5	13+ 3	2− 6	4
4	6	1	2	5	3
5	2	4	5+ 1	3	13+ 6
10+ 6	5	1− 3	28+ 4	1	2
1	3	2	6	7+ 4	5
3	4	6	5	2	1

168

20+ 4	3	6	1	2	28+ 5
5− 6	4− 5	1	4	3	2
1	14+ 2	4	17+ 6	5	3
2	1	9+ 3	5	6	4
5	25+ 4	2	3	1	6
3	6	5	2	4	1

169

24× 6	4	5÷ 1	5	48× 2	12× 3
2÷ 2	30× 3	5	4	6	1
1	2	2÷ 3	6÷ 6	5 5	4
60× 3	5	6	1	2÷ 4	2
4	30× 6	16× 2	3× 3	1	90× 5
5	1	4	2	3	6

170

12× 1	60× 3	4	5	48× 6	2
3	60× 2	5	6	4	5÷ 1
4	24× 6	12× 2	3	1 1	5
60× 6	4	1	2	15× 5	72× 3
2	5	2÷ 6	1	3	4
5÷ 5	1	3	2÷ 4	2	6

171

48× 4	2	6	6× 1	72× 3	5 5
30× 5	1	3	2	6	4
2÷ 1	6	60× 5	3	4	30× 2
2	4× 4	1	120× 6	5	3
2÷ 6	3	4	5	12× 2	1
30× 3	5	2	4÷ 4	1	6

172

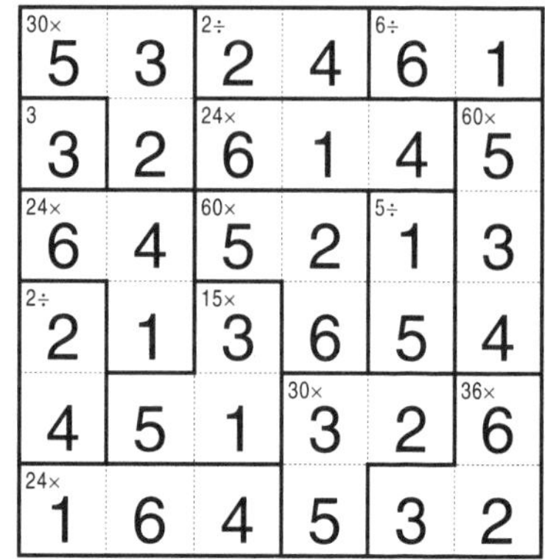

30× 5	3	2÷ 2	4	6÷ 6	1
3 3	2	24× 6	1	4	60× 5
24× 6	4	60× 5	2	5÷ 1	3
2÷ 2	1	15× 3	6	5	4
4	5	1	30× 3	2	36× 6
24× 1	6	4	5	3	2

173

120× 5	2	72× 1	360× 6	4	3
2	6	4	3	3÷ 1	5
288× 4	30× 1	6	40× 5	3	2÷ 2
6	3	5	4	2	1
3	4	2	1	180× 5	6
5÷ 1	5	6× 3	2	6	4 4

174

2÷ 6	50× 1	5	2÷ 4	24× 3	2
3	5	432× 6	2	4	1
5× 1	2	4	3	6	360× 5
5	144× 3	6÷ 1	6	10× 2	4
4	6	120× 2	1	5	3
2	4	3	5	1	6

175

540× 6	3	4× 4	1	96× 2	30× 5
2÷ 2	5	1	4	3	6
1	6	60× 5	2	4	3 3
120× 3	4÷ 4	2	180× 5	6	1
4	1	3	6	90× 5	2÷ 2
5	2	6	3	1	4

176

3÷ 3	1	40× 5	4	3÷ 6	2
40× 5	4	216× 3	2	1	120× 6
2	3	4	6	5	1
120× 6	5	2× 2	3÷ 1	3	4
4	216× 6	1	150× 5	2	3
1	2	6	3	4 4	5

177

12× 1	60× 3	4	10× 2	30× 6	5
3	4	1	5	48× 2	6
3÷ 2	6	5	3÷ 1	3	4
120× 6	5÷ 5	2÷ 2	4	72× 1	3
5	1	1080× 6	3	4	2
4	2	3	6	5	1

178

40× 2	4	15× 5	3	18× 1	6
5	1080× 6	2	1	24× 4	3
6	5	1	2	3	8× 4
1	36× 3	6	4800× 4	5	2
3	2	4	5	6	5÷ 1
4÷ 4	1	2÷ 3	6	2	5

179

120× 2	5	12960× 6	3× 3	1	19200× 4
3	1	2	5	4	6
1	3÷ 6	3	4	2	5
4	2	5	6÷ 6	15× 3	1
6	3	4	1	5	36× 2
20× 5	4	2÷ 1	2	6	3

180

96× 6	4	1080× 3	5	2÷ 1	2
4	1800× 2	5	1	3	6× 6
3	5	6	4	480× 2	1
2	2÷ 3	30× 1	6	4	5
20× 1	6	2	3	5	4
5	1	4	3÷ 2	6	3

181

36× 3	6	3840× 4	1	10× 2	5
30× 1	2	5	4	6	6480× 3
5	15× 3	1	2	4	6
6	5	30× 2	3	1	4
2÷ 2	4	2÷ 6	5	3	2÷ 1
4× 4	1	3	6	5	2

182

864× 2	4	3	30× 1	5	6
30× 5	2	6	3	120× 1	4
6	60× 1	14400× 4	5	3	2
1	5	2÷ 2	6	2÷ 4	3
3	18× 6	1	4	2	5
4	3	5	2	6÷ 6	1

183

20× 4	9720× 5	2	2÷ 3	6	6× 1
1	6	20× 5	2÷ 4	2	3
5	3	4	2	600× 1	3÷ 6
3	1	6	5	4	2
24× 6	2	3	1	5	60× 4
2	4÷ 4	1	6	3	5

184

30× 6	1	43200× 5	6× 3	2	12× 4
3÷ 1	5	6	2	1440× 4	3
3	6	4	5	1	2
96× 4	2	3	5÷ 1	5	6
10× 5	4	2	2÷ 6	3	1
2	3	4÷ 1	4	6	5

185

14+ 5	36× 3	6	2	3− 4	1
3	1− 5	4	2÷ 1	2	30× 6
6	9+ 4	2	3	1	5
6× 1	6	14+ 5	4	3 3	2÷ 2
8+ 2	1	18× 3	5	90× 6	4
4	2	1	6	5	3

186

2÷ 2	4	6× 3	25× 5	1	2− 6
90× 3	6	2	1	5	4
11+ 1	5	3− 4	2÷ 3	6	40× 2
6	3 3	1	60× 2	4	5
4	8+ 1	5	6	6× 2	3
5	2	13+ 6	4	3	1

187

4 4	1− 5	12× 2	6	9× 1	3
12× 2	6	60× 4	1	3	5÷ 5
6	3	5	9+ 2	120× 4	1
1	7+ 2	3	4	5	6
2− 3	1	60× 6	5	2	2÷ 4
5	4	10+ 1	3	6	2

188

36× 3	6	3÷ 1	1− 4	5	9+ 2
2	3− 5	3	6÷ 1	6	4
60× 4	2	180× 5	6	4× 1	3
5	3	6	12× 2	4	1
24× 6	1	4	3	2	5 5
7+ 1	4	2	14+ 5	3	6

189

4÷ 1	4	14+ 6	5	3	144× 2
2− 3	5	120× 2	8× 1	4	6
2	6	5	4	1	3
18+ 6	3	2− 1	2	14+ 5	4
4	1− 1	3	3÷ 6	2	5
5	2	72× 4	3	6	1

190

18+ 3	6	2÷ 2	1	15+ 5	4
12+ 2	3	6	3− 4	1	5
6	4	180× 5	3	2	1
100× 5	3÷ 1	3	6	432× 4	1− 2
4	1− 2	1	40× 5	6	3
1	5	4	2	3	6

191

13+ 6	1− 3	4	2÷ 2	5× 5	1
2	150× 5	6	1	180× 3	4
1	3÷ 2	5	144× 6	4	3
4	6	1− 1	3	2	5
13+ 3	4	2	60× 5	1	6 6
5	1	3	4	8+ 6	2

192

3− 3	12+ 2	5	6+ 4	6÷ 1	6
6	1	4	2	75× 5	3
120× 2	3	13+ 1	144× 6	4	5
4	5	2	2− 3	6	2÷ 1
90× 5	4	6	1	120× 3	2
1	6	3	5	2	4

193

1− 6	5	80× 4	17+ 3	1	24× 2
2÷ 2	4	5	1	6	3
1	12+ 2	3	6	8+ 5	4
4	3	240× 6	5	2	1
5÷ 5	1	2	4	360× 3	6
2÷ 3	6	1− 1	2	4	5

194

192× 4	2	2− 6	8+ 1	13+ 5	3
1	3	4	2	12+ 6	5
1− 6	4	2	5	3	1
5	2÷ 6	3	4÷ 4	1	2
30× 2	5÷ 1	5	19+ 3	4	6
3	5	5− 1	6	2	4

195

15+ 4	2	1200× 5	108× 3	1	6
6	5	4	1	2	3
2	4	36× 3	180× 6	5	5÷ 1
1	3	2	30+ 4	6	5
3÷ 3	1	6	5	4	2− 2
5	6	1	2	3	4

196

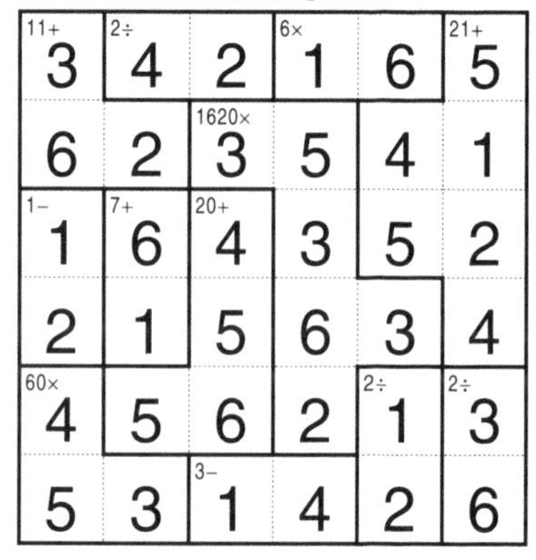

11+ 3	2÷ 4	2	6× 1	6	21+ 5
6	2	1620× 3	5	4	1
1− 1	7+ 6	20+ 4	3	5	2
2	1	5	6	3	4
60× 4	5	6	2	2÷ 1	2÷ 3
5	3	3− 1	4	2	6

197

2÷ 2	1	2÷ 3	6	23+ 5	2÷ 4
20× 1	1440× 5	9+ 4	3	6	2
4	3	5	2	1	6
5	2	6	3− 1	4	2− 3
15+ 6	4	2	20× 5	30× 3	1
3	6	1	4	2	5

198

720× 4	2	3	1	6	90× 5
60× 2	2− 4	6	5	1	3
6	5	1080× 4	3	2	1
3	1	5	24+ 6	4	3÷ 2
5÷ 1	3	2	4	5	6
5	6	1	2	7+ 3	4

199

6÷ 1	6	27+ 4	2	3	5
3600× 2	5	3÷ 3	1	120× 6	4
6	300× 2	1	4	5	3
3	72× 1	5	6	4	2
4	3	6	5	1− 2	1
5	4	12+ 2	3	1	6

200

18+ 3	2	4÷ 1	4	1− 6	5
2	1	4	7+ 5	18× 3	6
600× 5	6	1− 3	2	1	48× 4
1	5	2	2÷ 6	4	3
6	4	360× 5	3	8+ 2	2÷ 1
4	3	6	1	5	2

201

[6] 2	[25] 6	7	[8] 5	[8] 3	1	4
4	5	3	2	[20] 6	7	[4] 1
[11] 5	2	4	1	7	[20] 6	3
[6] 6	4	[17] 1	[16] 3	5	2	7
3	7	5	6	[10] 1	[6] 4	2
1	[5] 3	2	7	4	[16] 5	6
[8] 7	1	[10] 6	4	2	3	5

202

[3] 3	[11] 7	4	[9] 2	[25] 6	[13] 1	5
[23] 4	6	1	5	3	[10] 2	7
7	[11] 2	6	1	5	3	[10] 4
6	3	[12] 2	4	7	5	1
[7] 5	1	3	7	[22] 4	6	2
1	[17] 5	7	6	2	4	3
[6] 2	4	5	[17] 3	1	7	6

203

[7] 1	6	[12] 5	7	[4] 3	[6] 4	2
[12] 4	5	[14] 2	3	1	[25] 7	6
3	2	1	6	[15] 4	5	7
[13] 6	[24] 3	4	[18] 2	7	1	5
7	4	6	5	[20] 2	3	[8] 1
[18] 5	1	7	4	6	2	3
2	7	3	1	5	6	4

204

[16] 5	2	[23] 4	[7] 1	6	[16] 3	[13] 7
2	5	3	4	7	1	6
6	1	7	[7] 3	4	5	[11] 2
[7] 4	[12] 7	5	[8] 2	1	[13] 6	3
3	[10] 4	[6] 6	[25] 5	2	7	1
[8] 1	6	2	7	3	[10] 4	5
7	[4] 3	1	6	5	2	4

205

[11] 4	7	[14] 5	2	[10] 3	6	1
[4] 3	1	7	[10] 4	[13] 6	2	5
[16] 7	6	1	5	[9] 2	4	3
[15] 2	3	[5] 4	1	[37] 7	[18] 5	6
6	5	2	3	1	7	[13] 4
[8] 1	4	6	7	[9] 5	[4] 3	2
5	2	3	6	4	1	7

206

[9] 1	6	2	[14] 4	3	7	[10] 5
[19] 5	3	[26] 6	2	7	4	1
3	[10] 5	[17] 7	1	4	6	[8] 2
6	1	3	7	[14] 5	2	4
2	4	[15] 5	3	6	[8] 1	7
[24] 7	[2] 2	4	6	[3] 1	[8] 5	3
4	7	1	5	2	[9] 3	6

207

[17] 4	[39] 6	5	1	[8] 2	[13] 7	3
7	[8] 1	2	[16] 5	6	3	[16] 4
6	2	4	3	5	[14] 1	7
1	4	7	[19] 2	3	6	5
5	3	6	4	[7] 7	2	[9] 1
[14] 3	7	1	6	[9] 4	5	2
[7] 2	5	3	7	1	4	6

208

[8] 3	5	[28] 4	7	[3] 2	1	[21] 6
[12] 5	[6] 4	1	3	7	6	2
7	1	[18] 6	2	5	4	3
[9] 1	[21] 3	2	4	6	[16] 7	5
2	6	7	[8] 1	[11] 3	5	4
4	2	5	6	1	3	[14] 7
[13] 6	7	[8] 3	5	4	2	1

209

[10] 6	1	[30] 7	[9] 2	4	3	[15] 5
3	[10] 4	1	5	[12] 7	2	6
1	3	6	4	5	[25] 7	2
2	[14] 7	4	1	6	5	3
[11] 7	5	2	[9] 6	[5] 3	1	4
4	2	[19] 5	3	1	[13] 6	7
5	6	3	[14] 7	2	4	1

210

[9] 5	[19] 7	4	[11] 3	6	2	[11] 1
1	6	2	[21] 5	7	4	3
2	1	[19] 6	[25] 7	5	3	4
[17] 6	3	5	4	2	1	[20] 7
4	5	[4] 1	2	3	7	6
7	[9] 4	3	6	[13] 1	[18] 5	2
3	2	7	1	4	6	5

211

[12] 5	[16] 6	3	[7] 4	2	1	[11] 7
1	3	[25] 6	[31] 5	7	2	4
2	4	7	[4] 1	5	6	3
4	7	5	2	1	3	[19] 6
[11] 6	2	[33] 1	[16] 3	4	7	5
3	5	2	7	6	[11] 4	1
7	1	4	6	3	5	2

212

[20] 4	[20] 5	6	2	[12] 1	[12] 3	7
3	[25] 6	[24] 5	7	4	2	[9] 1
6	4	7	1	2	5	3
7	2	4	3	5	[7] 1	6
[7] 1	7	2	5	3	[10] 6	[11] 4
2	1	3	[30] 6	7	4	5
[8] 5	3	[1] 1	4	6	7	2

213

540 6	20 4	5	56 1	7	6 2	3
5	6	3	7 7	2	4	210 1
12 3	14 2	1	120 4	6	7	5
4	7	180 2	3	1	5	6
35 7	1	6	5	12 4	3	84 2
42 1	5	24 4	2	3	6	7
2	3	7	30 6	5	4 1	4

214

60 3	4	56 7	2	30 5	6	1
5	1	180 6	4	42 7	3	2
2	5	3	1	840 6	4	7
24 4	168 3	2	42 6	1	7	5
6	7	4	10 5	2	1	360 3
1	84 6	420 5	7	6 3	2	4
7	2	1	3	4	5	6

215

120 1	4	84 3	7	252 2	6	180 5
5	6 6	1	4	3	7	2
6	1	96 4	14 2	7	15 5	3
420 7	5	2	3	4	1	6
4	84 2	30 5	6	1	3	28 7
3	7	1260 6	40 1	5	2	4
2	3	7	5	6	4	1

216

96 4	2	35 1	5	7	54 6	3
2	168 4	7	1	180 6	3	480 5
6	245 7	3	2	5	1	4
7	1	5	3	2	4	6
15 5	90 3	288 6	56 4	1	2	98 7
3	6	2	7	60 4	5	1
1	5	4	6	3	7	2

217

840 3	2	210 7	5	432 1	4	6
4	5 5	48 1	6	3	392 2	7
5	1	3	2	6	7	4
7	420 3	2	4	720 5	6	1
72 6	7	5	3	4	70 1	2
2	6	4	168 1	7	5	45 3
1	4	6	7	2	3	5

218

210 5	126 7	3	6	1	960 4	2
7	3	2	420 4	42 6	5	1
8 2	30 6	1	5	7	6 3	4
4	5 1	5	7	3	2	6
18 3	5	336 6	24 2	4	1	420 7
1	4	7	3	2	6	5
6	2	4 4	1	105 5	7	3

219

42 3	40 2	5	24 4	6	1	28 7
2	140 5	4	756 6	3	7	1
7	1	60 3	5	2	6	4
4	7	1	2	160 5	3 3	900 6
1	84 6	2	7	4	5	3
30 6	504 4	7	21 3	1	2	5
5	3	6	1	7	4	2

220

150 2	5	3	504 6	28 7	4	1
5	3	1	7	4	48 2	6
588 7	2	6	6 3	5 5	1	4
72 6	4	7	2	1	105 5	3
3	1	960 4	180 5	6	7	42 2
28 1	6	5	4	2	3	7
4	7	2	1	3	30 6	5

221

60 5	4	84 7	6	2	18 3	1
24 2	3	5880 5	4	1	7	6
3	1	56 2	7	6	40 4	5
1	7	4	6300 3	5	6	2
4	1260 6	1	42 2	3	5	7
6	5	720 3	1	7	2	12 4
7	2	6	5	4	1	3

222

24 6	1	60 4	5	42 2	3	7
735 5	4	3	10 2	42 6	7	1
3	7	5	1	80 4	12 2	6
7	17640 3	6	4	5	10 1	2
1	2	9072 7	6	3	4	5
48 2	5	1	3	7	6	60 4
4	6	2	7	1	5	3

223

3360 4	7	12 3	60 2	5	6	2 1
6	1	4	105 5	3	7	2
5	4	18 6	1	42 7	2	3
84 7	6	2	3	960 1	4	5
48 2	105 3	210 5	7	4	18 1	6
1	5	7	6	2	3	140 4
3	2	1	4	6	5	7

224

25200 6	4	1	3	7	2	5
14 1	3 3	60 6	5	24 2	4	28 7
7	1	5	2	3	18144 6	4
2	140 5	24 4	7	6	3	1
4	7	2	6	1260 5	1	3
30 5	2	3	4	20 1	7	6
3	42 6	7	1	4	5	2

225

6− 1	12+ 7	5	2− 4	2	3− 6	3
7	8+ 6	12+ 1	3	4	3− 2	5
13+ 6	2	4	19+ 7	5	4+ 3	1
3	13+ 1	6 6	2	7	22+ 5	4
4	3	2	5	5− 6	1	7
3− 2	1− 5	6− 7	1	1− 3	4	6
5	4	19+ 3	6	1	7	2

226

5 5	11+ 6	3	2	13+ 1	11+ 4	7
15+ 6	1− 4	18+ 1	15+ 3	7	5	5+ 2
7	5	4	6	3+ 2	1	3
2	7	6	1	5	7+ 3	4
2− 1	3	5− 7	27+ 5	7+ 4	8+ 2	6
3− 4	1	2	7	3	1− 6	5
1− 3	2	5	4	6	6− 7	1

227

20+ 7	6	7+ 3	1	9+ 5	4− 2	2− 4
5 5	7	6− 1	3	4	6	2
1− 2	2− 3	7	5− 6	1	1− 4	5
3	1	1− 4	5− 2	28+ 6	5	7
23+ 6	4	5	7	1− 2	3	5− 1
5+ 1	5	11+ 2	4	3	7	6
4	2	6	5	11+ 7	1	3

228

7+ 2	11+ 4	7	24+ 6	1− 3	11+ 1	5
4	1	6	3	2	5	25+ 7
6− 1	16+ 7	8+ 2	5	1− 4	3	6
7	3	5	4	1 1	6	2
8+ 3	6	1	6− 7	24+ 5	5− 2	4
5	6+ 2	4	1	6	7	2− 3
14+ 6	5	3	2	7	4	1

229

38+ 6	3	1− 1	18+ 5	7	2− 2	4
4	5	2	6	5− 1	4− 3	7
6− 1	2	3	7 7	6	9+ 4	4− 5
7	13+ 6	4	2	6+ 3	5	1
9+ 3	7	5	4	2	1	15+ 6
5	1	13+ 6	3	4	7	2
2− 2	4	22+ 7	1	5	6	3

230

7+ 2	3	15+ 6	4	13+ 7	4− 1	5
32+ 3	2	5	5− 1	6	10+ 4	7 7
5	1	7	6	4	2	6+ 3
1	7	4	2− 5	3	1− 6	2
24+ 6	4	24+ 3	7	2	5	1
7	6	1	6+ 2	5	10+ 3	10+ 4
4	5	2	3	1	7	6

231

18+ 1	7	3	4	13+ 2	6	5
15+ 7	4	2	1	16+ 6	2− 5	3
4	11+ 5	6 6	3	7	6− 1	13+ 2
1− 3	6	9+ 1	3− 2	5	7	4
2	3	5	11+ 6	1	4	7
13+ 5	5+ 1	4	19+ 7	19+ 3	2	6
6	2	7	5	4	3	1

232

4+ 1	13+ 6	12+ 5	5+ 2	3	7 7	17+ 4
3	7	2	5	4− 1	10+ 4	6
12+ 2	3	11+ 4	1	5	6	7
7	1− 4	3	6	39+ 2	4− 1	5
4	1	7	3	6	16+ 5	2
6	5	9+ 1	18+ 4	7	2	2− 3
5	2	6	7	4	3	1

233

13+ 2	7	4	2− 3	5	9+ 6	7+ 1
6− 1	3− 6	2− 5	7	17+ 4	3	2
7	3	3+ 1	2	6	9+ 5	4
14+ 6	5	2− 2	4	7	1	3
3	2− 4	6	25+ 5	10+ 1	2	7
22+ 4	1	3	6	14+ 2	7	5
5	2	7	1	3	4	6

234

1− 4	18+ 7	6	5	33+ 3	8+ 1	4− 2
3	10+ 5	5+ 2	1	7	4	6
11+ 5	1	4	2	6	3	14+ 7
2	4	12+ 5	6	1	7	3
10+ 1	6	7	3	3− 2	5	4
13+ 6	3	6− 1	7	2− 4	2	12+ 5
7	14+ 2	3	4	5	6	1

235

2− 4	6	3− 5	8+ 2	3	6− 1	7
1− 5	4	2	3	20+ 7	6	8+ 1
16+ 2	14+ 1	4	1− 6	5	7	3
6	4− 3	1	5− 7	2	28+ 5	4
1	7	3	5	6	4	2
7	12+ 2	6	4	6+ 1	3	5
2− 3	5	12+ 7	1	4	2	6

236

23+ 1	16+ 7	3	6	11+ 5	4	2
5	10+ 1	2	7	9+ 4	21+ 6	3
7	4	11+ 6	2	3	5	1
7+ 2	6	1	3− 4	7	3	18+ 5
3	2	4	1− 5	6	1	7
1− 4	5	4− 7	3	4+ 1	2	6
14+ 6	3	5	1	2	3− 7	4

237

21× 3	120× 5	4	3÷ 2	6	7÷ 1	7
1	24× 4	6	168× 3	7	280× 2	5 5
7	6	1	4	2	5	432× 3
140× 2	3÷ 1	3	15× 5	4	7	6
5	2	7	1	3	6	4
24× 4	105× 7	84× 2	6	5× 5	3× 3	1
6	3	5	7	1	2÷ 4	2

238

126× 7	3	2	144× 4	6	5÷ 5	1
3	245× 7	5	6	4÷ 1	4	2÷ 2
240× 5	6	7	1	90× 3	2÷ 2	4
2	4	120× 6	3	5	1	126× 7
24× 1	5	4	210× 7	2	3	6
6	2÷ 2	1	5	588× 4	7	3
4	1	3	2	7	30× 6	5

239

15× 3	168× 6	7	2	210× 5	96× 4	1
5	2	12× 3	7	6	1	4
35× 7	1	4	90× 3	2	5	6
24× 6	5	1	4 4	196× 7	3	210× 2
1	168× 3	3÷ 2	150× 6	4	7	5
4	7	6	5	3÷ 1	3÷ 2	3
2	4	5	1	3	6	7

240

140× 5	7	1	2÷ 3	6	2÷ 4	252× 2
180× 6	3	4	175× 1	5	2	7
112× 4	2	5	7	3÷ 1	6	3
7	4	252× 2	5	3	30× 1	6
60× 2	1	7	96× 6	4	84× 3	5
3÷ 3	5	6	4	140× 2	7	1
1	6	3	2	7	5	4

241

24× 4	50400× 5	72× 6	21× 7	3	2÷ 1	2
3	2	4	6300× 1	5	6	7
2	1	3	2÷ 4	6	84× 7	5
5	6	7	2	35× 1	4	3
42× 6	4	2	5	7	3÷ 3	1
7	3	1	2÷ 6	16× 2	120× 5	4
1	35× 7	5	3	4	2	6

242

2÷ 4	2	5÷ 1	5	42× 6	7	120× 3
2100× 6	21× 3	7	6× 1	4	2	5
1	210× 6	5	3	2	84× 4	7
5	7	60480× 4	6	1	3	48× 2
2	5	216× 3	4	7	5÷ 1	6
7	1	6	28× 2	3	5	4
3	4	2	7	5	6	1

243

60× 4	5	3528× 1	2	6	7	15× 3
3	72× 4	6	7÷ 7	2÷ 2	20160× 1	5
6	3	7	1	4	5	2
15750× 5	4÷ 1	4	2÷ 3	7	2	6
7	2	5	6	3	4	1
2× 2	84× 7	3	5	1	6	1680× 4
1	6	2	4	5	3	7

244

15× 3	5	1512× 6	140× 4	7× 1	7	2÷ 2
60× 6	2	3	5	7	1	4
5	7	2	168× 6	420× 3	4	1
2	3	1	7	4	30240× 6	5
10080× 1	4	5	2	6	3	7
4 4	6	7	5÷ 1	5	2	2÷ 3
7	1	4	3	2	5	6

245

1260× 3	2	5÷ 5	252× 6	7	4÷ 4	1
5	7	1	35280× 3	6	2÷ 2	4
1	6	4	2	5	7	36× 3
480× 4	3	210× 7	5	2	5÷ 1	6
84× 7	4	6	1	3	5	2
6	1	2	7	12× 4	3	210× 5
2	5	12× 3	4	1	6	7

246

5040× 2	4	1	3	7	90× 6	5
28× 4	7	6	5	1	3	14× 2
30× 5	3× 1	3	24× 6	4	28× 2	7
6	90× 3	5	448× 4	2	7	4÷ 1
1	6	2	7	2÷ 3	5÷ 5	4
29400× 7	5	4	2	6	1	2÷ 3
3	2	7	1	5	4	6

247

7× 1	7	100× 5	4	42× 6	24× 3	2
15× 3	1	2÷ 2	5	7	37800× 6	4
5	3÷ 6	4	21× 1	420× 3	2	7
3360× 4	2	3	7	1	5	6
7	4	3÷ 6	2	5	1	3
6	5	7÷ 7	144× 3	2	4	1
6× 2	3	1	6	4	7	5

248

25200× 4	6	18× 3	7÷ 7	1	400× 5	2
7	5	6	2÷ 2	4	1	21× 3
5	51840× 3	4	1	2	2÷ 6	7
6	7× 7	2	4	5	3	4÷ 1
2÷ 2	1	70× 5	3	6	420× 7	4
1	2	7	6	3	4	5
12× 3	4	1	5	84× 7	2	6

249

294× 6	7	1	80× 4	5	2	2÷ 3
7	2– 5	3	2	2– 4	3× 1	6
3– 5	2	21+ 4	7÷ 7	6	3	1
3÷ 3	6	5	1	14× 7	2– 4	2
1	8× 4	6	17+ 3	2	700× 5	7
2	1	7 7	5	3	42× 6	4
9+ 4	3	2	6	1	7	5

250

19+ 4	5	7	6× 1	3	168× 2	6
4– 5	3	432× 6	4	1	7	2
1	21+ 7	2– 3	6	2	20× 5	4
2	6	5	3	672× 4	7÷ 1	7
6	1– 1	2	21+ 5	7	4	3÷ 3
1– 3	2	4	7	5	6	1
12+ 7	4	1	3÷ 2	6	2– 3	5

251

4– 1	5	20+ 7	6	70× 2	1– 3	4
42× 6	4	3	7	5	2÷ 2	1
7	1	120× 5	2	144× 6	4	4– 3
80× 5	2	1– 1	4	3	6	7
4	2÷ 6	2	15+ 3	7÷ 1	7	300× 5
2	3	4	1	7	5	6
630× 3	7	6	5	4÷ 4	1	2

252

3÷ 1	3	20+ 6	42× 7	2	20× 5	4
13+ 2	14+ 4	5	6	3	1	294× 7
5	2	3– 4	3	11+ 1	7	6
6	7	1	480× 4	5	2	3
1– 3	1	252× 7	5	6	4	10+ 2
4	6	2	2÷ 1	3– 7	3	5
2– 7	5	3	2	4	6÷ 6	1

253

3− 1	4	20× 5	10+ 3	7	3÷ 6	2
4200× 3	5	4	1	2÷ 2	21× 7	24+ 6
5	42× 7	2	19+ 6	4	3	1
2	360× 1	3	7	6	5	4
4	2	6	5	1800× 3	1	7
7	6	1	2	5	4	3
2÷ 6	3	3− 7	4	1− 1	2	5

254

21+ 1	3240× 3	5	2	6	19+ 4	7
2	5	3	6	1	7	2÷ 4
5	7	2− 1	3	4480× 4	2÷ 6	2
144× 6	1	5− 7	4	2	3	13+ 5
4	6	2	1	21× 7	5	3
4− 7	48× 4	6	5	3	2÷ 2	1
3	2	4	7	12+ 5	1	6

255

5÷ 5	4032× 4	6	98× 7	2	3÷ 1	3
1	60× 5	3	10+ 2	7	2− 4	6
2	6	4	5	3	4− 7	4÷ 1
3− 6	7	2	630× 1	26+ 5	3	4
3	1	5	6	4	2	7
7	3	1	84× 4	6	17+ 5	2
2− 4	2	7	3	1	6	5

256

12+ 4	3÷ 6	2	2− 7	5	14112× 3	4− 1
6	2	1− 3	4÷ 4	1	7	5
15× 3	5	4	13+ 1	6	2	7
6× 1	3	7	5	2	144× 6	4
2	17+ 1	5	3	12+ 7	4	6
245× 5	7	6	2	4	1	6× 3
7	4÷ 4	1	14+ 6	3	5	2

257

12+ 5	6	1	2520× 3	7	2	35+ 4
4÷ 1	4	6	2	5	7	3
28× 7	2	150× 5	6	1− 3	4	1
2	4− 7	3	5	4	1	6
1− 4	5	3− 7	28× 1	6	3	840× 2
2÷ 3	6× 1	4	7	2	6	5
6	3	2	4	5÷ 1	5	7

258

294× 7	6	3600× 3	1	5	4	2
5÷ 1	7	5	3− 3	1− 2	6	28× 4
5	30720× 4	2	6	3	1	7
34+ 6	1− 2	4	5	7÷ 1	7	2− 3
4	3	6	2	14+ 7	5	1
3	1	7	4	6	2	90× 5
2	5	7÷ 1	7	4	3	6

259

1− 6	7	240× 3	1	4	2	32+ 5
3÷ 3	7+ 4	1	5	2	7	6
1	2	30× 5	6	49× 7	3	84× 4
11+ 4	5	2	7	1	6	3
2÷ 2	1	30240× 4	3	6	5	7
2− 5	3− 6	7	2	3	4÷ 4	1
7	3	10+ 6	4	5	1	2

260

5÷ 1	98784× 2	6	7	15120× 3	11+ 5	4
5	7	1	2− 3	4	6	2
2− 4	2÷ 6	7	1	2	3	5
2	3	4	150× 6	5	1	7
26+ 3	4	2	5	10+ 1	3− 7	6÷ 6
6	5	3	2	7	4	1
7	1	120× 5	4	6	1− 2	3

261

(13) 7	6	(4) 4	(22) 1	(29) 2	5	8	(7) 3
2	5	6	3	8	(21) 1	7	4
(4) 1	(21) 7	5	(20) 8	6	4	(5) 3	2
3	2	(6) 1	5	7	6	(17) 4	8
(23) 6	8	2	(29) 7	4	3	(4) 1	5
8	4	3	6	(8) 5	(37) 7	2	1
5	1	8	4	3	2	6	(18) 7
4	3	7	2	1	8	5	6

262

(12) 8	(19) 3	5	1	(15) 7	(8) 2	(10) 6	4
4	1	7	2	8	6	(9) 3	(11) 5
(10) 3	(15) 8	2	(17) 7	4	5	1	6
7	5	(12) 3	(31) 8	6	4	(11) 2	1
(13) 5	4	1	6	3	7	8	(10) 2
6	2	4	3	(6) 5	1	(16) 7	8
(3) 1	(17) 7	6	4	(13) 2	8	5	(10) 3
2	(14) 6	8	(6) 5	1	3	4	7

263

(13) 7	1	5	(12) 8	(6) 2	4	(9) 6	3
(10) 6	2	(27) 7	3	1	(14) 8	(10) 4	5
2	4	8	5	3	6	1	(21) 7
(8) 3	5	(36) 4	2	(15) 7	(8) 1	8	6
5	6	3	1	8	7	(8) 2	4
(5) 4	8	(9) 1	(23) 7	6	(11) 3	5	2
1	7	2	6	4	(16) 5	3	(8) 8
(11) 8	3	6	4	5	2	(8) 7	1

264

(5) 3	(8) 1	(26) 7	8	(7) 5	2	(14) 4	6
2	6	1	7	(23) 8	(8) 5	3	4
(13) 6	(11) 2	3	4	7	8	(14) 1	(5) 5
7	(31) 3	6	(14) 2	(20) 1	4	5	8
8	5	4	1	6	3	(9) 2	7
(37) 5	7	(16) 2	3	4	6	(14) 8	1
4	8	5	6	2	1	(13) 7	3
1	4	8	5	3	7	6	2

265

(24) 3	8	(11) 5	(17) 2	7	(10) 4	6	(3) 1
5	(11) 7	6	8	(1) 1	(8) 3	4	2
8	4	(36) 2	3	6	7	1	(8) 5
(20) 4	6	7	1	8	5	2	3
(7) 6	1	(11) 3	4	(15) 5	2	(23) 8	7
1	2	4	5	3	(26) 6	7	8
(13) 7	3	1	(26) 6	2	8	5	(13) 4
2	5	8	7	(5) 4	1	3	6

266

(13) 2	(28) 7	5	(8) 1	4	3	(6) 6	(11) 8
4	3	7	(34) 5	8	6	2	1
1	(12) 5	3	7	(34) 2	8	(10) 4	6
3	1	6	(14) 8	5	(13) 4	7	2
(29) 7	4	2	6	1	5	(13) 8	3
6	8	(10) 1	(27) 4	3	2	5	7
8	(21) 6	4	2	7	1	3	5
5	2	8	3	6	7	(5) 1	4

267

(16) 2	5	(32) 6	4	8	7	(19) 1	(15) 3
3	6	(21) 2	7	(7) 1	8	4	5
(17) 8	4	5	3	2	1	6	7
5	2	4	(14) 8	3	(6) 6	(23) 7	1
4	1	(25) 7	6	(8) 5	3	8	(8) 2
7	3	8	(19) 1	4	5	2	6
(7) 6	(15) 8	(6) 1	5	7	2	(8) 3	(12) 4
1	7	3	2	(10) 6	4	5	8

268

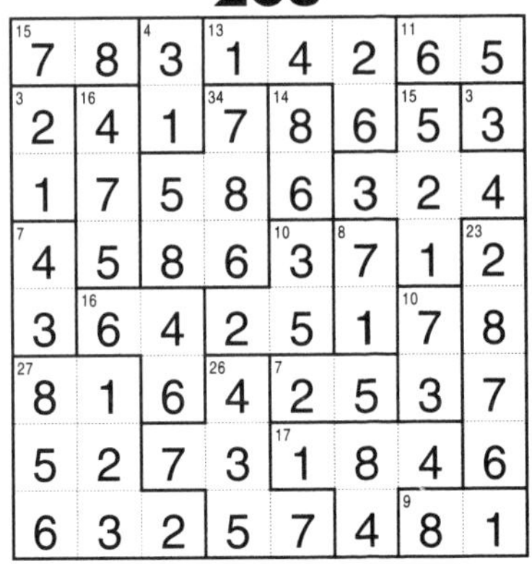

(15) 7	8	(4) 3	(13) 1	4	2	(11) 6	5
(3) 2	(16) 4	1	(34) 7	(14) 8	6	(15) 5	(3) 3
1	7	5	8	6	3	2	4
(7) 4	5	8	6	(10) 3	(8) 7	1	(23) 2
3	(16) 6	4	2	5	1	(10) 7	8
(27) 8	1	6	(26) 4	(7) 2	5	3	7
5	2	7	3	(17) 1	8	4	6
6	3	2	5	7	4	(9) 8	1

269

[210] 5	6	7	[10752] 8	3	1	4	2
[48] 4	3	1	7	[240] 5	6	[84] 2	8
[144] 3	4	[60] 2	5	8	7	6	1
8	[86016] 1	3	6	2	4	[35] 7	5
6	8	4	2	7	[30] 5	1	[63] 3
[35] 1	5	8	[8640] 4	6	2	3	7
7	[28] 2	5	1	4	3	[320] 8	[24] 6
2	7	6	3	1	8	5	4

270

[40] 8	[46080] 4	[42] 1	[280] 5	7	[6] 2	3	[72] 6
5	2	6	7	8	1	4	3
[42] 7	8	[36] 3	6	2	[16128] 4	[20] 1	5
2	1	5	[24] 8	3	6	7	4
3	6	2	1	[160] 4	5	8	[56] 7
4	3	[3136] 7	2	[6300] 5	8	6	1
[30] 1	5	4	[12] 3	6	7	2	8
6	7	8	4	1	3	5	2

271

[42] 2	7	[12] 4	1	3	[6720] 6	5	8
[72] 6	3	[34560] 8	5	[14] 2	4	1	7
4	8	3	6	7	1	[16] 2	[33600] 5
3	6	[12] 1	2	[35] 5	7	8	4
[5] 1	5	6	[192] 4	8	3	7	2
[39200] 7	1	[28] 2	[96] 8	6	5	[72] 4	[18] 3
5	2	7	3	4	8	6	1
8	4	5	7	[2] 1	2	3	6

272

[224] 7	[32] 8	1	4	[2016] 3	6	2	[35] 5
8	[96] 6	7	2	4	[90] 3	5	1
4	2	8	[24] 3	1	[30] 5	6	7
[30] 3	[140] 7	5	8	6	1	[48] 4	2
2	5	4	[56] 1	7	8	[48] 3	6
[18] 1	3	[69120] 6	[175] 7	5	2	8	[4] 4
6	4	2	5	8	[21] 7	1	3
5	1	3	6	2	[224] 4	7	8

273

[25] 1	5	[60480] 3	[24] 4	6	[224] 8	2	[224] 7
5	[35280] 1	6	3	2	7	8	4
[48] 8	4	1	7	5	2	[54] 3	6
6	2	5	8	7	[5] 1	[24] 4	3
[8] 4	3	7	2	1	5	6	[80] 8
2	6	[8960] 8	1	[288] 4	3	[35] 7	5
7	8	4	5	3	[24] 6	1	2
[21] 3	7	[12] 2	6	8	4	5	1

274

[60480] 6	[336] 7	8	[7680] 4	[6] 3	2	1	[1260] 5
1	8	6	5	2	3	4	7
[112] 7	2	4	8	6	[6720] 5	3	1
8	6	5	7	4	1	[24] 2	3
2	3	7	1	8	6	[240] 5	4
[60] 3	[5] 5	1	[36] 2	[28] 7	4	6	8
4	1	3	6	[35] 5	7	[96] 8	2
5	[24] 4	2	3	1	[56] 8	7	6

275

[126] 7	3	[40] 8	[48] 4	6	[120] 2	5	1
6	[1792] 7	5	[96] 8	2	1	3	4
8	4	6	2	[70560] 5	7	1	3
[5040] 4	8	[1] 1	[63] 7	3	[960] 5	2	6
5	6	7	3	1	8	4	2
3	[10] 5	2	1	4	6	7	[336] 8
2	1	[24] 3	[30] 5	[224] 8	4	6	7
1	2	4	6	7	[120] 3	8	5

276

[80] 5	2	[32] 4	8	[2240] 7	[8064] 1	6	[9] 3
8	[90] 5	6	2	4	7	3	1
[24] 2	3	[56448] 7	1	5	6	8	4
4	1	2	[240] 5	8	[882] 3	7	6
3	4	8	6	[80640] 2	[5] 5	1	7
[42] 7	8	[12] 1	3	6	2	[40] 4	5
6	7	3	4	1	8	[80] 5	2
1	6	5	7	3	4	2	8

277

6	2	1	8	7	4	5	3
3	5	7	1	2	8	6	4
8	7	2	3	6	1	4	5
5	6	3	4	8	2	1	7
4	3	6	5	1	7	2	8
7	1	4	2	3	5	8	6
2	8	5	6	4	3	7	1
1	4	8	7	5	6	3	2

278

6	1	2	4	5	8	7	3
2	5	4	1	3	7	6	8
5	6	8	2	4	3	1	7
1	3	7	5	8	4	2	6
7	4	1	3	6	5	8	2
8	7	3	6	1	2	4	5
3	8	6	7	2	1	5	4
4	2	5	8	7	6	3	1

279

8	2	5	1	7	3	6	4
4	5	2	7	6	8	3	1
1	7	3	5	2	6	4	8
2	8	4	6	5	7	1	3
3	1	6	2	4	5	8	7
7	3	8	4	1	2	5	6
5	6	1	3	8	4	7	2
6	4	7	8	3	1	2	5

280

3	7	5	6	1	8	2	4
7	5	6	3	4	1	8	2
8	1	2	4	7	5	6	3
5	3	8	2	6	4	1	7
2	4	3	5	8	6	7	1
1	2	4	8	5	7	3	6
6	8	1	7	3	2	4	5
4	6	7	1	2	3	5	8

281

23+ 6	1	1− 8	7	8+ 5	3	14+ 4	2
7	5	6+ 2	4	1 1	14+ 6	3	8
1	17+ 8	6	3	8+ 4	2	5	18+ 7
3	11+ 4	1	6	2	23+ 8	7	5
13+ 2	7	10+ 4	5	4+ 3	1	8	6
4	3− 2	5	1	37+ 8	16+ 7	6	3
19+ 5	6	13+ 3	8	7	2− 4	2	3− 1
8	3	7	2	6	5	1	4

282

1− 7	6	4+ 3	1	10+ 4	6− 8	2	31+ 5
1− 4	3+ 2	1	15+ 5	6	6+ 3	7	8
5	6− 8	2	3	7	1	6	2− 4
4+ 3	1	36+ 4	7	8	2	5	6
2	7	8	15+ 4	5	6	2− 3	1
18+ 6	4	2− 5	19+ 2	1	7	5− 8	3
8	2− 5	7	20+ 6	3	4	10+ 1	5− 2
1 1	3	6	8	2	5	4	7

283

8+ 5	10+ 1	7	2	7+ 3	4	14+ 6	8
3	2− 2	4	19+ 6	8	5	8+ 7	1
1− 1	1− 4	5	4− 3	8+ 6	2	15+ 8	7
2	17+ 6	7− 8	7	20+ 1	3	9+ 4	5
13+ 7	3	1	1− 5	4	8	2	6
6	8	1− 3	4	15+ 7	1	5	2
1− 4	5	14+ 6	8	13+ 2	11+ 7	1	7+ 3
1− 8	7	3+ 2	1	5	6	3	4

284

6 6	12+ 5	3	7+ 4	2	1	22+ 7	8
1− 2	1	4	11+ 3	33+ 8	18+ 5	6	7
4− 5	12+ 8	6	2	4	7	2− 3	1
1	4	8	7	6	6+ 3	2	7+ 5
18+ 8	3	13+ 5	6	17+ 7	4	1	2
14+ 3	7	2	4− 5	1	6	12+ 8	4
4	15+ 2	7	10+ 1	8+ 3	19+ 8	5	6
7	6	1	8	5	9+ 2	4	3

285

84× 6	7	2	8÷ 1	2÷ 3	224× 4	8	25× 5
2÷ 4	6× 2	3	8	6	7	5	1
8	30240× 1	210× 5	6	7	64× 2	2÷ 4	504× 3
7	3	5÷ 1	5	4	8	2	6
1	5	8	3	2	6	7	4
36× 2	6	7680× 4	280× 7	5	1260× 1	24× 3	8
3	4	6	2	8	5	1	7
5	8	28× 7	4	1	3	6	2

286

30× 5	224× 7	4	64× 2	8	2÷ 6	3	2940× 1
6	1	8	4	84× 3	7	4÷ 2	5
2÷ 2	1280× 5	90× 6	3	12× 1	4	8	7
1	8	5	90× 6	4	3	7	2
8	4	3	5	14× 7	2	1	6
3024× 4	3	7÷ 1	7	80× 2	5	240× 6	8
3	2	14× 7	48× 1	6	8	5	48× 4
7	6	2	8	5÷ 5	1	4	3

287

24× 8	10368× 6	1	8000× 2	5	4	21× 3	7
3	2	6	1120× 4	7	5	8	1
1	4	3	8	252× 6	7	5	40320× 2
4	3	70× 2	5	1	6	7	8
10× 2	1	5	7	16128× 3	4÷ 8	4÷ 4	6
210× 7	5	4	6	8	2	1	3
6	448× 8	7	3÷ 3	4	2÷ 1	2	5
5	7	8	1	36× 2	3	6	4

288

288× 8	6	35× 7	5	1	2÷ 2	4	36× 3
6	10× 5	61440× 8	2	336× 7	1	3	4
21× 7	2	21600× 5	3	4	6	1	8
3	1	6	4	8	5	98× 2	7
2÷ 2	4	3	6	5	8	7	40× 1
336× 4	7	2	8× 1	18× 6	3	8	5
40× 1	3	4	8	420× 2	7	5	3÷ 6
5	8	7÷ 1	7	12× 3	4	6	2

289

48× 6	53760× 2	4	5	8× 1	8	1260× 3	7
8	7	3÷ 3	1	60× 6	2÷ 2	4	5
84× 7	3	8	84× 6	2	1	5	4
3	8	2	7	40× 4	180× 5	6	1
4	7× 1	7	2	5	6	112× 8	3
10× 1	20× 5	2÷ 6	3	2÷ 8	4	7	2
2	4	30× 5	2÷ 8	378× 7	3	1	6
5	6	1	4	3	112× 7	2	8

290

24× 3	30× 5	6	2÷ 4	8	84× 7	2	4÷ 1
8	2÷ 1	2	75× 5	3	6	37632× 7	4
14× 7	2	10080× 1	6	5	3÷ 3	4	8
5040× 6	7	5	2	40× 4	1	8	3
1	4	3	8	2	5	2÷ 6	7
5	6	32× 8	7	4× 1	4	3	60× 2
24× 2	3	4	3× 1	84× 7	40× 8	5	6
4	56× 8	7	3	6	2	1	5

291

672× 3	7	2	10080× 1	4	6	40× 8	5
4÷ 1	2	8	30× 5	6	4	7	3
4	126× 3	7	6	1	5	16× 2	8
30× 6	1	5	9408× 8	8064× 3	7	40× 4	2
40× 2	6÷ 6	1	3	7	8	5	24× 4
5	4	2÷ 3	7	8	2	6	1
280× 8	5	6	4	30× 2	1	3	42× 7
7	2÷ 8	4	2	5	3	1	6

292

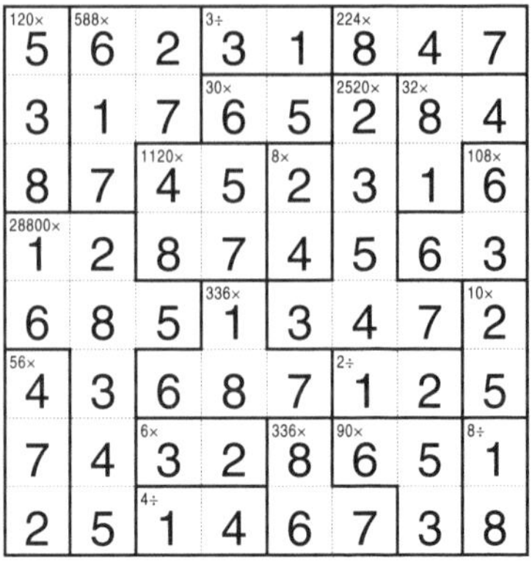

120× 5	588× 6	2	3÷ 3	1	224× 8	4	7
3	1	7	30× 6	5	2520× 2	32× 8	4
8	7	1120× 4	5	8× 2	3	1	108× 6
28800× 1	2	8	7	4	5	6	3
6	8	5	336× 1	3	4	7	10× 2
56× 4	3	6	8	7	2÷ 1	2	5
7	4	6× 3	2	336× 8	90× 6	5	8÷ 1
2	5	4÷ 1	4	6	7	3	8

293

4− 1	5	19+ 8	11+ 3	2	6	13+ 4	20+ 7
252× 7	6	2	1	3	4	5	8
6	9408× 2	7	8	4	9+ 3	1	5
4	7	2÷ 3	6	1	5	96× 8	2
3	38400× 4	5	16× 2	8	49× 1	7	6
5	8	1	4	6	7	1− 2	3
2	24× 1	17+ 6	175× 5	7	5− 8	3	4÷ 4
8	3	4	7	5	3÷ 2	6	1

294

30+ 5	168× 7	4	6	14× 1	48× 3	8	2
8	3	1	2	7	120× 4	6	5
4	288× 6	8	72000× 5	2	7÷ 7	1	36× 3
7	2	6	1	8	5	3	4
2− 3	1	12+ 2	7	5	6	19+ 4	8
2− 2	4	3	19+ 8	6	8÷ 1	60× 5	7
5÷ 1	5	7	4	180× 3	8	2	6
2− 6	8	5	3	4	10+ 2	7	1

295

30× 2	3	4480× 7	18+ 6	8	4	13+ 1	5
8+ 4	5	1	8	36× 3	6	2	7
3	1	2÷ 4	2	5	8	1− 7	6
14× 1	7	8	1− 5	6	6× 2	2160× 3	64× 4
7560× 7	2	16+ 5	4	1	3	6	8
5	6	3	1	4	7÷ 7	8	2
1536× 8	4	6	147× 7	2	1	5	3
6	8	2	3	7	20× 5	4	1

296

4− 8	48× 4	42× 7	2	3	5÷ 1	5	37+ 6
4	6	2	31+ 7	40× 8	5	144× 1	3
1	8	5	4	6	2	3	7
28× 7	2	3× 1	3	4	6	8	5
2	28× 7	4	1	22+ 5	2÷ 3	6	8
13+ 5	1	3− 3	6	2	29+ 8	7	2÷ 4
3	5	6	8	1	7	4	2
33+ 6	3	8	5	7	4	2	1

297

30× 5	5− 3	28+ 4	6	392× 8	7	6+ 1	2
6	8	2	2÷ 4	7	3× 1	3	15+ 5
20× 4	5	7	2	1	3	17+ 8	6
1	6	3	960× 8	5	2	7	4
1680× 8	7	5	1	6	1120× 4	2	3÷ 3
3	2	210× 6	7	4	24+ 8	5	1
2÷ 2	1	12+ 8	5	3	6	4	7
3− 7	4	1	3	2	5	14+ 6	8

298

40× 8	42× 3	28× 7	4	36+ 6	5	1	3÷ 2
5	2	35× 1	7	8	4	3	6
9+ 6	7	5	20160× 3	2÷ 4	2	8	1
3	1− 1	2	8	5	7	6	4
28× 4	192× 8	2÷ 3	6	4+ 2	1	14× 7	120× 5
7	4	3− 8	5	1	3− 6	2	3
1	6	8× 4	2	18+ 7	3	16+ 5	8
60× 2	5	6	1	3	8	4	7

299

8960× 2	8	4	7	9+ 3	1	11+ 6	5
8× 8	11+ 2	3	4	4− 6	5	8+ 7	1
1	80× 4	6	5	2	27+ 7	24× 3	8
4	5	6÷ 1	6	7	3	128× 8	2÷ 2
108× 3	6	20+ 7	2÷ 1	5	8	2	4
6	16+ 7	8	2	1	4	4− 5	16+ 3
2− 7	3	5	256× 8	4	48× 2	1	6
5	1	2	3	8	6	4	7

300

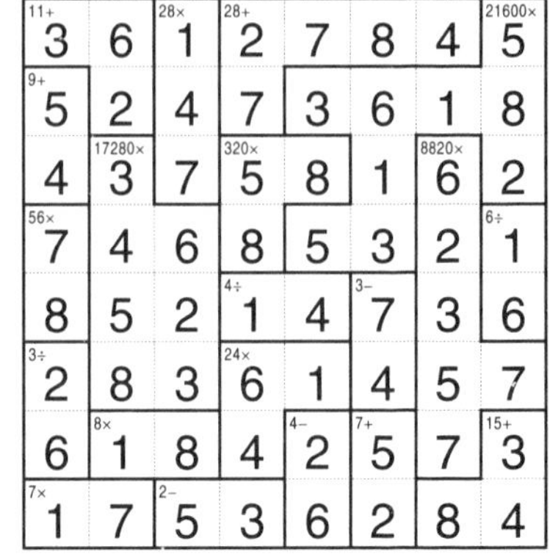

11+ 3	6	28× 1	28+ 2	7	8	4	21600× 5
9+ 5	2	4	7	3	6	1	8
4	17280× 3	7	320× 5	8	1	8820× 6	2
56× 7	4	6	8	5	3	2	6÷ 1
8	5	2	4÷ 1	4	3− 7	3	6
3÷ 2	8	3	24× 6	1	4	5	7
6	8× 1	8	4	4− 2	7+ 5	7	15+ 3
7× 1	7	2− 5	3	6	2	8	4

301

9	8	6	1	4	5	2	7	3
1	3	5	2	9	7	8	6	4
7	2	4	8	6	3	9	5	1
2	4	3	6	1	8	5	9	7
5	6	9	7	3	4	1	2	8
8	1	7	5	2	9	4	3	6
3	5	2	4	7	1	6	8	9
4	9	8	3	5	6	7	1	2
6	7	1	9	8	2	3	4	5

302

8	1	6	3	4	7	2	5	9
9	3	5	8	6	2	7	4	1
4	2	7	1	5	9	6	3	8
6	5	4	9	2	1	8	7	3
1	8	2	4	7	3	5	9	6
7	9	3	6	8	5	1	2	4
2	4	1	5	3	6	9	8	7
5	6	8	7	9	4	3	1	2
3	7	9	2	1	8	4	6	5

303

1	8	2	3	6	5	9	7	4
7	9	3	1	4	2	6	5	8
6	5	4	8	9	7	2	1	3
5	4	1	6	8	9	3	2	7
3	7	8	4	2	1	5	9	6
2	6	9	7	5	3	4	8	1
8	1	5	2	3	4	7	6	9
9	3	7	5	1	6	8	4	2
4	2	6	9	7	8	1	3	5

304

4	7	5	2	1	8	3	6	9
1	8	9	4	6	3	2	7	5
2	3	6	5	7	9	4	1	8
7	4	8	3	9	6	1	5	2
5	6	1	7	2	4	8	9	3
3	9	2	1	8	5	7	4	6
6	1	3	8	5	7	9	2	4
8	5	7	9	4	2	6	3	1
9	2	4	6	3	1	5	8	7

305

9	6	2	4	3	8	1	5	7
1	3	7	5	2	9	4	8	6
4	8	5	6	1	7	3	9	2
2	9	8	7	4	5	6	3	1
5	1	4	3	9	6	7	2	8
3	7	6	2	8	1	9	4	5
8	5	1	9	6	3	2	7	4
6	4	9	8	7	2	5	1	3
7	2	3	1	5	4	8	6	9

306

7	8	4	5	2	3	6	1	9
1	3	6	9	7	8	4	2	5
9	5	2	1	6	4	3	7	8
5	7	8	4	3	1	2	9	6
2	9	3	6	5	7	1	8	4
4	6	1	2	8	9	7	5	3
6	2	7	8	4	5	9	3	1
8	4	9	3	1	2	5	6	7
3	1	5	7	9	6	8	4	2

307

2	6	3	4	7	8	9	1	5
1	4	8	5	2	9	6	3	7
7	9	5	6	3	1	2	4	8
6	7	2	3	1	4	5	8	9
8	5	1	7	9	6	4	2	3
9	3	4	8	5	2	1	7	6
5	1	6	2	8	7	3	9	4
3	2	7	9	4	5	8	6	1
4	8	9	1	6	3	7	5	2

308

2	9	5	8	7	6	1	3	4
3	1	8	4	5	9	2	7	6
7	6	4	1	3	2	5	9	8
1	5	6	2	8	3	7	4	9
8	7	9	5	1	4	6	2	3
4	3	2	9	6	7	8	1	5
5	8	3	7	9	1	4	6	2
9	4	7	6	2	5	3	8	1
6	2	1	3	4	8	9	5	7

309

5	6	1	9	3	4	7	2	8
2	3	9	6	8	7	5	4	1
4	7	8	5	2	1	6	3	9
6	8	2	4	7	3	1	9	5
1	5	3	8	9	2	4	6	7
9	4	7	1	6	5	3	8	2
7	9	5	2	4	6	8	1	3
8	1	4	3	5	9	2	7	6
3	2	6	7	1	8	9	5	4

310

8	1	6	5	2	3	4	9	7
5	9	2	7	1	4	3	6	8
4	7	3	8	9	6	1	5	2
1	2	7	9	5	8	6	4	3
9	4	8	6	3	1	2	7	5
6	3	5	2	4	7	8	1	9
2	6	9	1	8	5	7	3	4
7	5	4	3	6	2	9	8	1
3	8	1	4	7	9	5	2	6

311

2	1	3	9	7	8	5	4	6
5	8	7	4	3	6	1	2	9
4	9	6	1	5	2	8	3	7
7	4	1	6	9	3	2	8	5
9	3	5	8	2	4	6	7	1
6	2	8	7	1	5	4	9	3
1	7	2	5	8	9	3	6	4
8	5	4	3	6	7	9	1	2
3	6	9	2	4	1	7	5	8

312

5	1	6	9	4	8	7	2	3
9	2	8	6	3	7	4	1	5
3	7	4	1	2	5	9	6	8
6	4	9	2	1	3	5	8	7
1	8	5	7	9	4	6	3	2
7	3	2	5	8	6	1	9	4
2	6	7	3	5	9	8	4	1
4	5	3	8	6	1	2	7	9
8	9	1	4	7	2	3	5	6

313

1	8	7	9	3	4	2	5	6
5	6	2	7	8	1	4	3	9
9	4	3	6	5	2	1	8	7
2	3	6	8	1	9	5	7	4
7	9	5	4	2	3	8	6	1
4	1	8	5	6	7	3	9	2
6	2	9	3	4	8	7	1	5
8	7	4	1	9	5	6	2	3
3	5	1	2	7	6	9	4	8

314

4	9	3	5	7	2	1	8	6
1	6	2	3	8	4	7	9	5
7	5	8	6	1	9	4	3	2
8	7	1	4	9	6	2	5	3
6	2	9	7	5	3	8	4	1
3	4	5	1	2	8	6	7	9
9	1	7	8	6	5	3	2	4
2	8	4	9	3	1	5	6	7
5	3	6	2	4	7	9	1	8

315

7	6	9	1	3	5	4	8	2
8	4	1	2	6	9	7	5	3
5	3	2	7	4	8	6	9	1
3	5	6	8	2	1	9	4	7
9	8	7	3	5	4	2	1	6
1	2	4	9	7	6	5	3	8
6	9	3	5	8	2	1	7	4
4	7	5	6	1	3	8	2	9
2	1	8	4	9	7	3	6	5

316

1	5	3	7	2	9	8	4	6
7	2	6	1	4	8	5	9	3
8	4	9	3	5	6	1	7	2
4	3	8	2	6	5	7	1	9
9	1	5	4	7	3	6	2	8
6	7	2	9	8	1	3	5	4
2	8	4	6	1	7	9	3	5
5	9	7	8	3	2	4	6	1
3	6	1	5	9	4	2	8	7

317

1	5	6	7	8	3	4	2	9
4	2	3	5	6	9	7	8	1
7	9	8	4	2	1	6	3	5
5	4	7	3	1	6	2	9	8
9	8	1	2	7	4	5	6	3
3	6	2	8	9	5	1	7	4
8	3	4	6	5	7	9	1	2
6	1	5	9	3	2	8	4	7
2	7	9	1	4	8	3	5	6

318

9	4	6	8	7	3	2	5	1
7	5	3	6	1	2	8	9	4
2	8	1	5	4	9	3	6	7
1	9	5	7	2	6	4	3	8
8	6	7	3	5	4	9	1	2
4	3	2	1	9	8	6	7	5
3	1	4	2	6	5	7	8	9
6	7	9	4	8	1	5	2	3
5	2	8	9	3	7	1	4	6

319

1	5	7	4	2	8	3	9	6
6	8	4	9	3	7	2	1	5
2	3	9	1	6	5	8	4	7
9	4	3	8	1	6	7	5	2
8	6	1	7	5	2	4	3	9
7	2	5	3	4	9	1	6	8
5	1	6	2	7	3	9	8	4
3	7	8	6	9	4	5	2	1
4	9	2	5	8	1	6	7	3

320

9	8	3	1	5	2	7	4	6
2	6	1	7	4	8	5	3	9
4	5	7	6	9	3	2	1	8
5	1	4	8	3	9	6	2	7
7	2	6	4	1	5	9	8	3
3	9	8	2	6	7	1	5	4
8	7	9	5	2	4	3	6	1
1	3	2	9	8	6	4	7	5
6	4	5	3	7	1	8	9	2

321

1	7	2	4	9	3	6	8	5
8	4	9	6	5	1	7	3	2
6	3	5	7	8	2	9	4	1
2	5	3	1	7	8	4	9	6
4	1	7	9	2	6	3	5	8
9	8	6	3	4	5	1	2	7
7	2	1	8	3	4	5	6	9
3	6	8	5	1	9	2	7	4
5	9	4	2	6	7	8	1	3

322

5	1	4	8	6	3	7	9	2
6	8	2	7	9	5	1	3	4
3	7	9	2	1	4	6	8	5
9	2	8	1	7	6	5	4	3
4	3	7	5	8	9	2	1	6
1	5	6	3	4	2	9	7	8
7	4	1	6	5	8	3	2	9
2	9	5	4	3	1	8	6	7
8	6	3	9	2	7	4	5	1

323

9	7	6	2	8	3	1	5	4
1	4	2	6	5	9	3	7	8
8	5	3	4	7	1	2	9	6
5	3	8	1	9	7	6	4	2
7	6	1	5	2	4	8	3	9
4	2	9	3	6	8	7	1	5
6	1	5	9	3	2	4	8	7
3	9	7	8	4	6	5	2	1
2	8	4	7	1	5	9	6	3

324

1	6	2	4	5	9	3	7	8
3	9	7	2	8	1	6	4	5
8	5	4	6	7	3	9	1	2
4	7	3	5	1	6	2	8	9
2	1	5	9	3	8	4	6	7
9	8	6	7	4	2	5	3	1
7	2	9	1	6	4	8	5	3
5	4	8	3	2	7	1	9	6
6	3	1	8	9	5	7	2	4

325

1	5	3	8	4	6	2	7	9
4	7	8	9	3	2	1	6	5
2	6	9	1	5	7	4	3	8
5	2	4	3	7	9	8	1	6
3	8	1	6	2	5	7	9	4
6	9	7	4	1	8	3	5	2
7	1	2	5	9	4	6	8	3
8	3	5	2	6	1	9	4	7
9	4	6	7	8	3	5	2	1

326

9	4	6	5	1	2	8	3	7
5	3	2	7	4	8	9	6	1
8	7	1	3	9	6	2	4	5
1	8	3	6	5	4	7	2	9
2	6	7	9	8	3	1	5	4
4	5	9	1	2	7	6	8	3
7	1	8	4	6	5	3	9	2
3	2	4	8	7	9	5	1	6
6	9	5	2	3	1	4	7	8

327

1	8	6	5	2	3	4	7	9
3	4	2	8	9	7	6	5	1
7	5	9	4	1	6	8	3	2
2	7	1	9	3	8	5	6	4
8	3	4	1	6	5	2	9	7
6	9	5	2	7	4	3	1	8
9	6	3	7	8	2	1	4	5
5	1	8	3	4	9	7	2	6
4	2	7	6	5	1	9	8	3

328

9	7	4	2	5	6	8	3	1
8	6	3	7	1	4	5	2	9
1	2	5	8	9	3	6	7	4
7	3	8	9	4	5	2	1	6
5	9	1	6	7	2	3	4	8
2	4	6	3	8	1	9	5	7
4	8	2	5	6	7	1	9	3
3	1	9	4	2	8	7	6	5
6	5	7	1	3	9	4	8	2

329

2	9	5	8	6	7	4	3	1
4	8	1	3	9	5	2	7	6
3	6	7	2	4	1	8	9	5
5	7	9	6	1	8	3	4	2
8	4	3	7	5	2	6	1	9
6	1	2	4	3	9	7	5	8
1	2	4	9	7	6	5	8	3
7	5	6	1	8	3	9	2	4
9	3	8	5	2	4	1	6	7

330

5	9	2	1	3	8	4	6	7
7	6	8	4	9	2	5	3	1
3	1	4	6	5	7	9	2	8
2	8	5	7	6	1	3	9	4
6	4	3	8	2	9	7	1	5
1	7	9	3	4	5	2	8	6
8	5	1	2	7	3	6	4	9
9	2	6	5	1	4	8	7	3
4	3	7	9	8	6	1	5	2

331

3	2	8	7	5	6	4	1	9
6	7	5	1	9	4	2	8	3
9	4	1	8	3	2	6	5	7
4	3	2	6	8	7	1	9	5
8	5	7	9	4	1	3	2	6
1	6	9	5	2	3	7	4	8
7	8	6	2	1	9	5	3	4
5	1	4	3	7	8	9	6	2
2	9	3	4	6	5	8	7	1

332

8	5	2	7	1	4	9	3	6
6	3	1	9	5	2	4	8	7
9	7	4	8	3	6	5	1	2
5	6	7	3	9	8	2	4	1
4	1	3	2	6	7	8	5	9
2	8	9	5	4	1	6	7	3
3	2	6	4	7	5	1	9	8
1	9	5	6	8	3	7	2	4
7	4	8	1	2	9	3	6	5

333

6	1	3	4	9	8	7	2	5
7	8	4	3	2	5	6	9	1
2	5	9	1	7	6	3	4	8
8	7	1	6	4	9	5	3	2
4	6	5	2	3	7	8	1	9
3	9	2	8	5	1	4	6	7
1	4	6	7	8	2	9	5	3
9	2	7	5	6	3	1	8	4
5	3	8	9	1	4	2	7	6

334

6	7	3	2	9	8	4	5	1
5	2	8	6	4	1	7	9	3
4	1	9	5	7	3	8	2	6
9	4	6	3	1	2	5	7	8
8	5	2	4	6	7	3	1	9
7	3	1	9	8	5	6	4	2
2	8	4	7	3	9	1	6	5
1	9	7	8	5	6	2	3	4
3	6	5	1	2	4	9	8	7

335

1	2	3	6	7	8	4	5	9
8	6	9	4	5	2	7	3	1
7	5	4	3	1	9	6	2	8
6	7	1	5	3	4	9	8	2
3	9	8	1	2	6	5	7	4
5	4	2	9	8	7	3	1	6
4	3	5	8	6	1	2	9	7
2	1	6	7	9	5	8	4	3
9	8	7	2	4	3	1	6	5

336

4	8	2	5	9	6	3	7	1
3	5	7	1	2	4	6	8	9
6	1	9	8	7	3	4	5	2
5	2	6	3	1	7	8	9	4
7	4	3	9	8	5	1	2	6
8	9	1	6	4	2	7	3	5
2	7	5	4	6	8	9	1	3
9	6	8	2	3	1	5	4	7
1	3	4	7	5	9	2	6	8

337

6	4	1	7	8	9	5	3	2
5	8	7	2	1	3	6	4	9
9	3	2	4	5	6	8	1	7
7	2	8	6	9	4	1	5	3
4	9	5	3	2	1	7	6	8
1	6	3	8	7	5	9	2	4
3	5	9	1	4	7	2	8	6
2	7	6	5	3	8	4	9	1
8	1	4	9	6	2	3	7	5

338

6	3	9	5	4	1	7	8	2
2	7	4	8	6	9	3	1	5
8	5	1	2	7	3	9	6	4
5	9	7	4	1	8	6	2	3
1	2	6	3	9	7	5	4	8
3	4	8	6	5	2	1	9	7
7	6	5	9	8	4	2	3	1
9	8	3	1	2	5	4	7	6
4	1	2	7	3	6	8	5	9

339

6	8	2	1	4	7	9	3	5
9	4	5	3	2	6	1	7	8
7	1	3	5	9	8	2	4	6
4	5	6	8	1	9	7	2	3
8	7	9	2	6	3	5	1	4
3	2	1	7	5	4	8	6	9
5	3	7	6	8	2	4	9	1
2	9	8	4	3	1	6	5	7
1	6	4	9	7	5	3	8	2

340

2	8	7	4	6	1	5	3	9
9	4	5	7	8	3	1	2	6
1	3	6	2	9	5	7	8	4
8	6	9	3	5	2	4	1	7
3	7	1	9	4	6	2	5	8
4	5	2	1	7	8	6	9	3
6	1	3	8	2	4	9	7	5
7	2	4	5	3	9	8	6	1
5	9	8	6	1	7	3	4	2

341

2	9	8	4	1	3	7	5	6
5	4	3	7	2	6	1	8	9
1	6	7	5	9	8	2	4	3
6	7	5	9	8	1	3	2	4
9	3	1	6	4	2	8	7	5
8	2	4	3	5	7	6	9	1
7	1	9	2	3	4	5	6	8
4	8	2	1	6	5	9	3	7
3	5	6	8	7	9	4	1	2

342

5	9	2	6	3	8	1	7	4
8	6	4	2	7	1	3	5	9
1	3	7	5	9	4	8	6	2
3	8	6	7	4	2	5	9	1
2	7	9	1	5	6	4	8	3
4	5	1	9	8	3	6	2	7
6	1	8	3	2	9	7	4	5
7	2	3	4	6	5	9	1	8
9	4	5	8	1	7	2	3	6

343

3	6	4	9	5	1	2	7	8
8	9	5	2	6	7	1	4	3
7	1	2	8	4	3	9	6	5
2	5	3	4	9	8	6	1	7
1	4	7	6	3	5	8	9	2
6	8	9	7	1	2	5	3	4
5	7	1	3	8	9	4	2	6
9	3	6	5	2	4	7	8	1
4	2	8	1	7	6	3	5	9

344

5	1	4	9	2	7	6	8	3
2	7	3	5	6	8	4	1	9
8	9	6	4	1	3	2	5	7
7	5	8	3	9	2	1	6	4
1	3	9	6	5	4	7	2	8
4	6	2	7	8	1	9	3	5
3	4	1	2	7	5	8	9	6
6	2	5	8	4	9	3	7	1
9	8	7	1	3	6	5	4	2

345

5	8	1	6	3	4	2	9	7
9	3	6	7	2	8	5	1	4
4	7	2	9	5	1	6	8	3
1	6	9	3	8	7	4	5	2
7	4	5	2	1	9	8	3	6
3	2	8	5	4	6	9	7	1
6	9	4	8	7	3	1	2	5
2	1	3	4	9	5	7	6	8
8	5	7	1	6	2	3	4	9

346

8	4	3	6	9	2	5	1	7
9	2	5	7	8	1	4	3	6
6	1	7	4	5	3	9	2	8
4	8	6	2	1	5	7	9	3
2	5	9	8	3	7	1	6	4
3	7	1	9	6	4	8	5	2
1	9	2	3	4	8	6	7	5
7	6	4	5	2	9	3	8	1
5	3	8	1	7	6	2	4	9

347

9	3	6	4	8	5	1	7	2
7	4	8	6	2	1	9	3	5
1	5	2	9	3	7	6	8	4
2	8	5	3	1	6	7	4	9
6	9	7	8	5	4	3	2	1
3	1	4	7	9	2	5	6	8
4	2	9	5	6	3	8	1	7
5	7	3	1	4	8	2	9	6
8	6	1	2	7	9	4	5	3

348

3	8	2	9	1	4	5	7	6
6	1	9	5	7	3	8	2	4
7	4	5	2	6	8	9	3	1
1	9	3	7	4	6	2	5	8
2	7	4	3	8	5	6	1	9
5	6	8	1	2	9	7	4	3
8	3	1	6	5	2	4	9	7
4	5	7	8	9	1	3	6	2
9	2	6	4	3	7	1	8	5

349

8	7	9	5	4	3	2	6	1
2	5	1	7	8	6	9	3	4
3	4	6	9	2	1	7	8	5
1	6	2	4	9	5	3	7	8
4	9	5	8	3	7	6	1	2
7	3	8	6	1	2	5	4	9
6	2	7	1	5	8	4	9	3
5	1	4	3	7	9	8	2	6
9	8	3	2	6	4	1	5	7

350

1	9	6	4	5	8	3	2	7
5	8	3	1	2	7	4	9	6
7	4	2	6	3	9	8	1	5
3	5	1	9	4	6	7	8	2
8	6	7	5	1	2	9	3	4
9	2	4	7	8	3	5	6	1
6	3	9	2	7	5	1	4	8
2	1	5	8	9	4	6	7	3
4	7	8	3	6	1	2	5	9

351

1	9	4	7	6	5	2	3	8
6	5	8	9	3	2	1	7	4
7	3	2	4	8	1	6	9	5
3	8	1	5	4	9	7	6	2
4	2	6	1	7	8	9	5	3
9	7	5	6	2	3	8	4	1
2	6	7	3	1	4	5	8	9
5	1	3	8	9	7	4	2	6
8	4	9	2	5	6	3	1	7

352

6	4	3	8	9	5	1	2	7
5	1	9	7	2	4	6	3	8
7	2	8	6	3	1	5	9	4
9	6	7	1	4	2	8	5	3
8	3	2	5	7	6	4	1	9
4	5	1	3	8	9	2	7	6
1	9	4	2	6	7	3	8	5
3	7	5	4	1	8	9	6	2
2	8	6	9	5	3	7	4	1

353

1	5	9	4	2	3	6	8	7
8	3	6	7	9	1	5	4	2
2	7	4	8	5	6	3	1	9
6	1	5	9	7	8	2	3	4
7	4	2	3	1	5	8	9	6
9	8	3	2	6	4	1	7	5
3	2	8	5	4	7	9	6	1
4	9	1	6	8	2	7	5	3
5	6	7	1	3	9	4	2	8

354

3	1	6	5	4	2	8	9	7
7	5	8	6	3	9	1	2	4
2	9	4	7	1	8	6	5	3
8	4	3	9	6	5	7	1	2
9	6	2	8	7	1	4	3	5
5	7	1	3	2	4	9	6	8
6	2	7	4	9	3	5	8	1
1	8	9	2	5	7	3	4	6
4	3	5	1	8	6	2	7	9

355

3	8	9	2	7	1	6	4	5
1	2	4	5	3	6	9	7	8
7	6	5	8	4	9	1	3	2
4	3	8	7	1	2	5	6	9
9	5	6	3	8	4	2	1	7
2	1	7	9	6	5	3	8	4
6	9	1	4	2	7	8	5	3
5	4	3	6	9	8	7	2	1
8	7	2	1	5	3	4	9	6

356

6	4	8	7	5	1	3	9	2
1	9	7	8	3	2	5	6	4
2	3	5	6	4	9	8	1	7
8	5	3	2	1	7	6	4	9
7	6	4	9	8	3	2	5	1
9	1	2	5	6	4	7	8	3
3	2	6	1	9	5	4	7	8
5	7	1	4	2	8	9	3	6
4	8	9	3	7	6	1	2	5

357

3	7	6	4	1	2	9	5	8
8	4	2	6	5	9	7	1	3
1	9	5	8	3	7	4	6	2
9	2	1	5	8	4	6	3	7
5	8	7	2	6	3	1	4	9
4	6	3	7	9	1	8	2	5
6	3	9	1	2	8	5	7	4
7	5	8	3	4	6	2	9	1
2	1	4	9	7	5	3	8	6

358

9	6	7	8	4	1	2	5	3
5	8	2	3	7	6	9	1	4
1	3	4	2	9	5	7	6	8
8	9	5	1	6	2	4	3	7
3	4	6	7	8	9	5	2	1
7	2	1	4	5	3	8	9	6
2	7	9	6	3	4	1	8	5
6	1	8	5	2	7	3	4	9
4	5	3	9	1	8	6	7	2

359

9	8	4	2	6	5	3	1	7
2	3	7	4	8	1	9	6	5
5	6	1	7	9	3	2	4	8
3	9	8	6	1	7	4	5	2
1	4	6	9	5	2	8	7	3
7	2	5	8	3	4	1	9	6
6	1	9	3	7	8	5	2	4
8	7	2	5	4	9	6	3	1
4	5	3	1	2	6	7	8	9

360

6	2	9	7	4	8	3	1	5
4	1	3	2	5	6	8	7	9
7	8	5	1	9	3	2	6	4
2	9	6	3	1	4	5	8	7
5	4	8	6	7	9	1	2	3
3	7	1	8	2	5	4	9	6
9	3	7	5	8	2	6	4	1
1	5	2	4	6	7	9	3	8
8	6	4	9	3	1	7	5	2

361

1	8	9	3	2	6	5	4	7
4	5	3	9	7	1	6	2	8
6	7	2	8	5	4	9	1	3
5	2	1	4	8	7	3	6	9
8	6	4	5	9	3	1	7	2
3	9	7	1	6	2	8	5	4
2	3	5	7	1	9	4	8	6
9	1	6	2	4	8	7	3	5
7	4	8	6	3	5	2	9	1

362

9	6	7	1	2	8	5	3	4
1	2	4	7	5	3	8	9	6
8	5	3	9	4	6	1	2	7
3	9	2	4	8	7	6	1	5
4	1	5	2	6	9	3	7	8
7	8	6	3	1	5	9	4	2
6	4	1	5	9	2	7	8	3
2	7	8	6	3	1	4	5	9
5	3	9	8	7	4	2	6	1

363

9	2	1	3	7	8	4	5	6
4	8	6	1	5	2	7	9	3
5	3	7	9	6	4	1	2	8
6	1	3	8	4	9	5	7	2
8	5	2	6	1	7	9	3	4
7	9	4	2	3	5	6	8	1
2	6	5	7	8	1	3	4	9
3	7	9	4	2	6	8	1	5
1	4	8	5	9	3	2	6	7

364

1	5	7	2	9	4	6	3	8
8	4	6	7	3	1	2	5	9
9	3	2	8	6	5	4	7	1
6	7	5	3	2	8	1	9	4
3	9	4	6	1	7	8	2	5
2	8	1	5	4	9	7	6	3
5	2	9	1	8	6	3	4	7
7	6	8	4	5	3	9	1	2
4	1	3	9	7	2	5	8	6

365

5	7	8	3	1	6	4	2	9
2	9	6	7	8	4	5	3	1
1	3	4	2	9	5	6	8	7
6	2	7	4	5	8	9	1	3
8	5	9	1	2	3	7	6	4
3	4	1	9	6	7	8	5	2
4	8	3	6	7	1	2	9	5
7	6	2	5	3	9	1	4	8
9	1	5	8	4	2	3	7	6

366

4	6	1	2	8	3	5	7	9
3	5	2	7	9	6	1	4	8
9	8	7	1	5	4	3	2	6
8	2	5	4	6	7	9	1	3
7	9	6	5	3	1	4	8	2
1	3	4	9	2	8	7	6	5
2	4	8	3	7	9	6	5	1
6	7	3	8	1	5	2	9	4
5	1	9	6	4	2	8	3	7

367

2	6	8	5	4	7	3	1	9
4	5	9	1	6	3	2	8	7
1	7	3	9	8	2	4	5	6
8	2	1	7	9	6	5	3	4
7	3	6	4	5	1	9	2	8
5	9	4	2	3	8	6	7	1
6	8	5	3	1	9	7	4	2
9	4	2	8	7	5	1	6	3
3	1	7	6	2	4	8	9	5

368

3	1	4	6	7	8	9	5	2
2	7	5	4	3	9	6	8	1
9	8	6	2	1	5	7	4	3
1	3	7	5	6	2	4	9	8
5	2	9	1	8	4	3	6	7
4	6	8	7	9	3	2	1	5
6	5	3	8	4	7	1	2	9
8	9	1	3	2	6	5	7	4
7	4	2	9	5	1	8	3	6

369

9	2	7	6	8	3	1	4	5
5	3	1	4	9	7	2	6	8
4	8	6	5	1	2	9	3	7
7	1	4	3	2	9	8	5	6
8	5	9	7	4	6	3	2	1
2	6	3	1	5	8	7	9	4
1	9	2	8	6	5	4	7	3
6	7	8	9	3	4	5	1	2
3	4	5	2	7	1	6	8	9

370

4	9	1	8	7	5	6	2	3
5	7	8	2	6	3	1	4	9
6	2	3	9	1	4	5	7	8
9	6	4	1	3	2	8	5	7
1	5	7	4	9	8	3	6	2
3	8	2	6	5	7	9	1	4
2	3	9	5	4	6	7	8	1
7	4	6	3	8	1	2	9	5
8	1	5	7	2	9	4	3	6

371

1	4	9	5	3	6	7	8	2
3	5	8	2	7	4	6	1	9
2	6	7	8	9	1	4	5	3
9	3	4	7	5	2	8	6	1
5	7	1	9	6	8	3	2	4
6	8	2	1	4	3	9	7	5
8	9	6	4	1	5	2	3	7
4	1	3	6	2	7	5	9	8
7	2	5	3	8	9	1	4	6

372

7	6	9	5	2	8	3	1	4
2	5	8	1	3	4	9	7	6
3	4	1	6	9	7	2	8	5
6	7	5	8	4	3	1	9	2
9	8	4	2	5	1	6	3	7
1	3	2	9	7	6	5	4	8
8	1	3	7	6	5	4	2	9
4	9	6	3	8	2	7	5	1
5	2	7	4	1	9	8	6	3

373

6	3	9	4	2	1	8	5	7
4	7	1	3	5	8	2	6	9
2	5	8	9	6	7	1	4	3
8	9	2	1	3	6	5	7	4
5	6	3	2	7	4	9	1	8
1	4	7	5	8	9	3	2	6
7	1	6	8	9	5	4	3	2
9	2	4	6	1	3	7	8	5
3	8	5	7	4	2	6	9	1

374

6	8	3	2	7	4	9	5	1
2	7	1	9	8	5	4	3	6
5	9	4	6	3	1	8	2	7
7	6	2	3	4	8	5	1	9
8	3	5	1	2	9	6	7	4
4	1	9	7	5	6	2	8	3
3	2	6	8	9	7	1	4	5
1	4	8	5	6	3	7	9	2
9	5	7	4	1	2	3	6	8

375

4	2	3	6	8	5	1	9	7
8	6	7	9	1	3	5	2	4
9	5	1	2	4	7	8	3	6
2	7	8	5	3	6	4	1	9
5	4	9	1	2	8	6	7	3
3	1	6	4	7	9	2	8	5
1	9	5	3	6	2	7	4	8
7	3	4	8	5	1	9	6	2
6	8	2	7	9	4	3	5	1

376

5	2	8	6	9	3	4	1	7
6	3	7	2	4	1	9	8	5
9	4	1	8	7	5	2	3	6
4	1	9	7	3	2	6	5	8
8	6	2	5	1	4	7	9	3
3	7	5	9	8	6	1	4	2
7	5	4	3	6	9	8	2	1
2	9	6	1	5	8	3	7	4
1	8	3	4	2	7	5	6	9

377

5	9	3	1	7	4	8	2	6
7	8	4	6	9	2	1	3	5
1	6	2	3	8	5	4	9	7
3	1	9	2	6	7	5	4	8
6	5	7	4	3	8	2	1	9
4	2	8	5	1	9	7	6	3
8	7	6	9	4	1	3	5	2
9	4	5	7	2	3	6	8	1
2	3	1	8	5	6	9	7	4

378

4	6	2	5	9	7	1	3	8
3	7	5	1	8	4	2	9	6
1	9	8	3	2	6	7	4	5
2	1	3	4	6	5	8	7	9
8	5	6	7	3	9	4	2	1
9	4	7	8	1	2	5	6	3
6	2	1	9	7	8	3	5	4
5	3	9	2	4	1	6	8	7
7	8	4	6	5	3	9	1	2

379

2	8	6	9	5	1	4	3	7
1	7	5	3	8	4	2	9	6
3	9	4	2	7	6	1	5	8
6	1	7	8	2	3	5	4	9
9	3	8	4	6	5	7	1	2
5	4	2	1	9	7	6	8	3
4	2	1	7	3	9	8	6	5
8	6	3	5	1	2	9	7	4
7	5	9	6	4	8	3	2	1

380

2	4	6	3	8	7	1	5	9
5	1	9	6	4	2	3	8	7
7	3	8	5	9	1	2	6	4
1	2	3	7	5	9	8	4	6
6	8	5	2	1	4	7	9	3
9	7	4	8	6	3	5	1	2
4	6	7	1	2	8	9	3	5
8	5	2	9	3	6	4	7	1
3	9	1	4	7	5	6	2	8

381

7	1	6	5	9	8	4	3	2
9	5	8	3	4	2	6	1	7
3	2	4	1	7	6	5	8	9
1	4	7	9	2	5	8	6	3
5	8	3	6	1	7	2	9	4
2	6	9	4	8	3	7	5	1
4	7	1	8	6	9	3	2	5
8	3	2	7	5	1	9	4	6
6	9	5	2	3	4	1	7	8

382

4	5	3	2	6	7	8	1	9
7	6	9	5	8	1	4	3	2
8	1	2	4	3	9	6	7	5
6	7	4	8	1	5	2	9	3
9	3	5	7	2	6	1	8	4
1	2	8	3	9	4	7	5	6
5	4	6	1	7	3	9	2	8
3	8	1	9	4	2	5	6	7
2	9	7	6	5	8	3	4	1

383

3	6	2	8	1	7	4	5	9
5	8	7	3	4	9	6	1	2
1	4	9	5	2	6	8	3	7
9	3	5	4	6	1	2	7	8
2	1	8	7	9	3	5	6	4
6	7	4	2	8	5	3	9	1
8	5	3	9	7	4	1	2	6
4	9	6	1	5	2	7	8	3
7	2	1	6	3	8	9	4	5

384

4	2	7	6	5	8	1	9	3
1	5	9	3	4	2	6	7	8
8	3	6	1	7	9	2	5	4
3	6	5	2	8	1	9	4	7
7	8	2	9	3	4	5	1	6
9	1	4	7	6	5	3	8	2
5	9	3	4	2	7	8	6	1
2	4	1	8	9	6	7	3	5
6	7	8	5	1	3	4	2	9

385

7	2	9	5	3	6	4	8	1
3	6	4	1	7	8	2	9	5
1	5	8	4	2	9	6	3	7
9	4	5	7	1	3	8	2	6
6	7	1	8	4	2	9	5	3
2	8	3	6	9	5	7	1	4
8	1	6	9	5	7	3	4	2
4	9	2	3	6	1	5	7	8
5	3	7	2	8	4	1	6	9

386

1	7	2	5	8	9	6	4	3
8	9	6	3	7	4	2	5	1
3	4	5	2	6	1	9	7	8
2	6	3	1	5	7	8	9	4
4	5	1	9	2	8	3	6	7
7	8	9	6	4	3	1	2	5
9	1	7	4	3	2	5	8	6
6	2	8	7	1	5	4	3	9
5	3	4	8	9	6	7	1	2

387

6	7	8	4	2	1	3	5	9
1	3	9	6	5	7	2	4	8
2	5	4	3	9	8	6	7	1
7	8	1	5	3	2	4	9	6
5	2	6	7	4	9	1	8	3
9	4	3	1	8	6	5	2	7
8	6	2	9	1	5	7	3	4
3	9	7	2	6	4	8	1	5
4	1	5	8	7	3	9	6	2

388

5	7	1	3	2	8	6	4	9
3	2	4	1	9	6	8	7	5
6	8	9	4	5	7	3	1	2
2	9	3	5	1	4	7	8	6
7	1	5	6	8	3	9	2	4
4	6	8	9	7	2	5	3	1
1	3	6	8	4	9	2	5	7
9	5	2	7	3	1	4	6	8
8	4	7	2	6	5	1	9	3

389

8	2	5	9	4	1	3	7	6
4	3	7	8	5	6	2	1	9
1	9	6	3	7	2	4	8	5
5	7	3	2	1	9	8	6	4
2	4	8	6	3	5	1	9	7
6	1	9	7	8	4	5	3	2
3	8	4	5	9	7	6	2	1
9	5	2	1	6	3	7	4	8
7	6	1	4	2	8	9	5	3

390

6	9	4	7	8	3	5	2	1
5	3	7	9	1	2	8	4	6
1	8	2	4	6	5	9	3	7
2	5	6	8	3	7	4	1	9
4	7	3	1	9	6	2	5	8
9	1	8	2	5	4	6	7	3
7	6	1	5	2	9	3	8	4
3	4	5	6	7	8	1	9	2
8	2	9	3	4	1	7	6	5

391

7	6	5	8	9	1	2	4	3
8	4	3	5	2	6	7	9	1
9	1	2	3	4	7	8	5	6
2	3	7	4	6	9	5	1	8
4	9	6	1	8	5	3	2	7
5	8	1	7	3	2	9	6	4
3	2	9	6	1	8	4	7	5
1	7	4	9	5	3	6	8	2
6	5	8	2	7	4	1	3	9

392

7	1	4	5	6	9	3	8	2
8	6	9	2	3	1	4	5	7
3	2	5	7	8	4	1	9	6
1	4	7	3	9	5	6	2	8
6	9	8	1	7	2	5	4	3
5	3	2	6	4	8	7	1	9
4	8	3	9	5	6	2	7	1
9	7	1	4	2	3	8	6	5
2	5	6	8	1	7	9	3	4

393

5	8	4	2	3	1	7	9	6
3	1	7	6	4	9	5	8	2
9	6	2	5	8	7	4	3	1
4	7	8	1	2	5	9	6	3
6	5	1	3	9	4	8	2	7
2	3	9	8	7	6	1	4	5
7	2	6	4	1	8	3	5	9
1	4	3	9	5	2	6	7	8
8	9	5	7	6	3	2	1	4

394

2	8	6	3	4	5	7	1	9
9	3	7	8	2	1	6	5	4
4	5	1	6	7	9	2	8	3
1	7	5	9	8	2	3	4	6
3	6	4	1	5	7	9	2	8
8	9	2	4	6	3	5	7	1
6	2	3	7	1	4	8	9	5
7	4	9	5	3	8	1	6	2
5	1	8	2	9	6	4	3	7

395

8	1	4	3	7	6	5	9	2
2	3	7	9	5	1	8	4	6
5	6	9	2	4	8	7	1	3
7	8	5	1	9	3	2	6	4
6	9	3	4	2	7	1	8	5
1	4	2	8	6	5	3	7	9
4	5	1	6	8	2	9	3	7
3	2	6	7	1	9	4	5	8
9	7	8	5	3	4	6	2	1

396

7	3	8	2	1	4	6	9	5
5	1	6	9	8	7	2	3	4
2	4	9	3	5	6	8	1	7
1	5	3	7	2	8	4	6	9
6	8	2	4	9	3	5	7	1
4	9	7	5	6	1	3	8	2
8	6	4	1	7	5	9	2	3
9	7	5	6	3	2	1	4	8
3	2	1	8	4	9	7	5	6

397

4	2	9	3	5	6	8	1	7
6	7	5	9	8	1	3	4	2
3	8	1	7	2	4	6	9	5
7	3	4	8	1	9	5	2	6
8	1	2	6	4	5	7	3	9
9	5	6	2	7	3	4	8	1
1	6	3	5	9	8	2	7	4
2	4	8	1	6	7	9	5	3
5	9	7	4	3	2	1	6	8

398

9	8	2	7	1	5	3	4	6
7	4	1	6	8	3	2	9	5
6	5	3	9	4	2	1	7	8
3	9	8	4	6	1	5	2	7
2	7	5	3	9	8	4	6	1
1	6	4	2	5	7	9	8	3
8	1	6	5	2	9	7	3	4
4	3	9	1	7	6	8	5	2
5	2	7	8	3	4	6	1	9

399

7	4	3	6	9	5	1	8	2
8	1	2	3	4	7	5	6	9
5	9	6	2	8	1	4	7	3
6	2	5	1	7	3	9	4	8
3	8	9	4	5	2	6	1	7
1	7	4	8	6	9	3	2	5
4	6	7	5	3	8	2	9	1
2	5	8	9	1	4	7	3	6
9	3	1	7	2	6	8	5	4

400

8	2	4	7	5	3	6	9	1
9	7	1	4	6	8	5	3	2
3	6	5	2	9	1	4	8	7
1	5	9	3	2	4	7	6	8
2	4	7	6	8	5	3	1	9
6	3	8	9	1	7	2	5	4
5	8	2	1	7	6	9	4	3
4	9	6	8	3	2	1	7	5
7	1	3	5	4	9	8	2	6

401

2	6	7	5	3	1	8	4	9
5	3	9	4	7	8	6	1	2
4	8	1	9	6	2	3	5	7
8	9	4	6	2	5	1	7	3
3	2	5	1	8	7	4	9	6
7	1	6	3	4	9	2	8	5
9	5	8	2	1	6	7	3	4
1	4	2	7	9	3	5	6	8
6	7	3	8	5	4	9	2	1

402

6	2	5	1	3	8	9	7	4
9	8	1	7	6	4	5	3	2
7	3	4	2	9	5	8	6	1
2	7	8	4	5	9	6	1	3
4	6	9	3	2	1	7	5	8
1	5	3	6	8	7	2	4	9
3	9	7	8	4	6	1	2	5
5	4	6	9	1	2	3	8	7
8	1	2	5	7	3	4	9	6

403

2	7	9	4	6	1	3	5	8
4	5	1	7	8	3	2	6	9
3	8	6	2	5	9	7	4	1
9	1	5	3	2	4	8	7	6
6	2	3	9	7	8	4	1	5
7	4	8	6	1	5	9	3	2
1	3	4	8	9	6	5	2	7
8	6	7	5	4	2	1	9	3
5	9	2	1	3	7	6	8	4

404

7	8	9	6	2	3	5	1	4
5	3	2	8	1	4	6	7	9
6	4	1	7	5	9	3	2	8
8	9	5	4	3	7	2	6	1
3	2	6	5	9	1	4	8	7
1	7	4	2	6	8	9	3	5
2	1	7	9	4	6	8	5	3
9	6	3	1	8	5	7	4	2
4	5	8	3	7	2	1	9	6

405

9	6	2	1	5	8	4	7	3
3	1	4	7	6	2	5	9	8
5	7	8	3	9	4	6	2	1
1	8	6	2	7	9	3	4	5
4	3	7	6	1	5	2	8	9
2	5	9	4	8	3	7	1	6
8	9	3	5	4	7	1	6	2
7	2	1	8	3	6	9	5	4
6	4	5	9	2	1	8	3	7

406

4	8	5	3	9	1	7	2	6
3	2	6	7	8	4	5	1	9
1	9	7	6	5	2	8	3	4
2	6	1	5	3	7	4	9	8
5	3	9	2	4	8	1	6	7
7	4	8	9	1	6	3	5	2
8	5	2	4	6	3	9	7	1
9	7	4	1	2	5	6	8	3
6	1	3	8	7	9	2	4	5

407

9	4	1	2	5	8	7	6	3
3	8	6	1	7	4	5	9	2
2	7	5	3	9	6	8	4	1
5	1	2	7	8	9	4	3	6
7	3	8	6	4	2	1	5	9
4	6	9	5	1	3	2	7	8
1	2	4	9	6	5	3	8	7
8	9	3	4	2	7	6	1	5
6	5	7	8	3	1	9	2	4

408

6	5	8	4	9	2	1	3	7
1	2	3	6	7	5	8	9	4
7	4	9	1	3	8	6	2	5
3	7	1	2	6	4	9	5	8
9	6	4	5	8	3	2	7	1
2	8	5	9	1	7	3	4	6
5	3	6	7	2	1	4	8	9
4	1	2	8	5	9	7	6	3
8	9	7	3	4	6	5	1	2

409

4	6	9	2	5	3	8	7	1
1	8	5	4	9	7	6	2	3
2	3	7	6	8	1	5	4	9
9	2	3	8	4	5	1	6	7
6	7	4	1	3	2	9	5	8
5	1	8	7	6	9	4	3	2
7	4	6	9	2	8	3	1	5
3	9	2	5	1	6	7	8	4
8	5	1	3	7	4	2	9	6

410

2	1	4	6	7	3	5	9	8
5	7	3	9	4	8	6	1	2
9	8	6	5	2	1	4	7	3
4	9	2	3	8	6	7	5	1
6	3	7	1	5	2	9	8	4
1	5	8	4	9	7	3	2	6
3	2	5	8	6	9	1	4	7
7	4	1	2	3	5	8	6	9
8	6	9	7	1	4	2	3	5

411

3	5	6	7	2	8	4	9	1
2	7	8	9	4	1	3	5	6
4	9	1	3	5	6	8	7	2
7	1	9	4	3	5	6	2	8
8	6	2	1	9	7	5	3	4
5	4	3	6	8	2	9	1	7
1	3	7	8	6	9	2	4	5
9	8	5	2	1	4	7	6	3
6	2	4	5	7	3	1	8	9

412

7	3	5	6	2	8	9	1	4
4	6	8	1	9	3	2	5	7
1	9	2	7	4	5	8	3	6
9	1	6	2	7	4	3	8	5
3	5	7	8	1	9	4	6	2
8	2	4	5	3	6	7	9	1
5	7	3	9	6	2	1	4	8
2	8	9	4	5	1	6	7	3
6	4	1	3	8	7	5	2	9

413

5	8	6	3	7	4	1	9	2
2	4	9	6	1	5	8	7	3
7	3	1	2	9	8	5	6	4
9	6	3	4	2	1	7	8	5
1	5	2	8	6	7	4	3	9
8	7	4	9	5	3	6	2	1
3	9	8	5	4	6	2	1	7
4	2	7	1	8	9	3	5	6
6	1	5	7	3	2	9	4	8

414

7	3	4	1	6	5	9	2	8
1	2	5	4	9	8	3	6	7
8	6	9	2	7	3	4	5	1
9	8	6	7	5	1	2	3	4
4	5	1	8	3	2	6	7	9
3	7	2	6	4	9	1	8	5
6	4	8	3	1	7	5	9	2
5	1	7	9	2	6	8	4	3
2	9	3	5	8	4	7	1	6

415

1	4	7	6	2	9	3	5	8
6	3	2	5	4	8	7	1	9
5	9	8	3	1	7	2	4	6
8	2	5	9	3	4	1	6	7
7	6	9	8	5	1	4	3	2
3	1	4	7	6	2	9	8	5
9	7	3	4	8	5	6	2	1
4	5	1	2	7	6	8	9	3
2	8	6	1	9	3	5	7	4

416

3	1	8	7	4	5	2	9	6
5	6	7	3	2	9	1	8	4
4	9	2	6	1	8	7	3	5
6	4	3	5	9	1	8	2	7
1	8	9	4	7	2	6	5	3
2	7	5	8	3	6	9	4	1
9	2	6	1	5	3	4	7	8
8	3	4	9	6	7	5	1	2
7	5	1	2	8	4	3	6	9

417

2	5	1	3	4	6	8	7	9
6	7	4	9	5	8	1	3	2
3	8	9	1	7	2	6	4	5
7	4	8	5	2	3	9	1	6
1	3	6	8	9	7	2	5	4
9	2	5	4	6	1	7	8	3
4	1	3	2	8	9	5	6	7
8	6	2	7	3	5	4	9	1
5	9	7	6	1	4	3	2	8

418

4	9	1	8	6	2	3	5	7
8	6	7	3	9	5	2	1	4
2	5	3	7	1	4	6	9	8
5	8	6	9	3	7	4	2	1
3	1	9	4	2	6	8	7	5
7	2	4	1	5	8	9	3	6
9	4	5	2	8	1	7	6	3
6	3	8	5	7	9	1	4	2
1	7	2	6	4	3	5	8	9

419

6	7	9	3	4	8	5	2	1
2	8	3	1	6	5	4	7	9
4	1	5	2	7	9	3	8	6
5	2	1	9	8	6	7	4	3
9	3	8	4	1	7	2	6	5
7	4	6	5	2	3	1	9	8
3	9	2	6	5	4	8	1	7
8	5	4	7	9	1	6	3	2
1	6	7	8	3	2	9	5	4

420

8	5	2	6	9	1	7	4	3
3	9	7	4	8	5	2	6	1
6	1	4	2	3	7	8	9	5
1	4	9	3	7	8	6	5	2
5	8	3	9	6	2	1	7	4
2	7	6	5	1	4	3	8	9
7	6	5	1	2	9	4	3	8
4	3	1	8	5	6	9	2	7
9	2	8	7	4	3	5	1	6

421

7	8	3	2	4	1	9	6	5
1	9	4	5	6	7	2	3	8
2	5	6	8	3	9	7	4	1
3	2	7	1	8	6	4	5	9
4	1	9	3	7	5	6	8	2
8	6	5	9	2	4	1	7	3
6	3	8	7	9	2	5	1	4
9	7	1	4	5	8	3	2	6
5	4	2	6	1	3	8	9	7

422

1	7	2	5	3	8	4	9	6
8	6	5	4	2	9	1	7	3
4	9	3	7	1	6	8	2	5
7	4	8	1	6	3	2	5	9
3	2	9	8	4	5	6	1	7
5	1	6	2	9	7	3	4	8
6	8	1	9	7	2	5	3	4
2	5	7	3	8	4	9	6	1
9	3	4	6	5	1	7	8	2

423

7	9	3	2	1	6	5	8	4
6	8	1	5	4	3	2	7	9
2	5	4	8	7	9	1	3	6
1	2	6	7	5	4	3	9	8
8	3	5	6	9	2	7	4	1
4	7	9	1	3	8	6	5	2
9	1	2	3	8	5	4	6	7
5	6	8	4	2	7	9	1	3
3	4	7	9	6	1	8	2	5

424

2	1	9	8	7	3	4	5	6
3	6	7	4	5	2	1	9	8
5	8	4	6	9	1	2	3	7
7	3	5	1	4	6	8	2	9
1	9	8	2	3	5	7	6	4
4	2	6	7	8	9	3	1	5
9	4	1	3	6	8	5	7	2
8	5	2	9	1	7	6	4	3
6	7	3	5	2	4	9	8	1

425

2	7	5	4	9	1	3	6	8
8	6	4	3	7	2	5	9	1
3	1	9	6	5	8	7	4	2
9	8	1	7	6	4	2	5	3
5	4	3	1	2	9	8	7	6
6	2	7	8	3	5	9	1	4
4	5	6	2	8	7	1	3	9
1	9	2	5	4	3	6	8	7
7	3	8	9	1	6	4	2	5

426

8	9	1	2	6	5	3	4	7
7	5	4	8	1	3	6	2	9
2	3	6	4	7	9	1	5	8
1	2	5	7	3	4	9	8	6
4	6	3	9	5	8	2	7	1
9	7	8	6	2	1	5	3	4
3	8	9	5	4	6	7	1	2
5	4	7	1	9	2	8	6	3
6	1	2	3	8	7	4	9	5

427

2	8	9	7	3	4	5	1	6
4	1	3	5	2	6	9	8	7
5	7	6	1	9	8	3	2	4
3	6	5	8	7	9	1	4	2
7	4	2	6	5	1	8	9	3
8	9	1	3	4	2	7	6	5
6	2	7	9	8	5	4	3	1
1	3	8	4	6	7	2	5	9
9	5	4	2	1	3	6	7	8

428

6	1	8	4	3	9	2	5	7
9	2	3	7	1	5	6	4	8
4	5	7	8	2	6	1	3	9
8	6	4	1	5	2	9	7	3
5	3	2	6	9	7	8	1	4
7	9	1	3	8	4	5	6	2
2	7	6	9	4	1	3	8	5
1	8	9	5	7	3	4	2	6
3	4	5	2	6	8	7	9	1

429

1	7	8	2	6	3	9	5	4
9	3	6	4	5	8	1	7	2
5	4	2	9	7	1	6	8	3
2	1	4	8	3	9	5	6	7
6	8	3	5	2	7	4	9	1
7	5	9	6	1	4	2	3	8
3	6	5	7	4	2	8	1	9
8	2	1	3	9	6	7	4	5
4	9	7	1	8	5	3	2	6

430

7	6	8	3	1	9	2	5	4
4	9	1	5	2	8	7	3	6
2	3	5	4	7	6	1	9	8
6	8	7	1	3	5	9	4	2
1	4	2	9	6	7	3	8	5
3	5	9	2	8	4	6	1	7
9	7	4	6	5	1	8	2	3
5	2	6	8	9	3	4	7	1
8	1	3	7	4	2	5	6	9

431

2	5	7	3	8	4	9	6	1
1	9	6	7	5	2	4	3	8
3	4	8	9	1	6	5	2	7
5	2	4	1	6	3	8	7	9
8	6	3	4	9	7	1	5	2
9	7	1	5	2	8	6	4	3
7	8	5	2	4	9	3	1	6
6	1	2	8	3	5	7	9	4
4	3	9	6	7	1	2	8	5

432

6	7	3	9	1	8	2	4	5
8	9	2	5	4	6	7	3	1
4	5	1	3	2	7	6	8	9
9	1	7	2	8	4	5	6	3
2	6	5	1	7	3	8	9	4
3	8	4	6	5	9	1	7	2
7	2	9	8	3	5	4	1	6
1	4	6	7	9	2	3	5	8
5	3	8	4	6	1	9	2	7

433

6	3	1	4	2	5	9	7	8
2	5	8	7	9	1	6	4	3
9	4	7	3	6	8	2	1	5
5	7	3	2	8	9	1	6	4
1	6	4	5	3	7	8	2	9
8	9	2	1	4	6	5	3	7
7	8	9	6	1	4	3	5	2
3	1	5	8	7	2	4	9	6
4	2	6	9	5	3	7	8	1

434

1	4	7	9	6	8	5	3	2
6	8	5	2	7	3	4	1	9
9	2	3	5	1	4	8	7	6
2	5	9	6	8	7	1	4	3
7	1	6	3	4	9	2	8	5
4	3	8	1	2	5	9	6	7
8	6	2	7	9	1	3	5	4
3	7	4	8	5	2	6	9	1
5	9	1	4	3	6	7	2	8

435

8	1	9	4	6	2	3	7	5
3	7	2	1	5	8	9	4	6
5	6	4	9	3	7	2	8	1
6	8	7	5	2	1	4	3	9
9	5	1	8	4	3	7	6	2
2	4	3	6	7	9	1	5	8
1	9	5	7	8	4	6	2	3
7	3	8	2	9	6	5	1	4
4	2	6	3	1	5	8	9	7

436

7	6	3	2	1	5	8	9	4
9	2	8	6	7	4	1	3	5
4	1	5	3	8	9	7	2	6
6	3	9	1	2	8	5	4	7
8	5	1	4	3	7	2	6	9
2	7	4	9	5	6	3	8	1
5	9	2	8	4	1	6	7	3
3	4	7	5	6	2	9	1	8
1	8	6	7	9	3	4	5	2

437

9	2	4	5	1	7	8	6	3
8	1	7	3	9	6	2	5	4
3	6	5	2	4	8	7	9	1
5	7	1	8	6	4	9	3	2
6	8	2	1	3	9	4	7	5
4	9	3	7	2	5	6	1	8
7	3	6	4	5	2	1	8	9
2	5	9	6	8	1	3	4	7
1	4	8	9	7	3	5	2	6

438

8	2	9	6	7	4	1	3	5
5	3	6	2	9	1	4	8	7
1	7	4	5	8	3	2	9	6
7	8	3	1	4	9	5	6	2
9	6	1	7	5	2	3	4	8
4	5	2	8	3	6	9	7	1
6	4	5	9	2	8	7	1	3
3	1	7	4	6	5	8	2	9
2	9	8	3	1	7	6	5	4

439

7	2	4	9	6	8	5	1	3
3	1	6	5	7	2	4	9	8
8	5	9	4	1	3	6	7	2
4	3	7	1	8	6	9	2	5
9	6	2	3	4	5	7	8	1
1	8	5	2	9	7	3	6	4
5	7	3	6	2	1	8	4	9
2	9	8	7	5	4	1	3	6
6	4	1	8	3	9	2	5	7

440

4	5	9	7	1	6	8	2	3
8	6	3	2	4	9	5	1	7
7	1	2	8	3	5	9	4	6
2	3	1	4	5	7	6	9	8
6	7	8	1	9	2	4	3	5
9	4	5	3	6	8	2	7	1
5	2	6	9	7	3	1	8	4
1	9	7	5	8	4	3	6	2
3	8	4	6	2	1	7	5	9

441

5	4	8	9	2	3	1	7	6
2	7	6	4	8	1	5	3	9
9	1	3	6	5	7	2	8	4
7	2	9	5	1	8	6	4	3
6	5	4	3	9	2	8	1	7
3	8	1	7	6	4	9	5	2
4	6	5	8	3	9	7	2	1
8	3	2	1	7	6	4	9	5
1	9	7	2	4	5	3	6	8

442

9	3	2	5	4	8	7	1	6
7	8	6	1	9	2	3	5	4
1	5	4	6	7	3	2	8	9
3	1	5	4	8	9	6	7	2
6	4	9	7	2	5	8	3	1
2	7	8	3	6	1	9	4	5
8	2	7	9	5	4	1	6	3
5	9	1	8	3	6	4	2	7
4	6	3	2	1	7	5	9	8

443

6	1	8	9	3	7	2	4	5
4	2	7	6	5	8	1	9	3
9	3	5	1	4	2	7	8	6
8	5	3	2	9	4	6	1	7
7	4	1	5	8	6	3	2	9
2	9	6	3	7	1	8	5	4
1	6	4	7	2	9	5	3	8
5	7	9	8	1	3	4	6	2
3	8	2	4	6	5	9	7	1

444

8	7	4	3	2	5	1	6	9
2	1	3	8	6	9	7	4	5
6	9	5	4	7	1	3	2	8
5	8	1	7	3	2	4	9	6
4	3	9	1	5	6	2	8	7
7	6	2	9	8	4	5	1	3
1	5	7	2	9	8	6	3	4
3	2	8	6	4	7	9	5	1
9	4	6	5	1	3	8	7	2